Hospitality Accounting

Second Edition

ManageFirst
PROGRAM®

NATIONAL
RESTAURANT
ASSOCIATION®

PEARSON

Boston   Columbus   Indianapolis   New York   San Francisco   Upper Saddle River
Amsterdam   Cape Town   Dubai   London   Madrid   Milan   Munich   Paris   Montréal   Toronto
Delhi   Mexico City   São Paulo   Sydney   Hong Kong   Seoul   Singapore   Taipei   Tokyo

Pearson

Editorial Director: Vernon R. Anthony
Executive Acquisitions Editor: Alli Gentile
NRA Product Development: Randall Towns and
  Todd Schlender
Senior Managing Editor: JoEllen Gohr
Associate Managing Editor: Alexandrina B. Wolf
Senior Operations Supervisor: Pat Tonneman
Senior Operations Specialist: Deidra Skahill
Cover photo: Trosamange/Dreamstime.com

Cover design: Karen Steinberg, Element LLC
Director of Marketing: David Gesell
Marketing Coordinator: Les Roberts
Full-Service Project Management: Barbara Hawk and
  Kevin J. Gray, Element LLC
Text and Cover Printer/Binder: LSC Communications
Text Font: Minion Pro, Myriad Pro Semicondensed

Photography Credits

Front matter: i Trosamange/Dreamstime.com; vii (left) Suhendri Utet/Dreamstime; (right) Meryll/Dreamstime; viii (top) Mtr/Dreamstime; (bottom) Stratum/Dreamstime; ix (bottom left) Aprescindere/Dreamstime; xv (bottom left) Petar Neychev/Dreamstime; 23, 77, 129, 155, 211, 239, 268 Nikada/iStockPhoto

All other photographs owned or acquired by the National Restaurant Association Educational Foundation, NRAEF

7 17

ISBN-10:   0-13-217524-X
ISBN-13: 978-0-13-217524-1

ISBN-10:   0-13-272487-1
ISBN-13: 978-0-13-272487-6

Contents in Brief

Contents

10 Accounting and Finance Issues for Restaurant Owners 240

About the National Restaurant Association and the National Restaurant Association Educational Foundation

Founded in 1919, the National Restaurant Association (NRA) is the leading business association for the restaurant and foodservice industry, which comprises 960,000 restaurant and foodservice outlets and a workforce of nearly 13 million employees. We represent the industry in Washington, DC, and advocate on its behalf. We operate the industry's largest trade show (NRA Show, restaurant.org/show); leading food safety training and certification program (ServSafe, servsafe.com); unique career-building high school program (the NRAEF's *ProStart*, prostart.restaurant.org); as well as the *Kids LiveWell* program (restaurant.org/kidslivewell) promoting healthful kids' menu options. For more information, visit www.restaurant.org and find us on Twitter @*WeRRestaurants*, *Facebook*, and *YouTube*.

With the first job experience of one in four U.S. adults occurring in a restaurant or foodservice operation, the industry is uniquely attractive among American industries for entry-level jobs, personal development and growth, employee and manager career paths, and ownership and wealth creation. That is why the National Restaurant Association Educational Foundation (nraef.org), the philanthropic foundation of the NRA, furthers the education of tomorrow's restaurant and foodservice industry professionals and plays a key role in promoting job and career opportunities in the industry by allocating millions of dollars a year toward industry scholarships and educational programs. The NRA works to ensure the most qualified and passionate people enter the industry so that we can better meet the needs of our members and the patrons and clients they serve.

What Is the ManageFirst Program?

The ManageFirst Program is a management training certificate program that exemplifies our commitment to developing materials by the industry, for the industry. The program's

EXAM TOPICS

ManageFirst Core Credential Topics

Hospitality and Restaurant Management
Controlling Foodservice Costs
Hospitality Human Resources Management and Supervision
ServSafe® Food Safety

ManageFirst Foundation Topics

Customer Service
Principles of Food and Beverage Management
Purchasing
Hospitality Accounting
Bar and Beverage Management
Nutrition
Hospitality and Restaurant Marketing
ServSafe Alcohol® Responsible Alcohol Service

most powerful strength is that it is based on a set of competencies defined by the restaurant and foodservice industry as critical for success. The program teaches the skills truly valued by industry professionals.

ManageFirst Program Components

The ManageFirst Program includes a set of books, exams, instructor resources, certificates, a new credential, and support activities and services. By participating in the program, you are demonstrating your commitment to becoming a highly qualified professional either preparing to begin or to advance your career in the restaurant, hospitality, and foodservice industry.

These books cover the range of topics listed in the chart above. You will find the essential content for the topic as defined by industry, as well as learning activities, assessments, case studies, suggested field projects, professional profiles, and testimonials. The exam can be administered either online or in a paper-and-pencil format (see inside front cover for a listing of ISBNs), and it will be proctored. Upon successfully passing the exam, you will be furnished with a customized certificate by the National Restaurant Association. The certificate is a lasting recognition of your accomplishment and a signal to the industry that you have mastered the competencies covered within the particular topic.

To earn this credential, you will be required to pass four core exams and one foundation exam (to be chosen from the remaining program topics) and to document your work experience in the restaurant and foodservice industry. Earning the ManageFirst credential is a significant accomplishment.

We applaud you as you either begin or advance your career in the restaurant, hospitality, and foodservice industry. Visit www.nraef.org to learn about additional career-building resources offered by the NRAEF, including scholarships for college students enrolled in relevant industry programs.

MANAGEFIRST PROGRAM ORDERING INFORMATION

Review copies or support materials

FACULTY FIELD SERVICES
Tel: 800.526.0485

Domestic orders and inquiries

PEARSON CUSTOMER SERVICE
Tel: 800.922.0579
http://www.pearsonhighered.com/

International orders and inquiries

U.S. EXPORT SALES OFFICE
Pearson Education International Customer Service Group
200 Old Tappan Road
Old Tappan, NJ 07675 USA
Tel: 201.767.5021
Fax: 201.767.5625

For corporate, government, and special sales (consultants, corporations, training centers, VARs, and corporate resellers) orders and inquiries

PEARSON CORPORATE SALES
Tel: 317.428.3411
Fax: 317.428.3343
Email: managefirst@prenhall.com

For additional information regarding other Pearson publications, instructor and student support materials, locating your sales representative, and much more, please visit www.pearsonhighered.com/managefirst.

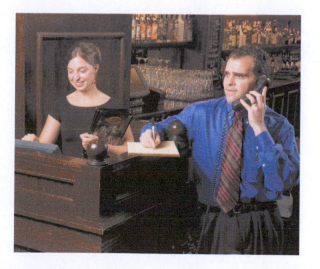

Acknowledgements

The National Restaurant Association is grateful for the significant contributions made to this book by the following individuals.

Mike Amos
Perkins & Marie Callender's Inc.

Steve Belt
Monical's Pizza

Heather Kane Haberer
Carrols Restaurant Group

Erika Hoover
Monical's Pizza Corp.

Jared Kulka
Red Robin Gourmet Burgers

Tony C. Merritt
Carrols Restaurant Group

H. George Neil
Buffalo Wild Wings

Marci Noguiera
Sodexo—Education Division

Ryan Nowicki
Dave & Busters

Penny Ann Lord Prichard
Wake Tech/NC Community College

Michael Santos
Micatrotto Restaurant Group

Heather Thitoff
Cameron Mitchell Restaurants

Features of the ManageFirst books

We have designed the ManageFirst books to enhance your ability to learn and retain important information that is critical to this restaurant and foodservice industry function. Here are the key features you will find within this book.

BEGINNING EACH BOOK

Real Manager

This is your opportunity to meet a professional who is currently working in the field associated with the book's topic. This person's story will help you gain insight into the responsibilities related to his or her position, as well as the training and educational history linked to it. You will also see the daily and cumulative impact this position has on an operation, and receive advice from a person who has successfully met the challenges of being a manager.

BEGINNING EACH CHAPTER

Inside This Chapter

Chapter content is organized under these major headings.

Learning Objectives

Learning objectives identify what you should be able to do after completing each chapter. These objectives are linked to the required tasks a manager must be able to perform in relation to the function discussed in the book.

Case Study

Each chapter begins with a brief story about the kind of situations that a manager may encounter in the course of his or her work. The story is followed by one or two questions to prompt student discussions about the topics contained within the chapter.

Key Terms

These terms are important for thorough understanding of the chapter's content. They are highlighted throughout the chapter, where they are explicitly defined or their meaning is made clear within the paragraphs in which they appear.

THROUGHOUT EACH CHAPTER

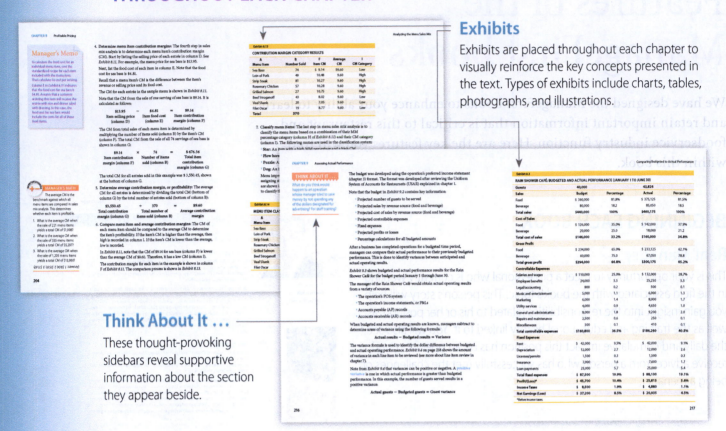

Exhibits

Exhibits are placed throughout each chapter to visually reinforce the key concepts presented in the text. Types of exhibits include charts, tables, photographs, and illustrations.

Think About It ...

These thought-provoking sidebars reveal supportive information about the section they appear beside.

AT THE END OF EACH CHAPTER

Application Exercises and Review Your Learning

These multiple-choice or open- or close-ended questions or problems are designed to test your knowledge of the concepts presented in the chapter. These questions have been aligned with the objectives and should provide you with an opportunity to practice or apply the content that supports these objectives. If you have difficulty answering the Review Your Learning questions, you should review the content further.

AT THE END OF THE BOOK

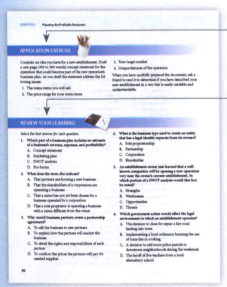

Field Project

This real-world project gives you the valuable opportunity to apply many of the concepts you will learn in a competency guide. You will interact with industry practitioners, enhance your knowledge, and research, apply, analyze, evaluate, and report on your findings. It will provide you with an in-depth "reality check" of the policies and practices of this management function.

Geoffrey Hill
Vice President
Roark Capital Group

REAL MANAGER

Philosophy: **Focus on great results and solid personal relationships and everything else will take care of itself.**

MY BACKGROUND

I grew up in Buffalo, New York, and I'm a product of the Buffalo public school system. My dad was a mechanical engineer and my mom had her own drapery and window treatment business. We were not a privileged family, but my parents worked very hard to make sure we had a good situation.

My first job in hospitality was in high school, when I was a dish washer. Before that, I didn't know much about the industry—other than as a consumer. Looking back, the experience with that first job is what got me interested in the industry. It taught me teamwork, humility, and hard work—all things I enjoyed from playing team sports. I also loved the vibrancy of the restaurant and foodservice industry, seeing it firsthand in the kitchen. I found myself "charged up" by the energy and passion. The industry often has a bad rap as an entry-level employer, but many successful business leaders started the same way I did—washing dishes and busing tables.

MY CAREER PATH

I really didn't decide on a "career" until I started looking at colleges. I was being recruited by several Ivy League schools to play football. During my research and school visits, I discovered the Hotel and Restaurant School at Cornell. After digging into the program and meeting the faculty, I was hooked.

My first management experience was during one of my college summers. I was an evening shift manager-on-duty at a Holiday Inn. There, I learned firsthand how important leadership is to success in this field. We are an employee-intensive industry that still focuses more on people than technology to achieve results. Having someone turn over the keys to a business every night—as a young and inexperienced person—was a challenge. By treating the people I was working with correctly—with dignity and respect—I found that they wanted to help me be successful.

Remember: **Our industry is filled with people from very diverse backgrounds— all with different views, experiences, educational levels, and interests. If you can't lead this type of diversity, you should find a different industry.**

I took all of the basic classes in college, but after that, I focused on operations and development. From my job as a hotel general manager to that of president of the worldwide brand, Cinnabon, I could see how important it was to understand the principles of finance and accounting. Three years ago, I moved over to Roark Capital Group, the private equity owner of Cinnabon. Since then, I have been involved with acquisitions of restaurant companies—Wingstop, Corner Bakery, Il Fornaio, Auntie Anne's Pretzels, and Arby's—through our private equity fund.

Since arriving at Roark, I have come to appreciate even more the importance of finance and accounting. Instead of just looking at an operating P&L to see how the business is performing, I am now looking at everything from acquisition modeling and finance to credit leverage scenarios across our large portfolio of restaurant investments. While there are many more traditional private equity finance experts here at Roark, the experience I have had running businesses is invaluable. Having operating intuition allows me to look at financial scenarios differently than those who have had only financial and accounting experience. I would strongly suggest that anyone interested in hospitality finance or accounting make sure he or she truly understands how the business works.

Something I always think about: **Be true to the real outcome and never stop asking "why?" You can analyze the numbers in so many different ways that the results can almost say anything you want them to say. Use the numbers to tell the *real* story, not just the outcome you want.**

WHAT DOES THE FUTURE HOLD?

Technology will change our industry for the better. Operators will have more access to financial information quicker than ever before because of software developments. This will also eliminate the need for a large number of traditional accounting positions. However, what we *will* need are finance and accounting people who can make sense of the numbers and interpret the technology to help produce better results in the business.

MY ADVICE TO YOU

I was not able to continue my formal education after graduating from Cornell. While I would have liked to pursue my MBA, I was not in the financial position to do so after graduating. What I *did* do was focus on three basic things that have served me very well.

First, focus on results. Those who perform in this world get ahead. Of course, it goes without saying that those results must be developed with honesty and integrity. First, you have to perform; then you can expect to be given more responsibility.

Second, build great relationships inside and outside the organization. Find a mentor from whom you can learn and create internal fans who will want to help you succeed.

Third, keep learning. Just because you can't continue your formal education doesn't mean you have to stop learning. Use the people and other resources available to you to continue your education. Don't be afraid to say "I don't understand; please teach me."

1

Introduction to Accounting and Finance

INSIDE THIS CHAPTER

- **What Is Accounting?**
- **The Uniform System of Accounts**
- **Accounting Ethics**
- **Accounting Fundamentals**

CHAPTER LEARNING OBJECTIVES

After completing this chapter, you should be able to:

- Explain the purpose of accurate accounting.

- Describe the difference between cash accounting and accrual accounting.

- State the purpose of a Uniform System of Accounts.

- Describe the three components of the accounting equation.

- Explain the importance of Generally Accepted Accounting Principles (GAAP).

KEY TERMS

CASE STUDY

"How did the meeting go, Ted?" asked Veronica, the assistant manager of Walker's Gameday Steakhouse. Ted, the manager of the Gameday, had just returned from the monthly meeting with the restaurant's co-owners.

"Well, they were pleased our sales were up from last year," Ted said.

"So they were happy?" asked Veronica.

"Well, not exactly," said Ted. "Our costs were up, too."

"But our costs have to be up. We served more guests this year," said Veronica.

"I agree," replied Ted. "And I explained that. But they felt the costs were higher than they should have been, even with the extra guests we served. We didn't make as much profit as they had hoped."

1. What could cause a busy establishment to make less profit than it should?

2. How important do you think it is for managers to know exactly how much money is spent to generate an operation's weekly, monthly, and annual sales? What do you think could happen if they do not know?

WHAT IS ACCOUNTING?

The term accounting simply means "to count." Based on that definition, everyone who can count already is, or can be, an accountant. **Certified public accountants (CPAs)** are those who have been specially trained and, by passing a test, are certified as highly competent in the field of business accounting. For managers in the restaurant and foodservice industry, however, accounting simply means counting, or accounting for, the money received and spent operating a restaurant or foodservice facility or company.

Accounting is based on mathematics. Some managers who find mathematics to be difficult may likewise find accounting to be challenging at first. But all managers must understand how to perform important accounting tasks. Effective managers learn how to perform them well.

The Purpose of Accounting

The purpose of accounting is to provide useful information. If it is to be useful, accounting information must possess specific characteristics:

- It must be easy to obtain.
- It must be accurate.
- It must be timely.
- It must be easy to understand.

In the restaurant and foodservice business, accounting is used to keep track of an operation's cash and other valuable property, known as assets. Assets are the things (including cash) that have value. This means accounting for the operation's **revenue**, which is the amount of money generated from the sale of products and services. It also means accounting for **expenses**, which are costs incurred in the operation of the business, as well as liabilities, which are the debts the business incurs in the process of doing business. When a business knows its revenue and its expense, it can determine its profits using the following formula:

$$\textbf{Revenue} - \textbf{Expense} = \textbf{Profit}$$

Accounting for a business begins long before it opens its doors to customers. For example, if a new businessperson needs to get a loan to begin operations, he or she may need to ask a bank or other lenders for money (see *Exhibit 1.1*). Before agreeing to a loan, the lender will likely want to know several things:

- How much money will be borrowed?
- What will the money be used for?
- Where will the money come from to repay the loan?
- How quickly will the loan be repaid?

THINK ABOUT IT . . .

You are an accountant every time you consider how much money you earn and have in the bank. What would happen if you stopped keeping track of your personal income and spending?

Exhibit 1.1

To answer each of these questions, business owners must add up all the business expenses that will be incurred, and then subtract that amount from anticipated business revenue or other money available to spend. In so doing, the owners are counting, or accounting, by using basic mathematical rules of addition and subtraction. The ways that accountants add, subtract, multiply, and divide numbers is the same way any other person performs these same tasks. The specific numbers that are added, subtracted, multiplied, and divided are carefully selected by accountants to help them better understand particular parts of their business.

Performing accounting tasks accurately is important to many who are involved in a business:

- Owners are interested in the current financial condition of their operations. They are also interested in what future business will be like.
- Lenders to a business are interested in the ability of a business to repay its loans.
- Investors are interested in the amount to be earned on their investments.
- Managers are interested in the best way to efficiently run the business.
- Suppliers are interested in the ability of a business to pay its bills.

Accounting is an important tool of business used to gather information. Like the use of many tools, increased use of the tool makes the user more comfortable and skilled when using it.

It is important to understand that it is not the purpose of accounting to *make* management decisions. Managers make management decisions. Managers use accounting information to help them make *better* decisions for their businesses. To understand the value of accounting, consider the kinds of information that would be needed in each of these situations:

- A manager wants to put a new item on the menu and must decide the price at which it will be sold.
- A manager wants to buy a new piece of equipment and wants to know if the operation can afford to purchase it.
- A manager wants to know if raises can be granted to employees and still permit the operation to meet established profit targets.
- A manager wants to know how much profit is made each time one serving of an operation's best-selling menu item is purchased by a guest.
- A manager wants to know if it makes good business sense to open the establishment one hour earlier and close it one hour later.
- A manager wants to know if it is better to clean the operation's windows with current staff or hire an outside cleaning company to do it instead.

In each case, accounting data will not make the manager's decision, but they will provide the manager with needed decision-making information.

Manager's Memo

Few restaurants and foodservice operations have the luxury of having a full-time accountant on-site. While a professional accountant may be employed to file the taxes of a business or to prepare other required accounting documents, managers perform many important accounting tasks.

Like many other management skills, the ability to understand and apply accounting concepts will improve with experience. Pleasing guests and preparing great food and beverage products are critical tasks essential to success in a restaurant or foodservice business. Knowing how to properly account for the income and expenses associated with performing those critical tasks is also essential to business success.

THINK ABOUT IT . . .

Accounting information must be accurate, timely, and easy to understand. What would happen if information about the amount of money currently reported in your bank accounts was not accurate?

How Managers Use Accounting

Managers use accounting in a variety of ways. In fact there are even unique fields, or branches of accounting, that are of special importance to managers:

- Financial accounting
- Cost accounting
- Managerial accounting

FINANCIAL ACCOUNTING

Financial accounting is the branch of accounting that specializes in recording business transactions. A **business transaction** occurs when a product or service is purchased or sold. In a restaurant or foodservice operation, the sale of a meal or a beverage is a business transaction. In a beverage operation, the sale of a drink is a business transaction. The purchase of a needed supply item is yet another transaction. Restaurant and foodservice operations conduct hundreds of business transactions each day:

- Raw ingredients are purchased to make menu items (*Exhibit 1.2*).

- Employees are paid to prepare food and serve guests.

- Energy used to power the operation is purchased from utility companies.

- Food and beverage sales are made to guests.

- Taxes due are collected and paid.

Financial accountants record and report on all types of an operation's business transactions.

Exhibit 1.2

COST ACCOUNTING

Cost accounting is the branch of accounting that specializes in recording the expenses of a business. Recall that a business expense is a cost incurred in the operation of the business. Managers of food and beverage operations incur costs when they purchase the ingredients for those menu items and beverages they sell to guests. But managers also incur many other costs, both large and small. Some examples are easy to recognize:

- Building rent
- Utilities
- Advertising
- Employee labor

- Uniforms
- Dishware and glassware
- Equipment

Other examples are less obvious:

- Insurance premiums
- Property taxes
- Payroll taxes
- Internet access fees
- Office expenses
- Cleaning supplies (*Exhibit 1.3*)
- Menu printing costs

The specific types and the amounts of expense incurred by hospitality businesses differ based on the business. For example, if an establishment has a fireplace, firewood would be an operating expense. An establishment without a fireplace would not have that expense. While the specific expenses incurred by businesses are many and are varied, cost accountants carefully record and report on all of them.

MANAGERIAL ACCOUNTING

Managerial accounting is the field of accounting that addresses the specific financial information managers need to make good decisions about how to operate their businesses. Managerial accounting, which is also known as management accounting, is the branch of accounting of greatest importance to most restaurant and foodservice managers.

The types of questions that can be answered by information gathered by managerial accountants are many:

- How much money is spent by each guest visiting an operation?
- At what time of the day does an operation generate the majority of its revenue?
- What were the total costs of operating the business last month? Last year?
- Are sales increasing or decreasing? By how much?
- Should menu prices be increased? Decreased?
- Is the operation spending an appropriate amount for food? Beverages? Labor? Other expenses?

In each of these cases, managerial accounting information can help managers better understand their businesses.

Another important area of accounting is tax accounting, or the recording and reporting of taxes to be paid. A fifth area is auditing, which is the independent verification of a business's financial records. Each field of accounting is important because it provides business owners and managers with the critical information they need to do a good job operating their businesses.

Accounting Systems

Depending on the size of a business, the owners may choose to implement a centralized or a decentralized system of accounting. In a centralized accounting system, financial information from a business is transmitted—for example by mail, email, or network, or by posting to the Web—to a central location, where it may be recorded and then analyzed by management. It may also be combined with other operations for analysis about a group of businesses.

To illustrate why some businesses operate under a centralized system, assume a person owns 10 establishments in California. The owner's office is in New York City. If the owner wanted to know, on a daily basis, the combined revenue for the 10 operations, the owner would likely want each of the operations to report its previous day's sales to the New York office. When the information is received, the revenue of the 10 operations would be added together to yield one number that represents the previous day's total sales.

Centralized accounting is most used in chain-operated or multiunit restaurant or foodservice companies. When managers operate in a centralized accounting system, it is their job to provide accurate financial information, in a timely manner, to the central accounting office.

In a decentralized accounting system, the manager usually takes a larger accounting role. When operating with a decentralized accounting system, a manager collects accounting data from the operation and then records, reports, and analyzes those data at the same site.

Regardless of whether a centralized or decentralized accounting system is in place, businesses use either a cash accounting method or an accrual accounting method to record and report their financial information. A cash accounting method recognizes business income as it is received and business expenses as they are paid. An accrual method does not. An accrual accounting method recognizes and records revenues when they are earned, rather than when the cash is received.

To illustrate the cash accounting method, assume the owner of a restaurant had revenue of $2,000 on a specific day. On that same day the manager wrote a check for $800 for food. When using the cash accounting method, the revenue would be reported as $2,000. Business expense for the same time period would be recorded as $800. This would be true even if all the food purchased that day was not sold on that day.

Under the accrual accounting method, expenses are matched with the revenues they have generated rather than the time when the expenses are paid.

To be even more precise, under the accrual method, managers recognize revenue when all the events that establish their rights to receive the revenue have occurred and when the amount of income to be received is known with reasonable accuracy. Then, if the amount actually received differs from the estimated revenue, an adjustment to revenue is made when the payment is actually received.

To illustrate, if a guest purchases $100 worth of food and pays by check, the accrual accounting method calls for recording the $100 in revenue on the day of the guest's purchase. Assume, however, that the check is later rejected by the bank. It is returned to the establishment because of insufficient funds. In that case a correction, or adjustment to revenue, would be made in the operation's financial records.

Similarly, the accrual accounting method recognizes an item of expense when the operation becomes liable for it, not when they pay for it. Becoming liable means that all events have occurred that establish the expense obligation. For example, products like food and beverages have been delivered or services, such as lawn mowing or snow plowing, have been performed.

To illustrate, assume a manager buys food and has it delivered in December. The manager does not pay the bill for the food until January. In this case, the entire food expense would initially be recorded as a December expense, not a January expense, because it was received in December.

However, to enhance reporting accuracy, when preparing this operation's end-of-month or end-of-year financial reports, the rules of accrual accounting require that only the cost of food actually used in December be reported as a December expense. In most cases, restaurant or foodservice operations are required to use the accrual accounting method, and doing so makes good business sense.

Manager's Memo

A cash accounting method is the type most people use to manage their personal finances. Income is recorded as it is received in paychecks or other sources. Expenses for food, clothing, or entertainment are recognized and recorded when they are paid. The system is simple to use but sometimes does not do a very accurate job of reporting true income and expense.

For example, assume your rent is $1,000 per month. You pay it on the first of the month. Do you think you had $1,000 of rent expense on that single day, but no rent cost for any of the other days in the month? How would you go about determining your actual daily rent cost?

RESTAURANT TECHNOLOGY

Today's restaurant and foodservice managers can choose from a variety of accounting system vendors. These vendors supply complete accounting systems that help managers electronically record and report the revenue and expenses of a business.

In increasing numbers of cases, these systems allow managers to upload their financial data to the cloud. Cloud computing is the delivery of computing services where shared resources, software, and information are provided over the Internet. Managers can upload data to a secure cloud-based Web site. The data can then be remotely accessed by anyone with access to the same Web site and proper login credentials. In this way, important accounting information can be easily shared with those who need access to it and at any time they wish.

Exhibit 1.4

THE UNIFORM SYSTEM OF ACCOUNTS

Owners and managers of businesses are not usually required by law to record their financial transactions in only one way. They are free to use the accounting systems and procedures they prefer and that help them most. These may be systems they develop themselves or that they buy from companies that supply complete accounting systems.

While owners and managers are not required to use standardized accounting systems, there are very specific requirements about the information their records must contain. This information relates to the taxes a business has collected on sales made to customers as well as the taxes owed by the business. Federal, state, or local governments can levy these taxes. Each of these governmental entities may require businesses to supply very specific information that is used to calculate the amount of taxes that must be paid.

Because the reporting and paying of taxes is so important, business owners typically require that their managers collect and report financial information in a way that consistently makes it easy to comply with all applicable tax requirements. They can better do so when they use uniform accounting procedures designed especially for their businesses. The **Uniform System of Accounts for Restaurants (USAR)** is one such system in wide use.

An account is a device accountants use to record specific information about a business. For example, a revenue account is used to record information about revenue, or money collected. Similarly, expense accounts are used to record the costs incurred in the operation of a business.

The number and name of the accounts used varies by establishment. For example, in a typical establishment serving alcoholic beverages the operation's owner might want to have one revenue account for recording food sales and another account for recording alcoholic beverage sales (*Exhibit 1.4*). In a quick service restaurant that offers drive-through service, the owner may want to have a revenue account for drive-through sales and another for sales made to guests who come into the restaurant.

The number of different revenue and expense accounts that can be created and used is determined by an operation's owners and managers. Each account should be created to provide valuable financial information and must make good sense for the business.

The USAR was developed for the National Restaurant Association by a professional accounting firm. The system helps managers by providing a format that can be used in nearly all restaurant and foodservice operations. Its use also allows owners and managers to use information from two or more different operations to compare the financial performance of one to the other. Its consistent use also allows managers to compare their performance in one time period to that of a previous time period.

ACCOUNTING ETHICS

Ethics refers to the behavior of one person toward another person. Ethical behavior is based on a person's view of what is right or wrong. A manager's view of right, wrong, good, or bad actions are shaped by his or her personal life experience. As a result, ethical views can be influenced by others, but ultimately they come from a person's sense of honesty, integrity, and fairness.

A manager's ethics will likely be similar to those of many people they know, but can be very different from some others they encounter. All managers interact with owners, co-workers, employees, customers, and suppliers. Today's workforce features a greater diversity than perhaps any time in the past. That means diversity of race, age, nationality, religion, gender, sexual orientation, and even ethics.

In fact, many of the same characteristics that make people different also make their views of right and wrong behavior different. Managers are likely to encounter individuals whose opinions about right and wrong behavior may be quite different from their own. Managers may feel challenged to hold firm to their own ethical views while at the same time acknowledging and respecting those individuals who may hold valid ethical views that are different from their own.

Society expects all professionals to act responsibly and ethically. This is true of doctors, lawyers, and those in many other professions. In fact, some professional groups have detailed ethical codes of conduct to which their members must adhere. A **code of conduct** is a document explaining employee behavioral expectations including company values, rules, principles, confidentiality, and loyalty. Some companies have employees read and sign an agreement that they will uphold the company's ethical code of conduct.

Restaurant and foodservice managers are professionals. Because they are professionals, they are expected to perform their duties, including their accounting duties, in ways that are ethical whether or not their companies have a formal code of conduct in place.

Several factors can contribute to ethical failures when reporting financial information:

- Self-interest
- Failure to be objective
- Poor judgment
- Lack of information
- Poor training
- Improper direction from leadership or ownership

Manager's Memo

In the restaurant and foodservice industry most managers use the terms *revenue, income,* and *sales* interchangeably.

A manager may state:

Our revenue yesterday was $1,000.

or

Our income yesterday was $1,000.

or

Our sales yesterday were $1,000.

All the statements mean that customers spent $1,000 yesterday in the business.

The terms *revenue, income,* and *sales,* however, can have slightly different meaning to accountants:

Revenue: This generally refers to income achieved from the business's normal operations.

Income: Some managers use this word interchangeably with *revenues.* Others use the word to signify a "net," or final amount of income from normal business operations. When used this way, revenue minus expenses equals net income.

Sales: Some managers use this word interchangeably with *revenues.* Others use the word to signify a specific number of units sold—for example, "we sold 10 orders of sirloin steaks last night."

Manager's Memo

The importance of reporting financial information in a uniform way can be easily illustrated. Assume you have a job and are paid every week. You are asked "How much money did you make last week?" Is the correct answer to this question the amount you were paid before taxes or after taxes? What would happen if one week you answered the question the first way, but the next week you answered it the second way?

Similarly, imagine what would happen if managers of two different restaurant or foodservice operations did not use the same "language" when talking to each other while using words such as *sales*, *revenue*, *costs*, and *expenses*.

In all cases, and regardless of their backgrounds, managers must exhibit ethical behavior when performing accounting work. The very nature of accounting requires a high level of ethics. Owners, lenders, managers, employees, and suppliers rely on a company's accurate financial records to make many decisions. Readers of a company's financial documents know that the ethics of the person preparing the documents is the most critical factor in determining the truthfulness and reliability of the information they contain. For that reason, lawful and ethical behavior on the part of those preparing financial documents is essential.

ACCOUNTING FUNDAMENTALS

Owners and managers who prepare financial documents for a business must understand key accounting fundamentals:

- Bookkeeping versus accounting
- The accounting equation
- Generally Accepted Accounting Principles (GAPP)
- Accounting arithmetic

Bookkeeping versus Accounting

Financial managers make a distinction between bookkeeping and accounting. Bookkeeping means the recording, but not the analyzing, of financial transactions. Bookkeeping produces critical information that will be used in accounting and analyzed by managers. When, for example, a manager records the revenue achieved by a business on a specific day, he or she is performing a bookkeeping function.

Exhibit 1.5

In most cases, the revenue figures from each day's sales would be summed for a week, a month, or a year. The resulting numbers would be analyzed by managers as they perform their managerial accounting functions (*Exhibit 1.5*). From accurate bookkeeping entries managers can assess important facts:

- Did revenue meet prior expectations?
- Is revenue increasing or decreasing?
- Is revenue higher or lower than a previous time period?
- Is revenue sufficient to meet profit goals?

Note that the bookkeeping entry itself did not provide the answer to these key questions. But accurate bookkeeping is essential. If the proper bookkeeping entry was not made, the answers to these and other key management questions will not be known. If the entry was made incorrectly, the answers to key questions may also be incorrect.

Sound bookkeeping provides the foundation for sound accounting decisions. It is not possible to make a meaningful analysis of a business's financial position if the data supplied by bookkeepers are not accurate. In most restaurant and foodservice operations, managers perform both bookkeeping and accounting tasks and they must do each well.

The Accounting Equation

To properly portray the financial standing of a business, accountants record information about assets, the items the business owns. These can include items such as land, buildings, supplies, and cash in the bank. Accountants also record the liabilities of a business. Liabilities are what a business owes to others. The difference between what a business owns (assets) and what it owes (liabilities) is called owner's equity:

Assets − Liabilities = Owner's equity

Owner's equity is the claim that owners of a business have on the business assets.

Accountants use the accounting equation to express the relationship between a business's assets, liabilities, and owner's equity:

Assets = Liabilities + Owner's equity

Using basic algebra the same accounting equation can also be expressed as:

Assets − Owner's equity = Liabilities
Assets − Liabilities = Owner's equity

To illustrate the use of the equation, assume Sara is the owner of an establishment. The operation has total assets of $1,000,000. This includes land, the building, and the equipment in the building. It also includes the food, beverages, and supplies owned by the establishment.

Sara owes her bank $700,000. She owes her suppliers $50,000. Her total liabilities are $750,000:

$700,000	+	$50,000	=	$750,000
Owed to bank		Owed to supplier		Total liability

Manager's Memo

News organizations consistently report cases of businesspeople who act unethically or even illegally in preparing financial documents. Managers trying to determine whether an action they might take when reporting financial information is ethical or not can ask themselves some key questions:

- Is the action legal?
- Does the action follow company policy?
- Does the action make the information reported easier or harder to understand?
- Am I being honest?
- Am I trying to disguise the truth?

How managers answer each of these key questions can help them decide whether their own actions are ethical.

THINK ABOUT IT . . .

You buy a car for $10,000, putting $2,000 down and taking a bank loan for the remaining $8,000. You will repay the loan over three years. How much of the car do you actually own on the day that you purchase it?

MANAGER'S MATH

Calculate the missing portion of each accounting equation in the examples presented:

1. _____ = $500,000 + $1,000,000
    Assets   Liabilities   Owner's equity

2. $1,500,000 = _____ + $1,250,000
    Assets   Liabilities   Owner's equity

3. $1,000,000 = $500,000 + _____
    Assets   Liabilities   Owner's equity

Note that when any two of the formulas' components are known, the third component can be calculated.

(Answers: 1. $1,500,000. 2. $250,000. 3. $500,000)

Using the accounting equation, Sara has $250,000 owner's equity in her business.

Liabilities + Owner's equity = Assets

Or

($700,000 + $50,000) + $250,000 = $1,000,000
Owed to bank   Owed to supplier   Owner's equity   Total assets

Or

$750,000 + $250,000 = $1,000,000
Total liability   Owner's equity   Total assets

Generally Accepted Accounting Principles (GAAP)

Managers who read financial information must have faith that the collection and reporting systems used to prepare it were accurate, consistent, and logical. If the system of collecting and reporting information is inconsistent or unclear, the reader of the information may be confused or misled and may make poor management decisions as a result.

Because one important aspect of accounting information is that it must be easily understood, financial information is recorded and reported using **Generally Accepted Accounting Principles (GAAP)**. GAAP are standards and procedures that have been widely adopted and used by those responsible for preparing business financial statements.

GAAP are designed for the purpose of ensuring clarity and uniformity in financial reporting. In the United States, GAAP are developed by the Financial Accounting Standards Board (FASB). The goal of FASB is to improve accounting practices and make financial records easier to understand.

There are many accounting principles in GAAP. Some are especially important to restaurant and foodservice owners and managers:

- Distinct business principle
- Cost principle
- Consistency principle
- Matching principle
- Time period principle
- Full disclosure principle

DISTINCT BUSINESS PRINCIPLE

The **distinct business principle** is important because it states that a business's financial records cannot be mixed with the personal financial records of its owners. Regardless of the size of a business, its records must reflect only the financial transactions of that business. This is true even when the business is owned by a single individual.

To understand the importance of the distinct business principle, imagine that an establishment operates in a state in which taxes are due on the profits achieved by each business. Assume further that the owners of this operation routinely purchased steaks. Some of the steaks were sold to the establishment's guests, and some were taken home to be eaten by the operation's owners and by members of their families. In this scenario, the profits of the establishment would be reduced by the value of the steaks taken for the owners' personal use.

Recall that in this example the state in which this establishment operates assesses taxes on profits. As a result, the tax due to be paid would appear lower than it really should be. If the owners of this operation paid taxes on the reduced profits shown, they could be in violation of the tax laws of their state. By carefully using the distinct business principle, those preparing the financial records of this establishment could help ensure that its owners were not in violation and that the records accurately reflected only the actual expenses of the business.

COST PRINCIPLE

The cost principle is important because it states that accountants must value the assets and liabilities of a business at their actual cost. To better understand the critical nature of this principle, assume an establishment purchases steaks from a meat supplier. The steaks are purchased for $5 each. The steaks will be sold for $20 each. What is the value of the steaks to this establishment?

Clearly, the operation hopes to sell each of the steaks to customers for $20 each. From that perspective, the value of the steaks is $20 each. The establishment, however, paid only $5 per steak. From that perspective, the steaks have a value of $5 each. The cost principle comes into play in this situation and states that the steaks should be valued at $5.

It is important to note that the use of this or any other GAAP is not required by law. The use of GAAP, however, does help business owners comply with the many laws that are based on a business's financial performance. The cost principle is one such way of helping to ensure compliance.

Manager's Memo

Another related GAAP states that the value of an asset or liability be expressed in the currency that is primarily used by the business. For example, in the United States, most businesses record their financial information in dollars. International restaurant and foodservice companies, those companies operating units in China, Russia, and the Middle East, for example, may have to convert financial information from operating units in those countries into U.S. dollars before reporting it.

CONSISTENCY PRINCIPLE

The cash and accrual methods of accounting record revenue and expense in different ways. Most businesses use the accrual accounting method. The consistency principle states that regardless of the method used, the same method should be used each time financial information is recorded.

To illustrate why, consider the operation manager who must pay a fire insurance premium to an insurance company once per year. Assume the premium is $12,000. Under the cash accounting method the expense would be recorded on the day of the year the premium was paid. If the premium was paid on January 1 of the year, the expense would be recorded as a January expense.

When using the accrual accounting method, the premium would be recorded as an equal cost each month, so that the total premium amount would be divided by 12 to reflect the fact that the cost of fire insurance is actually incurred monthly. Under the two systems, the reporting of the business's monthly expenses would vary as shown in *Exhibit 1.6*.

Exhibit 1.6

EXPENSE REPORTING: CASH ACCOUNTING METHOD VERSUS ACCRUAL ACCOUNTING METHOD

Fire Insurance Expense	Cash Accounting Method	Accrual Accounting Method
January	$ 12,000	$ 1,000
February		1,000
March		1,000
April		1,000
May		1,000
June		1,000
July		1,000
August		1,000
September		1,000
October		1,000
November		1,000
December		1,000
Total	**$12,000**	**$12,000**

Mixing the use of the cash accounting method and accrual accounting method is not permitted under the consistency principle. Only when the consistency principle is followed can readers of a business's financial information truly understand the revenue generated and costs incurred by a business during a specific time period.

MATCHING PRINCIPLE

The matching principle applies only to those operations using the accrual accounting method. That accounting method requires revenue to be recorded when earned and expenses to be recorded when incurred. The purpose of the matching principle is to match revenues achieved with the costs required to earn the revenue.

To illustrate, when the owners of a restaurant or foodservice operation purchase tables, it is with the expectation that the tables will help generate business income over the entire useful life of the tables (*Exhibit 1.7*). It would not make sense to record as an expense the entire cost of the tables on the day they were purchased, as would be done under the cash accounting method.

Exhibit 1.7

Rather, a portion of the cost of the tables might be charged for each month the tables were used. Thus, if a table had a useful life of 10 years, then 1/10 of the cost of the table might be recorded as an expense each year to match the cost of the table with the yearly revenue the table would help generate. That amount could be divided by 12 to calculate the monthly cost of purchasing the tables.

While the rules are very detailed, in certain cases, and if an expense is very small, the matching principle can be disregarded. For example, assume a manager buys a pen for $1 and the pen is expected to last for several months before it runs out of ink. In this case, the amount of money involved is so small that it makes little sense to try to match the monthly costs of the pen to its expected life.

The rules related to matching revenues to expenses can be complex. In all cases, however, the matching principle encourages those who record financial information to do their best to tie their revenues directly to the costs of creating the revenue.

Managers can prepare financial reports that summarize business transactions that occurred in one day, one week, one month, one year, or longer. The time period principle states that a business must clearly identify the time for which business transactions have been reported. For example, if a business wishes to issue a financial report for a single month of activity, the month and year of the activity should be clearly stated on that financial report.

In many cases, businesses report their financial transactions on a monthly basis as well as on a fiscal year basis. A **fiscal year** is any consecutive 12-month period. In many cases, a business will define its fiscal year as being a January to December traditional calendar year. Fiscal years, however, need not follow calendar years. In all cases, a year-end fiscal report summarizes the financial transactions that have occurred in the prior 12 months.

Financial reports that address less than a fiscal year are very common. For example, owners and managers may want to know about their revenue achieved and expenses incurred on a weekly, monthly, or quarterly basis. Regardless of the accounting period addressed, the time period principle requires that it be clearly stated.

FULL DISCLOSURE PRINCIPLE

The goal of all good financial reporting is to give the report's readers as clear an indication as possible of the actual information reported. For that reason, reported revenue should be accurate. Reported expenses should also be accurate and should be reported according to the appropriate GAAP. Doing so is good, but those who prepare financial reports for a business must do even more.

The full disclosure principle requires those who prepare financial reports to include any financial or other information a reader may need to *fully* understand the report being read. As a result, those who prepare financial summaries should include in those summaries all information that would affect a reader's understanding of the statements. The interpretation of this principle can be subjective at times because the amount of information that *could* be provided is potentially very large.

To reduce the amount of disclosure, it is customary for accountants to disclose only the information about events that are likely to have a material, or significant, impact on the business's financial position or financial results. Examples of items to disclose include any changes from prior accounting methods used, the existence of pending lawsuits, or the existence of significant tax liabilities that are in dispute but may need to be paid in the future. Any disclosed items may be included in the financial documents themselves or added to the documents as supplemental notes or reports.

GAAP of all types are the rules, procedures, and standards that preparers of financial documents use to make their work clear to others. Restaurant and foodservice managers and business owners are not typically professional accountants. As a result, they are not usually familiar with all of the details of GAAP and accurate financial reporting. Fortunately, for those situations when managers are unfamiliar with some aspect of report preparation, CPAs are readily available to provide needed help and guidance.

Manager's Memo

Auditing is the branch of accounting that independently verifies the accuracy of an organization's financial reports. When those persons conducting the audit are employed by the organization, it is called an internal audit. When those conducting the audit are not directly employed by the organization, it is called an external audit. Both internal and external auditors can play valuable roles in improving an organization's accounting and reporting procedures.

All audits are designed to strengthen an organization's accounting systems. External audits, because they are performed by those outside an organization, are especially helpful in detecting fraud or unethical behavior on the part of employees.

Accounting Arithmetic

Managerial accountants use the same basic math skills as restaurant and foodservice managers. A quick review of some basic terms and techniques used by both groups may be useful.

ADDITION

Addition is one of the four basic arithmetic operations. The others are subtraction, multiplication, and division. *Summing*, *plus*, *adding*, and *totaling* are all terms commonly used by managers to describe addition. In accounting work, addition is designated by the use of the plus sign (+).

Some examples of objects added by restaurant and foodservice managers include revenue amounts, costs, wages paid to employees, and quantities of foods and beverages. It is important to recall that, when using addition, the order in which the objects are added does not matter. Thus, $4 + 6 + 8 + 10 = 28$ and $10 + 8 + 6 + 4 = 28$.

SUBTRACTION

Minus, *subtracting*, *taking away*, and *reducing* are terms commonly used by managers to describe the subtraction process. Subtraction is designated by the use of the minus sign (−). When using subtraction, managers begin with a known value and remove a second known value from it. The amount remaining is known as the difference. Thus, in the formula $10 − 6 = 4$, 10 is the first known value, 6 is the amount removed, and 4 is the difference.

Like addition, typical examples of values subtracted by managers include revenue amounts and costs and quantities of foods and beverages. It is important to recall that, when using subtraction, the order in which two values are listed *does* matter. Thus, $10 − 6 = 4$, but $6 − 10 = −4$.

MULTIPLICATION

Multiplying and *times* are terms commonly used by managers to describe the multiplication process. Multiplication is designated by the use of the times sign (×). On most computer keyboards and keypads the asterisk (*) designates multiplication.

When using multiplication, managers begin with two known values, called *factors*, and calculate a result known as the *product*. Thus, in the formula $4 \times 8 = 32$, 4 is a factor, 8 is a factor, and 32 is the product. When multiplying, the order of the factors does not affect the product. Thus, $4 \times 8 = 32$ and $8 \times 4 = 32$.

DIVISION

Dividing or *divided by* are terms commonly used by managers to describe division. The division of two numbers is typically designated in one of two ways. The division sign (÷) is used in, for example, the formula $8 \div 4 = 2$.

A second way to write the same formula is to signify that one number, called the *numerator,* or dividend, is above or on top, of the other number, called the *denominator,* or *divisor.* The number resulting after division is the quotient, or remainder:

$$\frac{8}{4} = 2 \quad \text{or} \quad 8/4 = 2$$

In these examples, 8 is the numerator, 4 is the denominator, and 2 is the quotient. When dividing, the placement of a number as the numerator or denominator does affect the quotient. Thus, $32 \div 8 = 4.0$, but $8 \div 32 = 0.25$

Because division often results in fractional or less than whole numbers as the quotient, an understanding of fractions, percentages, and ratios is also helpful to most restaurant and foodservice managers.

PERCENTAGES AND RATIOS

As managers use addition, subtraction, multiplication, and division in their accounting work, they frequently encounter fractional numbers. The methods used to add, subtract, multiply, and divide fractional numbers are beyond the scope of this review. Managers should, however, be familiar with the various ways fractional numbers are presented when performing accounting tasks.

The simplest form of expressing a fractional number is in its decimal form. Other forms include the percentage and ratio forms. For example, if the fractional number to be expressed is one-half, these are the ways that value can be written:

> ½ **(fraction form)**
>
> 0.50 **(decimal form)**
>
> 50% **(percentage form)**
>
> 1:2 **(ratio form)**

In each case, the fractional value expressed equals one-half. Accountants commonly use each of these fractional forms when completing various aspects of their work. The following list indicates the types of percentages and ratios that managers will encounter in this book:

- Market share ratios (chapter 2)
- Revenue source percentages (chapter 3)
- Food and beverage cost percentages (chapter 3)
- Other expense percentages (chapter 4)
- Labor cost percentages (chapter 7)
- Pricing methods, including ratio pricing (chapter 8)
- Percentage variance calculations (chapter 9)
- Returns on investment (chapter 10)

SUMMARY

1. **Explain the purpose of accurate accounting.**

Accurate accounting is important to all business owners and managers. Major fields of accounting include financial, cost, managerial, tax, and audit. Accurate financial information is critical to the precise reporting of business transactions. Cost accountants can report precise cost information only if their work is accurate. Managers depend on truthful and easy to understand managerial accounting information to make good decisions about operating their businesses. Tax accounts must have the information they need to pay only the taxes legally due by a business. Auditors must do their work carefully if they are to ensure the overall accuracy of a business's accounting systems.

2. **Describe the difference between cash accounting and accrual accounting.**

Cash and accrual are the two main accounting methods. A cash accounting method is one in which managers record income as it is physically received and business expenses as they are physically paid. In the accrual accounting method, income is recognized and recorded when it is earned, regardless of when the resulting cash is received. Similarly, under the accrual accounting method, expenses are matched with the revenue they have generated and are recorded at the time they are incurred, rather than the time when the expense is paid. Most restaurant and foodservice operations use the accrual method of accounting.

3. **State the purpose of the Uniform System of Accounts.**

All businesses are required to report and pay taxes due. As a result, business owners record and report financial information in a way that consistently makes it easy to comply with all applicable taxing authorities. Doing so is simplified when they choose to use a "uniform" system of accounts. Different businesses have different financial reporting needs. The Uniform System of Accounts for Restaurants (USAR) was developed specifically for restaurants and foodservice operations. When it is used, owners and managers can share and analyze financial information across businesses and across time, as well as know about the taxes they must pay.

4. **Describe the three components of the accounting equation.**

The accounting equation is Assets = Liabilities + Owner's equity. Assets are those things owned by a business. They can include items such as land, buildings, equipment, and supplies. Liabilities are the debts of the business. These can include loans that must be repaid as well as other obligations for payment. Owner's equity is the amount of assets less the amount owed to others for the assets. Stated another way, owner's equity less a business's assets is the total amount a business owes to those who do not own the business.

5. **Explain the importance of Generally Accepted Accounting Principles (GAAP).**

Readers of financial information must be convinced that the reporting systems used are accurate, consistent, and logical. If the system is not, the reader may be confused or misled. To help ensure that those who prepare financial documents do so in a proper way, the use of Generally Accepted Accounting Principles (GAAP) is recommended. GAAP are designed for the purpose of ensuring clarity and consistency in the reporting of financial information.

APPLICATION EXERCISE

On December 31 of last year Armando calculated the following information for his business, the J-Town Bar and Grill. Using the data provided, create the profit formula and the accounting equation that reflects his operation's financial results and standing at the end of that year.

Assets (at year-end)	$3,650,000
Revenue (for the year)	1,235,500
Expenses (for the year)	1,006,250
Liabilities (at year-end)	2,175,000

REVIEW YOUR LEARNING

Select the best answer for each question.

1. Which branch of accounting primarily addresses the specific information managers need to make good decisions about how to operate their businesses?

   A. Managerial accounting

   B. Cost accounting

   C. Tax accounting

   D. Auditing

2. Which branch of accounting primarily addresses the recording of business transactions?

   A. Tax accounting

   B. Managerial accounting

   C. Financial accounting

   D. Cost accounting

3. Which accounting method recognizes expenses when they are paid rather than when they are incurred?

   A. Accrual

   B. Cash

   C. Cost

   D. Expense

4. Which person is primarily responsible for ensuring the accuracy of financial documents?

   A. The one reading the documents

   B. The one preparing the documents

   C. The one analyzing the documents

   D. The one paying taxes based on the documents

5. Rhamey owns his own establishment. His assets are $5,000,000 and his liabilities are $3,500,000. What is his owner's equity?

   A. $150,000

   B. $1,500,000

   C. $1,800,000

   D. $8,500,000

6. Adrianna owns her own operation. Her liabilities are $50,000 and her owner's equity is $450,000. What are the assets of the business?

   A. $40,000

   B. $50,000

   C. $400,000

   D. $500,000

7. Lawrence owns his own establishment. His assets are $750,000 and his owner's equity is $450,000. What are the liabilities of the business?

   A. $30,000

   B. $120,000

   C. $300,000

   D. $1,200,000

8. Which GAAP would be violated if the manager of an establishment valued bottles of a rare and expensive wine at the prices listed on the operation's menu rather than the price the manager actually paid for the wine?

   A. Cost principle

   B. Matching principle

   C. Consistency principle

   D. Time period principle

9. Which GAAP would be violated if the manager of a high-volume operation purchased a large dish machine and recorded the entire cost of the machine as an expense in the month it was purchased?

A. Time period principle

B. Matching principle

C. Consistency principle

D. Distinct business principle

10. Which GAAP would be violated if an owner purchased carpet for his home but charged the cost of the carpet to his establishment?

A. Cost principle

B. Matching principle

C. Time period principle

D. Distinct business principle

FIELD PROJECT

Visit a local commercial or noncommercial restaurant or foodservice operation.
Talk to the manager and determine the following:

1. Does the operation use the cash accounting method or the accrual accounting method?

2. Who is responsible for performing bookkeeping tasks related to recording revenue?

3. Who is responsible for performing bookkeeping tasks related to recording expenses?

4. How important are computers in tracking day-to-day business transactions and generating end of accounting period reports?

5. Does the operation use a centralized or decentralized accounting system?

6. What is the time frame of the operation's fiscal year?

7. Who is primarily responsible for creating the operation's monthly financial reports?

8. Who is primarily responsible for creating the operation's annual financial reports?

2 Planning the Profitable Restaurant

INSIDE THIS CHAPTER

- **Business Plans**
- **Analyzing Market Conditions**
- **Analyzing Financial History**

CHAPTER LEARNING OBJECTIVES

After completing this chapter, you should be able to:

- Explain the goal of a business plan.

- List and describe the tasks required to develop a business plan.

- Identify the main purpose of a financial plan.

- Identify the areas assessed when analyzing market conditions.

- Describe the major factors affecting market conditions.

- Explain the role demographics play in defining target markets.

- State the steps required to conduct a financial history analysis.

KEY TERMS

alternative revenue source (ARS), p. 37

benchmark, p. 47

benefit, p. 34

brand, p. 36

business plan, p. 26

co-branding, p. 37

concept statement, p. 28

corporation, p. 30

dba, p. 30

demographics, p. 35

executive summary, p. 27

feature, p. 34

financial plan, p. 26

finance, p. 27

market conditions, p. 40

market share, p. 44

market size, p. 44

partnership, p. 30

partnership agreement, p. 30

pro forma, p. 39

shareholder, p. 30

sole proprietorship, p. 29

SWOT analysis, p. 31

target market, p. 34

value, p. 36

CASE STUDY

"Well, what do you think?" asked Dan. "Are you in or not?"

Dan was talking to his longtime friend Darla. He just finished explaining his idea for a new restaurant he wanted to open, in which he wanted her to invest.

Darla agreed to meet with Dan when he told her over the phone that he had a great opportunity for her. After patiently listening to Dan's presentation, Darla asked him if he wrote down his ideas for the new business so she could review them later in detail.

"No," replied Dan. "I have all the ideas in my head. I don't need to write them down. I just need the money to get started! So are you in or not?"

1. Why do you think Darla wanted to see detailed plans for Dan's new restaurant?

2. Assume Dan approaches a banker to lend him money for the new business. What specific information might the banker want to see prior to making a lending decision?

BUSINESS PLANS

A **business plan** is a formal statement of business goals. It is an explanation of how the goals can be achieved, and the detailed steps for reaching the goals. A business plan may also contain background information about the organization or individuals associated with the proposed business.

A well-written business plan includes clear information about many important business issues, particularly financial matters. New restaurant or foodservice operations require a business plan, and they are also very helpful for improving existing businesses.

In nearly all cases, an effective business plan will include a detailed financial plan. A **financial plan** is an estimation of the cash needed to open a new business or buy an existing business, and to keep it operating until it becomes financially stable. A financial plan includes information about the amount of money an owner currently has available. It also includes information about start-up funds, which represent the total amount needed to open a new business. If a financial plan includes the use of borrowed money, the plan also includes how and when the money will be paid back.

For a new business, a well-developed business plan can help minimize the risk of failure. It can do the same for those that are already in operation. Business plans detail the goals a business seeks to achieve. Managers responsible for developing the financial portion of a business plan should understand how the overall business plan is developed, and the important information it contains. When they do, they are better able to use information found in business plans to help guide the development of the operation's financial activities.

There are many challenges associated with opening new operations. Owners and managers who wish to open a new establishment must give a great deal of thought to the business even before beginning to write a business plan. While the development of every new business will be unique, there are issues all owners must address when starting a new restaurant or foodservice business:

- **Location:** Where will the operation be located?
- **Facilities:** What building, parking, interior, and other space requirements must be met?
- **Menu:** What will the operation sell to its guests (*Exhibit 2.1*)?
- **Marketing:** How will customers find out about the business?
- **Financing:** How much money will be needed to start a business and where will it come from?

THINK ABOUT IT . . .

Lenders are nearly unanimous in requiring companies seeking start-up funding to submit a business plan. Would you want to see a business plan before you lent money? What information would you expect in the plan?

Exhibit 2.1

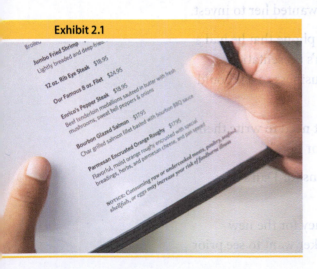

Not surprisingly, various parts of a comprehensive business plan address these issues and more. Accountants and others with a financial interest in the operation will, of course, be particularly interested in the finance portion of the business plan. **Finance** is the term managers use to describe the management of a business's money and other assets. As a result, issues related to financing actually affect every part of a business plan's development.

Creating a comprehensive business plan takes time. Typically, the more time devoted to the process, the better the final plan. A well-developed business plan will do four things:

- It communicates a clear understanding of the establishment's concept and proposed location.

- It serves as an operating tool that establishes a timeline for the establishment's development and financial targets for its ongoing operation.

- It assists in fund-raising, if required, by describing the establishment's need for financing and how any money to be borrowed will be repaid by the business.

- It serves as an operating guide to aid in decision making after the establishment has been opened.

There is no legally mandated requirement for the information that must be included in a business plan. However, an effective business plan includes several components:

- Executive summary
- Concept statement
- Operating plan
- Competitive assessment
- SWOT analysis
- Vendor assessment
- Marketing plan
- Financial plan

Executive Summary

An **executive summary** provides readers of a business plan with the highlights of the plan. While it appears first in the printed document, most business plan developers write the executive summary near the end of the business plan writing process. This is necessary because the summary typically includes information taken from other sections of the plan. Put another way, a writer cannot summarize something that has not yet been written.

> ### Manager's Memo
>
> In addition to its key role of explaining an owner's vision for a business, a business plan is used extensively in the actual operation of a business.
>
> In fact, every time a major business decision is to be made, the business plan is one of the major factors managers consider. When making a major decision, the owner or manager can ask "Is this in our business plan?" Related questions could be "How will the decision we make on this issue affect our business plan?", "Will our decision support the plan's goals?", and "Will it detract from our ability to meet our goals?" Frequent reference to an operation's business plan helps ensure owners and managers are going down the path originally set forth in the plan.

Producing a clear and compelling case for a restaurant or foodservice establishment in the executive summary portion of a business plan is critical. The author must convince readers at the outset that the rest of the plan is worth reading.

The executive summary portion of the business plan is usually brief, generally no more than one to two pages. Major points in the business plan are presented in this section, along with short supporting statements of one or two sentences.

In a typical restaurant or foodservice business plan, the first paragraph of the executive summary generally includes the following:

- Business name
- Business location
- Brief description of the establishment
- Purpose of the plan

The next paragraph should highlight important points such as projected revenue, expenses, and profits, as well as keys to the operation's success.

Concept Statement

The **concept statement** is the part of a business plan that details exactly what type of establishment will be created. The concept statement allows plan developers to be very specific about the customers they will seek to attract. This section of the plan addresses various key topics:

- Menu items
- Proposed selling prices
- Unique or distinguishing features

MENU ITEMS

A variety of individuals will read the business plan. It is therefore important to clearly explain the products and services the proposed establishment will offer. For example, suppose an owner seeks to open a casual restaurant featuring "American fare." Readers of the business plan will want to know what "American fare" means to this owner. The owner should explain what this description means from both a menu item and a service perspective and why this type of fare answers the needs of the target market. Providing specific menu examples helps provide a clear picture of what the proposed establishment will offer.

PROPOSED SELLING PRICES

Menu prices can range from very inexpensive to quite expensive, even when the menu items sold are very similar. For example, steaks can be sold at menu prices ranging from $5 to $50. As a result, if an owner plans to open an establishment featuring steak, he or she should explain whether the proposed pricing structure will place it in the lower, middle, or higher range of its competitors' pricing structures. Competitor's prices can be obtained simply by visiting these operations and comparing their prices with those of the operation described in the business plan. Developers of business plans specify where in the range of possible prices their establishment would fall.

Exhibit 2.2

UNIQUE OR DISTINGUISHING FEATURES

Defining a restaurant or foodservice operation in terms of what makes it unique in the eyes of customers differentiates it from its competitors. It also gives those prospective financial backers a clear idea of why the business is needed and why it will be popular with customers. For example, a plan developer might highlight that his or her establishment will feature low-cost fried seafood items served in a casual setting, Or, it will offer elegant meals on the top of a large downtown building that takes advantage of the spectacular lights of the city at night. Maybe the operation will highlight features such as video and other games for children that make the operation a fun place for families to eat (*Exhibit 2.2*).

Operating Plan

The operating portion of a business plan details the business structure of an operation and explains who will own and operate the establishment. It also addresses why these individuals are qualified to do it.

Many restaurants and foodservice establishments are operated as a sole proprietorship. A **sole proprietorship** is an operating business structure in which one individual owns, and frequently operates, the business. A sole proprietorship is the least complex business structure available to restaurateurs, as the proprietor is held personally responsible for all of its debts.

A sole proprietorship can be legally used as the operating structure of any size establishment. Under this structure, the owner is responsible for all debts incurred by the operation. From a potential lender's perspective, it is critical that the individual seeking funding is clearly identified in this portion of the plan. This portion of the plan should also establish that the owner would take personal responsibility for and have the financial ability to repay any loans given to the business.

In many instances, a sole proprietor's business is operated under a different name. When that is the case, both the name of the business and the individual owning it will be legally registered with the appropriate governmental agency. This is usually done in the state in which the business is operated. This practice allows those who will be doing business with the operation to know the identity of its owner. For example, consider Sharmey Larson who opens an establishment using the sole proprietorship business structure. She names it "Larson's Grilled Chicken," so the legal name of the business would be "Sharmey Larson dba Larson's Grilled Chicken." Here, **dba** means "doing business as."

Many restaurants and foodservice establishments are operated by partners in the business. A **partnership** is a business structure consisting of two or more owners who agree to share in the profits and losses of a business. While a partnership may be formed orally, it is best formed by a written contract. The terms of the contract, also called a **partnership agreement**, detail the rights and responsibilities of each co-owner of the business.

A partnership agreement should include how much time and money each owner will contribute to the business and who will operate it. It may also address how profits will be split among the owners, and who is responsible for any losses that may be incurred by the business.

The issue of responsibility for losses is especially important. This is because, as is true in a sole proprietorship, the partners in a general partnership are held personally responsible for any debts incurred by their business. For this reason, potential lenders to a new operation will want to know the identity of each partner as well as each partner's proposed contribution to the business. Also, as with a sole proprietorship, lenders will want to know which partners are committing to the repayment of any loans made to the business.

In many cases, restaurant and foodservice operations are operated as a corporation. A **corporation** is a formal business structure recognized as a legal entity having its own privileges and liabilities separate from that of its owners. When a corporation is formed, its owners are called shareholders or stockholders, because they share in the ownership of the business. A **shareholder** is an individual or group that owns one or more portions, or shares, of a corporation.

A corporation can legally borrow money, own property, hire employees, sue, and be sued. Corporations are different from sole proprietorships and partnerships because the corporation itself, not its shareholders, is responsible for all of its debts. This structure is a great advantage to shareholders because it removes them from individual liability for the debts of a business operated by the corporation. Lenders reading a business plan submitted by a corporation, however, will want to know a great deal about the financial stability of the corporation for this same reason.

After the business structure has been clearly identified, the operating portion of a business plan should detail the education and experience of the establishment's owners. Again, lenders will look for experience in the industry that assures them that the operation will not only survive, but also provide a return on their investment. It should include the education and experience of the operation's managers as well, if known when the business plan is prepared.

Competitive Assessment

This section of the business plan describes the businesses that the proposed operation will compete against. It may be tempting to state that the proposed operation will have no competition because its food, service, or location will be superior to all other operations. However, regardless of how good it is, nearly every business will face some form of competition.

A competitive assessment often mentions a specific establishment (e.g., Bill's Chicken will be the biggest competitor of Larson's Grilled Chicken). It also will include information about how the proposed business will compete to win its fair share of customers.

SWOT Analysis

Increasingly, restaurant and foodservice operation owners and investors like to see a SWOT analysis included in a business plan. A **SWOT analysis** identifies an operation's strengths and weaknesses and examines its opportunities and threats (see *Exhibit 2.3*). This analysis helps managers set goals and focus on plans that maximize the business's strengths, and capitalize on its greatest opportunities.

SWOT analysis considers the proposed establishment's strengths, weaknesses, opportunities, and threats from the viewpoints of the owners, managers, employees, and customers. A realistic SWOT analysis also considers strengths and weaknesses of a business in relation to its competitors. For example, if all of the competitors in the QSR segment offer speedy service, then speedy service is an operational necessity, not a strength.

STRENGTHS

In this part of the SWOT analysis, an owner or manager indicates all of the strengths of the operation. These are areas in which the business excels. Examples of strengths include a well-trained staff, a good location, well-kept and clean facilities, strong marketing abilities, high food quality, and service that consistently exceeds customer expectations (*Exhibit 2.4*).

Exhibit 2.3

| Strengths | Weaknesses |
| Opportunities | Threats |

Exhibit 2.4

RESTAURANT TECHNOLOGY

Increasingly, the ability of a manager to use advanced technology is viewed as a competitive strength. Sometimes it is even listed as such in a SWOT analysis. These managers can apply advanced technology to market their menu items and services to their guests, as well as to create custom-made in-house promotion materials. The impact of these actions is often reduced costs and increased profits.

Sophisticated financial management software programs are available to help prepare budgets and financial projections. In addition, tech-savvy managers can use technology such as cell phone apps to receive real-time revenue updates from their operations. This allows them to better recognize where they stand financially at all times.

Managers who know how to apply advanced technology solutions to their business are able to work faster and smarter, often giving them a real advantage over their competitors.

WEAKNESSES

This part of the SWOT analysis identifies any weaknesses in a business. This analysis is done so that the weaknesses can later be eliminated or turned into strengths. Some examples of weaknesses are an uninteresting menu, dirty premises, limited abilities or resources for marketing, undifferentiated products, poor-quality products, poor service, high staff turnover, and poor reputation.

In addition to weaknesses, there may be certain barriers to success, or things outside the operation's control, that might cause a weakness. For example, if the products to be produced take a high degree of skill to prepare properly or take a very long time to prepare because of a lack of skilled labor, the establishment will not easily be able to prepare high-quality products.

Many weaknesses are opportunities for improvement. Some barriers can be overcome by proper planning and execution. For example, to overcome the lack of skilled labor, an owner or manager might implement a new employee training program, modify recruiting efforts, or even change menus or recipes.

OPPORTUNITIES

In this section of the SWOT analysis the plan developer should address realistic opportunities to either increase revenue or decrease expenses. Examples of such opportunities include extending operating hours, adding additional locations, or launching a new delivery or takeout service. One way to determine opportunities is to look at strengths with an eye for building on them, and to look at weaknesses to see if eliminating them can create opportunities.

THREATS

Threats can come from a variety of sources. Identifying possible threats to a business is important to ensure that the threats are addressed or controlled before they can do damage to the business. Examples of possible threats in the SWOT analysis portion of a business plan include an increased number of competitors, increased taxes, poor economic conditions, changing desires of potential customers, or road construction that disrupts current traffic patterns.

To conduct a successful SWOT analysis, owners and managers must be realistic about the strengths and weaknesses of their operations, as well as the opportunities and threats they face. *Exhibit 2.5* presents an example of possible characteristics that different businesses might identify as they complete a SWOT analysis.

Exhibit 2.5

POSSIBLE SWOT ANALYSIS FINDINGS

Strengths	Weaknesses
• Prime intersection location for the operation • Good capabilities of management and staff • Being a new operation that offers a diverse level of service and products • High quality of meals and service • Few or no competitors	• Weak location due to the operation's poor visibility from the street • Poor capabilities of management and staff • Lack of marketing expertise • Poor quality of meals and service • Numerous competitors • Older operation with out-of-date menu
Opportunities	**Threats**
• Ability to expand services • Ability to increase number of menu items offered • New customer groups • Competitors closing • New promotional campaigns • Technology • Competitor changing concept	• Competitor offering lower prices • Competitor coming in with new or innovative menu and service • Negative publicity • Competitor mimicking a certain aspect of an operation's service or menu • Competitor changing concept

Vendor Assessment

Vendor assessment is an important part of a business plan if the operation's products are subject to shortage of supply or wide fluctuation in price. For example, an establishment that wishes to feature a locally produced wine as one of its distinguishing features would likely need to address the issue of steady product supply. In addition, the payment terms required by vendors often vary. These terms can directly affect an operation's financial ability to meet the terms.

The vendor assessment section assures plan readers that its developer has thought about possible vendors, necessary products and services and their prices, and how the vendors will be paid. In smaller communities, the number of vendor options available to a manager may be limited. In such a case, the consideration of alternative supply sources takes on great importance.

Marketing Plan

A marketing plan guides an operation's marketing efforts. As such, the marketing plan is a detailed listing of specific activities designed to reach the operation's revenue goals. The plan describes what, and when, specific marketing activities will be used to drive the operation toward its revenue goals.

Managers preparing this part of the business plan will address these key marketing concerns:

- Target customers
- Brand development
- How the market plan was developed
- The size of the marketing budget
- How the marketing plan will be implemented

TARGET CUSTOMERS

Many business experts believe that the primary role of any manager is to attract and keep customers. If there are too few customers, most businesses will not achieve the revenue levels they need to survive. When considered in this way, it is easy to see that restaurant and foodservice managers must always focus their efforts on pleasing their guests.

Successful managers identify what their potential customers need and want from a restaurant or foodservice operation. An establishment's **target market** is simply those potential customers whose specific needs and wants the organization will seek to meet.

It is important to recognize that not all guests want the same things from their dining experiences. Customers' desires can vary based on their circumstances:

- A couple going out for a romantic dinner to celebrate the anniversary of their first date
- A group of office workers stopping at a fast casual restaurant on their one-hour lunch break
- A father buying carry-out fried chicken to feed his family at home
- A salesperson entertaining an important client
- A doctor eating lunch in a hospital
- A first-year college student living in a residence hall and eating all of her meals in the university's central dining hall
- A delivery driver purchasing breakfast to go during a fuel stop

In each of these cases, the needs and wants of these customers likely will be very different.

To be effective, managers must recognize that the menu items they sell will have features and benefits for customers. In the restaurant and foodservice business, **features** are the characteristics of the actual menu items and services sold to guests. **Benefits** are the advantages or favorable results obtained from purchasing the feature.

To better understand the difference between features and benefits, consider a salesperson who sells vacuum cleaners to establishments. To be effective, he or she must understand that potential customers do not really want to buy a vacuum as much as they want to buy the benefits that come from having clean carpets (*Exhibit 2.6*). A feature is what the vacuum cleaner salesperson offers customers: the vacuum itself. The benefits are what the customers gain: clean floors, a pleasant environment, happy customers, and increased profits.

Similarly, consider the traveling family who has almost reached their ski vacation destination. This family stops at a highway interchange and buys dinner at an establishment offering drive-through window service. The family is certainly buying food and drinks. Just as important, however, it is purchasing convenience, the ability to use clean restrooms, menu variety, speed-of-service, and the ability to quickly continue on the way to its destination. These are the benefits that the customers actually get when they buy features, and these benefits are likely of great importance to this family.

The best managers focus on the specific characteristics of guests they hope to attract to their restaurants. This includes **demographics**: information about customers such as their age, gender, race, marital status, geographic location, or other personal characteristics. Demographics allow potential customers to be identified as part of a target market. Demographic information about customers helps managers more clearly identify their unique target markets. When that is done, products and services can be developed to appeal directly to those with specific demographic characteristics. *Exhibit 2.7* shows examples of demographic areas.

Different operations appeal to different target markets. An important role of owners and managers, then, is to carefully identify the target markets of their establishments and to clearly and consistently communicate the features and benefits to target markets.

Managers of various restaurant and foodservice establishments serve different target markets and often serve them differently. However, it is important to know that all customers share some important characteristics:

- All expect to be served safe food and beverages.
- All expect to be served in a clean environment.
- All expect to be served professionally.
- All expect to be treated with respect.
- All expect to receive good value for the money they spend.

Exhibit 2.6

Exhibit 2.7

EXAMPLES OF DEMOGRAPHIC AREAS

• Age	• Household size
• Education level	• Income
• Ethnicity	• Nationality
• Family life cycle	• Occupation
• Family status	• Race
• Gender	• Religion
• Geography	• Sexual orientation
• Home ownership	

THINK ABOUT IT . . .

Consider a good establishment that does not attract many customers. What happens if the establishment cannot pay its bills? Who is responsible for ensuring that the business draws enough customers in the future?

Value is the difference between what customers get when they buy a product or service and what they pay to get it. All customers desire good value, but good value is not the same as low price. In fact, when products or services are sold at prices so low that it becomes impossible to deliver good quality, it is similarly difficult to deliver good value. Effective managers ensure their operations provide good value to existing guests and communicate that fact to their potential guests.

BRAND DEVELOPMENT

Not all restaurant and foodservice operations are alike. For that reason establishments need to tell potential customers exactly who they are. This message of identity should be clearly stated in the marketing plan. Issues to address may include the way an operation looks on the outside, its décor, the menu items it will serve, its proposed pricing structure, and even the uniforms its staff will wear. **Brand** is the single term owners and managers use to describe an establishment's distinguishing features. Brand includes the operation's name, logos, signs, décor, and other characteristics that, when taken together, make one operation different from another.

Readers of a business plan know that effective marketing is an essential ingredient in an operation's success. In the marketing portion of the business plan, owners describe exactly what they will do to market their operation, how much it will cost, and when they will do it.

Financial Plan

While location is often mentioned as the single most important ingredient in an establishment's success, proper financing is considered by many to be the second most important. In the financial plan section of a business plan, owners assess estimated income and expense to reach conclusions about the overall viability of their concepts. It is important to recognize, however, that a new operation's expenses begin long before it opens and begins to make a profit. Financing includes providing the money the establishment needs during this initial period of unprofitability.

In nearly every case, an establishment that lacks enough start-up funding will not be able to pay its bills until it becomes profitable enough to do so. Start-up costs incurred vary based on a business's location and type of facility needed. However, all operations typically incur pre-opening costs related to the following:

- Land and building acquisition or lease
- Legal fees
- Required licenses
- Insurance

- Utility deposits and pre-payments
- Kitchen equipment and tools
- Dining-room furnishings
- China, flatware, and glassware (*Exhibit 2.8*)
- Employee uniforms
- Initial food and beverage inventories
- Pre-opening marketing costs
- Pre-opening payroll costs

Exhibit 2.8

Even after a new establishment is open, it may take many months before it reaches targeted levels of profitability. As a result, an establishment must have access to enough cash or credit to pay its bills in a timely manner starting from the very first day it opens.

Personal savings, family assistance, short-term and long-term loans, and available government grants are among the most commonly used sources of financing. The decision regarding which of these sources will be used and how much money must be secured from them must be known before writing the business plan. Additionally, realistic estimates of how quickly the establishment will reach its targeted level of profitability must be developed. These estimates are integral parts of the business plan.

One of the first steps that should be taken when considering the development of the financial section of a business plan is to learn about alternative revenue sources available. An **alternative revenue source (ARS)** generates money in addition to that raised from other funding sources such as loans and personal savings.

ARS opportunities can be classified as follows:

- Co-branding partnerships
- Grant opportunities
- Potential new sources of revenue

CO-BRANDING PARTNERSHIPS

Co-branding is what happens when two companies join together to share the expense of marketing the products and services each company offers to its own customers. Working together, each company can do a better job of marketing than they could do working alone.

The business term *co-branding* is a relatively new one. The most common co-branding arrangement involves two or more businesses that can help each other. For example, an establishment near a water park may choose to market itself to families who might visit the operation before or after going to the waterpark. Similarly, the waterpark seeks to market its admission tickets to the establishment's diners. By joining forces, both of these organizations may be able to reach a larger number of potential customers because each offers something both of these businesses' customers may want to buy. In some co-branding arrangements, two different establishments may even share a building or parking lot.

It is often helpful for managers to evaluate co-branding opportunities by answering four questions:

- Which co-branding opportunities offer the best chances for success?
- What will the co-branding arrangements consist of?
- How can the co-branding arrangements best be implemented?
- How will the effectiveness of the arrangements be evaluated and when?

GRANT OPPORTUNITIES

Restaurant and foodservice operation owners and managers who want to market effectively to grow and expand their businesses are sometimes surprised to learn there are others who want to help them do just that. Government grant and loan programs often target exactly the types of activities managers undertake to market their establishments. In other cases, restaurant and foodservice operations may qualify for grant assistance in nonmarketing areas.

The number and size of available grants and low-interest loans can change quite often, so it is important that managers stay up-to-speed on their availability. Examples of currently available grant, tax credit, and loan programs include the following:

American Recovery and Reinvestment Act (ARRA) Grants

The U.S. Department of Labor's Education & Training Administration offers several grant opportunities under the American Recovery and Reinvestment Act (ARRA) of 2009. Projects under these grants provide training and placement services in the energy efficiency and renewable energy industries for workers impacted by national energy and environmental policy, as well as other unemployed workers. In many cases, these unemployed workers can make excellent employees.

Work Opportunity Tax Credits (WOTC)

The Work Opportunity Tax Credit (WOTC) is a federal tax credit granted to businesses that hire individuals from 12 target groups that have consistently faced significant barriers to employment. The main objective of this program is to enable the targeted employees to gradually move from economic dependency into self-sufficiency as they earn a steady income, learn new skills, and become contributing taxpayers.

Manager's Memo

In many cases, a restaurant or foodservice operation will be owned and managed by the same person. In other cases, owners hire professional managers who will run their operations for them. Regardless of the arrangement it is essential that owners and managers work together to ensure the success of their operations.

Owners know the financial goals they have set for their businesses. Managers know how to satisfy guests. When owners and managers work closely together, financial goals can be met and guests can be pleased. That helps the business grow and helps ensure the long-term success of the operation.

Participating employers are compensated by being able to reduce their federal income tax liability. In many cases, these unemployed workers can make excellent employees. Tax credits secured by employing workers in these targeted groups can also free up other money that can then be made available for the establishment's marketing efforts.

Special Small Business Administration (SBA) Loans

The U.S. Small Business Administration (SBA) dedicates its energy and resources to providing support to small businesses and small-business owners across the nation. The SBA does not make grants, but it does offer a variety of loan programs. Because of its focus on small businesses, in many cases these loans are made to owners.

Like tax credits, loans secured from special SBA loan programs can free up an owner's other funds so that money can be made available for the operation's other activities.

Owners and managers can stay informed about grant, loan, and tax credit programs for which they may qualify by consulting their tax accountants and attorneys, as well as by their active membership in groups such as the National Restaurant Association, the professional trade association for members of the restaurant and foodservice industry.

PRO FORMA

Because potential lenders may place different requirements on businesses, the information needed in the financial portion of a business plan may vary somewhat. However, the plan will almost always include a three-year financial pro forma. A **pro forma** is a detailed estimate of the revenue, expenses, and profits to be achieved by a business over a specific time period. The pro forma financial documents will include other important information about a business's estimated assets, liabilities, and available cash over the time period indicated by the pro forma. If money will need to be borrowed, the financial plan included in the business plan will address how and when the business will pay back that money.

Putting It Together

While each business plan is as unique as the operation it describes, *Exhibit 2.9* details one suggested format for a restaurant or foodservice business plan. Note that this template suggests potential areas to be addressed. Other areas to address as needed may include items such as owners' and managers' resumes, sample copies of menus, or copies of leases and building plans.

THINK ABOUT IT . . .

Assume you were preparing a business plan for an establishment you want to own. Would you have difficulty actually writing the plan? Where would you look for help?

Exhibit 2.9

SAMPLE BUSINESS PLAN CONTENT CHECKLIST

- ☐ Cover sheet with establishment name and plan preparer's contact information, as well as the date of the plan's preparation
- ☐ One- to two-page executive summary
- ☐ Table of contents
- ☐ Description of the restaurant or foodservice operation's concept
- ☐ Legal description of the organization developing the establishment
- ☐ Vendor assessment
- ☐ Competitive assessment
- ☐ Marketing plan
- ☐ Financial projections
  - ☐ Pre-opening financing
    - ☐ Required amount
    - ☐ Use of money
    - ☐ Source of money
    - ☐ Loan repayment plan
  - ☐ Three-year operating pro forma

Manager's Memo

Some business owners need help when writing their business plans. The U.S. Small Business Administration (SBA) is a governmental agency that provides help to those who are preparing business plans. Its template for a business plan can be accessed at the following:

www.sba.gov/content/ templates-writing-business-plan

Many community colleges, universities, and nonprofit groups such as SCORE also provide business plan assistance. SCORE is a nonprofit association dedicated to educating entrepreneurs and helping small businesses start, grow, and succeed nationwide. SCORE is a resource partner with the SBA and has been mentoring small-business owners for more than 40 years.

THINK ABOUT IT . . .

When a local economy is weak, the residents of the area may have less money to spend. What can operations in economically depressed areas do to maintain strong revenue levels in difficult economic times?

ANALYZING MARKET CONDITIONS

Owners and managers must know a great deal about the market conditions in which they will be operating. **Market conditions** include the economic, legal, and competitive conditions faced by a business at a specific point in time. The competitive conditions in a market also include detailed information about the customers an operation seeks to attract.

To make good decisions about how to best open and operate their establishments, managers need sources of current and factual information. The information is related to these key areas:

- Economic conditions
- Legal requirements
- Competitive conditions

Economic Conditions

The economic condition of an area directly affects the ability of operations in that area to be successful. During the 1980s and early 1990s, the U.S. economy was extremely robust. The result was that many new establishments were built and the amount of food purchased away from home increased rapidly. Fueled in part by federal tax reductions, rising real estate values, and increased easy term borrowing, U.S. consumers spent a great deal on meals away from home. When the economy is strong, restaurant and foodservice operations are among the most favored places for spending money.

The recession that began in December of 2007 caused many Americans to be more careful with their spending. As a result, growth rates in overall restaurant and foodservice sales have slowed. The boom years of the 1980s and the more cautious years of the late 2000s exemplify how the economy can directly affect overall spending for an operation's products and services. Managers should continually monitor their local economies to ensure they can attract enough customers to succeed.

Legal Requirements

There are a large number of local, state, and federal laws and regulations that affect the operation of a restaurant or foodservice business. Because these laws change regularly, it is essential that managers monitor them.

Managers have specific legal responsibilities:

- Responsibilities to all guests
- Responsibilities related to serving food
- Responsibilities related to serving alcoholic beverages

RESPONSIBILITIES TO ALL GUESTS

An establishment that does not satisfy its guests will not stay in business. Despite the importance of guests, there are specific legal challenges that arise any time guests are served. From a legal perspective, a guest is anyone using an operation's services. This means guests include all diners, regardless of the person paying the bill for any purchases made in the establishment.

In all areas of the country, laws have been established that require managers to treat all guests fairly. For example, federal law makes it illegal to deny service to anyone on the basis of his or her race, color, religion, or national origin.

It is also a violation of federal law to segregate customers, such as by restricting their seating to predesignated sections of an establishment, based on those same characteristics. In addition, many towns and cities prohibit discriminatory practices such as those in privately owned and operated country clubs or city clubs.

Laws related to guest service may be made at the federal, state, or local level. In some cases the laws passed, such as laws prohibiting smoking or prohibiting the use of specific food ingredients, may cause a significant change in the way an establishment is managed and the services it can provide. As a result, managers must monitor these laws very closely.

RESPONSIBILITIES RELATED TO SERVING FOOD

Restaurant and foodservice managers have a legal obligation to sell only food that is wholesome and to deliver it to guests in a way that is safe. As a result, an establishment must handle and serve the items it sells in a way that protects guests from foodborne illnesses or other harm.

To help owners and managers do that, local health departments conduct routine and mandatory inspections of kitchens (*Exhibit 2.10*). They may also offer training or certification classes for employees. Establishments can be held responsible for food-related illnesses they cause their guests. To minimize the risk of causing harm to their guests, managers should show they are exercising reasonable care by providing food safety training to employees who handle or serve food.

RESPONSIBILITIES RELATED TO SERVING ALCOHOLIC BEVERAGES

Throughout history, alcoholic beverages have been manufactured, served, and enjoyed in nearly every society, including the United States. However, in 1920 the U.S. Congress passed the Eighteenth Amendment to the Constitution that prohibited the manufacture, sale, and transport of all alcoholic beverages in the United States.

Exhibit 2.10

Not surprisingly, the law known as Prohibition stopped only the legal manufacture and sale of alcoholic beverages. Many people still drank, but they drank alcoholic beverage products that were illegally made, poor-tasting, and in many cases actually dangerous to drink.

In 1933, Congress recognized the failure of Prohibition and repealed the Eighteenth Amendment. This allowed individual states and municipalities to pass their own laws restricting or even prohibiting the sale and consumption of alcohol within their boundaries. As a result, there are a wide variety of alcohol-related laws existing in the United States, and managers must know which apply to their own businesses. There are many types of laws regulating alcoholic beverage sales:

- **Who may sell it:** In all states, a state-issued liquor license is required before a business is permitted to sell alcohol. Many communities also restrict the number of liquor licenses that are granted.

- **When it may be sold:** Most communities have laws that restrict the specific hours or, in some cases, the days on which alcohol may be sold.

- **Where it may be sold:** In most states, businesses that serve alcohol are prohibited from operating near schools or churches. In addition, the terms of a liquor license may restrict the sale of alcohol to limited or very clearly defined areas of an establishment's building or grounds.

- **Who may serve it:** It is common for states to impose minimum age requirements for those who serve alcoholic beverages. The majority of states permit adults age 18 or older to serve alcoholic beverages in an establishment, but these laws do vary.

- **Who may buy it:** In the United States, guests must be 21 to purchase alcohol, but not all guests over 21 can be served legally. For example, establishments cannot sell alcohol to visibly intoxicated persons, those without proper identification, or those suspected of buying alcohol for the purpose of giving it to a minor.

- **How it may be served:** Many localities prohibit the service of more than one alcoholic beverage to a single guest at the same time. Others restrict the manner in which promotions, specials, or discounts on the selling price of alcohol may be offered to guests.

Laws related to alcohol service are an excellent example of the impact of the legal environment on foodservice and restaurant operations. Managers should monitor this important area carefully.

Competitive Conditions

To be successful a restaurant or foodservice operation must meet the needs of its customers better than its competitors. Managers must understand who their competitors are and how much of a threat they pose to the success of their own operations.

There are various ways to identify or categorize competitors. For example, competitors can be grouped based on the threat they pose to the success of an establishment. In such a case, an establishment that opens 30 miles away would be a smaller threat than a similar operation opening nearby.

Another way to categorize competitors is by what an establishment considers to be its direct competition. There are different types of direct competitors:

- **Establishments that sell similar products and services:** For example, a fine-dining establishment featuring the highest-quality food and beverages with expensive menu items would consider other similar operations in its vicinity to be competition. It would not likely consider a smaller, very casual and inexpensive QSR to be a direct competitor (see *Exhibit 2.11*).

Exhibit 2.11

- **Establishments that sell similar products but at different service levels:** For example, an establishment that specializes in home-delivered pizza might also consider an operation that sold pizza in a traditional dining-room setting to be one of its competitors.

After managers have identified their competitors, they can begin to research them. They can visit these establishments, observe how they operate, and study their menus. Their goal should be to find out what these direct competitors offer customers and to learn from them. When doing an assessment, managers should pay close attention to a variety of areas:

- Menu selections
- Pricing structure
- Décor
- Service levels
- Reputation

Most establishments have direct competitors, so managers must be concerned about how best to attract the customers they need in ways that are superior to their competitors.

MARKETS

An operation's target market must be large enough to ensure that an adequate number of customers will be attracted to the business. **Market size** refers to the number or value of units sold to an entire group of customers in a given time period. For example, in a town where 200,000 takeout chicken dinners are sold in one year, the market size of the takeout chicken dinner business in that town would be 200,000 units.

If the average takeout chicken dinner in the town sold for $10, then the market size for takeout chicken dinners could also be expressed in monetary terms as $2,000,000:

$$200,000 \quad \times \quad \$10 \quad = \quad \$2,000,000$$

200,000	$10	$2,000,000
Takeout chicken dinners sold	Per dinner	Market size

If a manager operated a takeout chicken dinner establishment in that town, it is easy to see why it is important to know about, and to continually monitor, the size of the takeout chicken dinner market in the town. Estimating a market's size precisely can be challenging. However, experienced managers know that a good estimate of market size must be obtained to calculate an establishment's market share.

Market share is the number or value of units sold by a business during a given period and is expressed as a percentage of the total market size. Like market size, market share can be expressed either as the share of units sold or as a share of revenue.

For example, in the town whose market size for takeout chicken dinners was 200,000 units and $2,000,000 per year in sales, a specific establishment sold 30,000 takeout chicken dinners. That operation's market share would be 15 percent:

$$30,000 \quad \div \quad 200,000 \quad = \quad 15\%$$

30,000	200,000	15%
Chicken dinners sold	Market size units	Market share

Similarly, the takeout chicken dinner revenue generated by the operation would have been $300,000:

$$30,000 \quad \times \quad \$10 \quad = \quad \$300,000$$

30,000	$10	$300,000
Chicken dinners sold	Per dinner selling price	Revenue

As a result, the operation's market share, expressed in terms of revenue, would also be 15 percent:

$$\underset{\text{Revenue}}{\$300{,}000} \div \underset{\substack{\text{Market size}\\\text{revenue}}}{\$2{,}000{,}000} = \underset{\substack{\text{Market share}\\\text{revenue}}}{15\%}$$

If a market's size is known or can be closely estimated, an establishment can closely estimate its own market share.

ANALYZING FINANCIAL HISTORY

Planning for profitable operations is often made easier when a business is already open (*Exhibit 2.12*). This is because a business that has been operating for a period of time has produced a financial history. A financial history is the record of a business's past revenues, expenses, and profits or losses.

In some cases an existing business's financial records are accurate and complete. In other situations some or all of the records may be missing or incomplete. In general, however, any accurate historical information available to a manager is useful in future planning.

To better understand why, consider the manager who needs to estimate the costs of heating and cooling an operation for one year. If the operation has not yet opened, the manager may still estimate heating and cooling costs. The manager could use a variety of information sources to make the estimate:

- Personal experience
- Estimates obtained from energy providers and utility companies
- Estimates provided by restaurant or foodservice experts
- Costs incurred in similar local operations
- Costs based on statewide or national industry averages for similar operations

In each case, data provided would be helpful if data are readily obtained and accurate. It would be more helpful, however, if the business had operated for the past year and the manager had actual copies of the operation's heating and cooling bills for the prior year.

Similarly, when managers can review accurate data related to all of an existing operation's past revenues, expenses, and profits or losses it can make future planning easier and more precise. The purpose of analyzing historical data is simple. It is to improve the planning and forecasting of future business

Exhibit 2.12

MANAGER'S MATH

OPEN FOR BUSINESS

Assume you are analyzing sales data for an establishment that has been open for four years. The data are presented as follows:

Time Frame	Revenue
Year 1	$1,268,000
Year 2	1,155,000
Year 3	1,102,500
Year 4	985,000
Total	

1. What was the total revenue generated in these four years?

2. What was the four-year average revenue per year achieved by this business?

3. What was the average revenue per year in the first two years of this business's operation?

4. What was the average revenue per year in the last two years of this business's operation?

5. Which average revenue figure do you think would be most helpful to you in estimating future yearly sales for this business?

(Answers: 1. $4,510,500; 2. $1,127,625; 3. $1,211,500; 4. $1,043,750; 5. The most recent are most important.)

performance. Managers who use historical data for future planning can do so by using five basic steps:

1. Determine the time frame
2. Collect the data
3. Establish benchmarks
4. Review the data
5. Analyze the findings

Step 1: Determine the Time Frame

In some cases a business may have a tremendous amount of historical operating data. This would be true, for example, if an operation had been in business for many years. In other cases, a business may have been in operation for only a short period of time. In all cases, a manager's first task is to determine the time frame for which the historical data will be analyzed.

Managers assessing historical data for use in future planning are concerned with several aspects of the data:

• The completeness of the data
• The accuracy of the data
• The format in which the data are available
• The time frame addressed by the data

Data that are complete, accurate, and available in an easy-to-use format are best. In most cases, data that address a more recent period are more useful than data that address times periods far in the past. In all cases, managers must establish the detail, format, and time frame addressed by the historical data to be analyzed.

Step 2: Collect the Data

Step 2 in the use of historical financial data for planning purposes is to actually collect and organize the data identified in step 1. Revenue data must be organized into the time periods in which they were achieved. Expenses must be organized in a way that is meaningful for assessment. Profit and loss data should also be collected and organized. Many managers use similar major categories in the collection and organization of financial data:

• Revenue
• Food and beverage costs
• Labor costs
• Other expenses
• Profits

Step 3: Establish Benchmarks

The third step in the analysis of historical financial data is to establish benchmarks. Benchmarks are descriptions of desired performance. Financial benchmarks are descriptions of desired financial performance. For example, an owner or manager may establish a financial benchmark for profits to be achieved. The benchmark for profits may be established on a weekly, monthly, or annual basis.

Similarly, benchmarks may be established for desired expense levels. The benchmarks for these expenses may be established as a fixed monetary amount or as a percentage of revenue achieved by the business.

The sources of information used for establishing benchmarks are varied, and can include the following:

- Owner's financial goals
- Experience gained from operating similar establishments
- Advice from industry consultants
- Published industry averages

Step 4: Review the Data

After collecting and organizing financial data and establishing benchmarks, compare the operation's actual financial results to the benchmarks. For example, the operation's actual historical sales results can be compared to the benchmark to determine if achieved sales were less than, equal to, or greater than the established benchmark.

Step 5: Analyze the Findings

Restaurant and foodservice managers can draw reasonable conclusions after comparing actual financial results to established benchmarks. This step can help with future financial planning and the preparation of business plans. Managers completing this step can answer many important questions:

- Were revenue benchmarks achieved? How often?
- Were food and beverage cost benchmarks achieved?
- Were benchmarked labor costs achieved?
- Were other expenses at benchmarked levels? Which ones?
- Were profit targets achieved?

OPEN FOR BUSINESS

MANAGER'S MATH

A potential owner has established a benchmark profit target of $2,000 per month for a business she is considering purchasing. In analyzing the financial history of the business she reviews the following profit data from last year:

Month	Profit Achieved
January	$1,400
February	1,100
March	1,600
April	2,250
May	2,900
June	2,350
July	2,900
August	3,100
September	2,200
October	1,850
November	1,700
December	1,600
Total	

1. What was this operation's total profit for the year?

2. Did this operation make an average monthly profit of $2,000?

3. What monthly profit target concerns might this potential owner have if she purchases the business?

(Answers: 1. $24,950. 2. Yes [$24,950 ÷ 12 = $2,079.17 per month]. 3. Does not meet profit target in 6 of the 12 months. That could cause issues with available cash.)

Answers to questions such as these guide managers in the investigation of possible problem areas and their remedies. If weaknesses in past financial performance are identified, these should be addressed in the Weakness section of the business plan's SWOT analysis. Possible solutions to these problems can be identified in the Opportunities section of the SWOT analysis. Doing so helps managers and readers of a new business plan understand the historical financial performance of an existing operation, and determine what may be done to maintain or improve it to ensure profitable operations in the future.

SUMMARY

1. **Explain the goal of a business plan.**

   The goal of a properly conceived, thorough, and well-written business plan is to help minimize the risk of failure for a business. When creating a business plan, owners and managers assess key areas that influence operational success. These include plans for marketing the operation, as well as the business's strengths and weaknesses. Business plan developers also assess an operation's known opportunities to improve and grow, as well as potential threats to its success. When a business plan includes well-thought-out marketing and financial plans, the business plan is a powerful tool for helping ensure the success of a new or existing operation.

2. **List and describe the tasks required to develop a business plan.**

   A business plan is a formal statement of business goals. To develop a business plan, owners first identify their concept and their target markets. Next they develop a menu designed to attract that specific market, and establish their menu prices. They identify the financial and other resources needed to open the business, and then create revenue and expense estimates that indicate all of the financial resources that will be needed to begin operations. They then develop their brand and a SWOT analysis is completed, as well as an analysis of the competitors, suppliers, and legal and marketing environments that affect the business. After reaching a positive conclusion about the viability of the concept, owners commit their business plans to writing.

3. **Identify the main purpose of a financial plan.**

   The main purpose of a financial plan is to detail the sources and uses of money needed to open or purchase a business, and to then operate it. Since a new operation's expenses begin before it opens, a detailed plan for how these expenses will be paid is needed. If money must be borrowed to open the business, the financial plan shows who will lend the money and how the money will be repaid.

   After a new establishment is open, it may take several months before the operation creates significant profits. The financial plan explains how immediate expenses will be paid until revenues are adequate to meet the financial obligations of the business. For this reason pro forma financial information is always included in the financial plan.

4. **Identify the areas assessed when analyzing market conditions.**

The analysis of market conditions requires the assessment of several key areas. The first is the competitive environment, so managers begin by identifying their competitors. A competitive assessment may mention specific establishments or groups of restaurant or foodservice operations. It directly addresses how a business will compete to win its fair share of customers by using its menu selections, pricing, décor, and service levels to obtain and retain a strong customer base.

Because the demographics of customers can vary a great deal, information such as the age, gender, race, marital status, geographic location, and other personal characteristics of the operation's target market are carefully assessed. Last, market condition assessment also includes an analysis of the economic and legal conditions faced by a business at a specific point in time.

5. **Describe the major factors affecting market conditions.**

There are three major factors that affect market conditions: economic conditions, legal requirements, and competitive conditions, including target markets. The economic conditions of an area directly affect an establishment's success. When the economy of an area is strong, business most often is strong as well. A weak economy often means reduced sales levels. The legal restrictions placed on a business directly impact its financial success. For that reason, managers must continually monitor their legal responsibilities toward guests. Managers must also monitor changing laws related to the service of food and beverages.

Finally, the presence of competitors and the size of an operation's target market directly affect market conditions. They also affect business profitability. Therefore market size, the number of direct competitors, and an operation's market share are examples of information that must be carefully monitored.

6. **Explain the role demographics play in defining target markets.**

Demographics are important to managers. Managers use customer demographics to identify their target markets. Important demographic factors include a target market's age, ethnicity, and marital status. Gender, sexual orientation, and religion are among additional customer-defining demographics. Experienced managers know that the features and benefits sought by guests vary largely on guests' demographic characteristics. When the demographics of a target market are known by managers, they can promote the features and benefits they sell to those targeted guests who most seek those same features and benefits.

7. **State the steps required to conduct a financial history analysis.**

To conduct a financial history analysis of an existing business, managers follow five steps. Step 1 is to determine the time frame to be analyzed. In step 2, appropriate data from the designated time frame are collected and assembled into the desired format for review. The third step in the analysis of historical financial data is the determination of benchmarks, goals, or financial targets. When that has been completed, step 4 calls for the actual analysis of the data. In the final step, managers review the analysis to draw reasonable conclusions about past performance and identify opportunities for improvement. The findings from an analysis of historical financial data from an existing operation become an important part of the operation's business plan for future profitable operations.

APPLICATION EXERCISE

Consider an idea you have for a new establishment. Draft a one-page (300 to 500 words) concept statement for the operation that could become part of the new operation's business plan. As you draft the statement address the following issues:

1. The menu items you will sell

2. The price range for your menu items

3. Your target market

4. Unique features of the operation

When you have carefully prepared the document, ask a friend to read it to determine if you have described your new establishment in a way that is easily readable and understandable.

REVIEW YOUR LEARNING

Select the best answer for each question.

1. **Which part of a business plan includes an estimate of a business's revenue, expenses, and profitability?**

    A. Concept statement

    B. Marketing plan

    C. SWOT analysis

    D. Pro forma

2. **What does the term *dba* indicate?**

    A. That partners are forming a new business

    B. That the shareholders of a corporation are operating a business

    C. That a name has not yet been chosen for a business operated by a corporation

    D. That a sole proprietor is operating a business with a name different from the owner

3. **Why would business partners create a partnership agreement?**

    A. To sell the business to new partners

    B. To explain how the partners will market the business

    C. To detail the rights and responsibilities of each partner

    D. To confirm the prices the partners will pay for needed supplies

4. **What is the business type used to create an entity that has a legal identity separate from its owners?**

    A. Sole proprietorship

    B. Partnership

    C. Corporation

    D. Shareholder

5. **An establishment owner just learned that a well-known competitor will be opening a new operation very near the owner's current establishment. In which portion of a SWOT analysis would this fact be noted?**

    A. Strengths

    B. Weaknesses

    C. Opportunities

    D. Threats

6. **Which government action would affect the legal environment in which an establishment operates?**

    A. The decision to close for repair a key road leading into town

    B. Implementing a local ordinance banning the use of trans fats in cooking

    C. A decision to add more police patrols to downtown neighborhoods during the weekends

    D. The layoff of five teachers from a local elementary school

7. **Which management decision targets customers based on a specific guest demographic?**

   A. Promoting a daily "Buy one appetizer and get the second appetizer at half price" special

   B. Offering an "Early Bird" special to senior citizens every day between 4:00 p.m. and 6:00 p.m.

   C. Offering free soft drink refills from 11:00 a.m. to 1:00 p.m. each day

   D. Implementing a "Two for One" dinner special on Mondays

8. **What is an example of a feature purchased by establishment customers?**

   A. Freshly baked pizza

   B. Nearness to home

   C. Easy accessibility

   D. Speedy service

9. **A pizza establishment earned $640,000 in revenue last year. The market size for pizza last year was $1,600,000. What was the operation's market share last year?**

   A. 25%

   B. 40%

   C. 50%

   D. 80%

10. **Which step in an assessment of historical financial data comes immediately before data analysis?**

    A. Establishment of profit targets

    B. Determination of time frame

    C. Drawing of conclusions

    D. Data collection

3

Income Statements (P&Ls)

INSIDE THIS CHAPTER

- **The Importance of Income Statements**
- **The Income Statement Format**
- **Reading the Income Statement**

CHAPTER LEARNING OBJECTIVES

After completing this chapter, you should be able to:

- Explain the purpose of an income statement.

- Identify the three major types of financial information included in an income statement.

- Identify operating costs as controllable, noncontrollable, fixed, variable, or semivariable.

- Explain how managers read and analyze an income statement.

KEY TERMS

accounting period, p. 58	fixed costs, p. 67	noncontrollable costs, p. 66
beverage cost percentage, p. 64	food cost percentage, p. 64	payment terms, p. 57
budget, p. 70	gross profit, p. 64	prime cost, p. 65
controllable costs, p. 66	income statement, p. 54	profit and loss (P&L) report, p. 54
cost of sales, p. 63	investor, p. 56	revenue source, p. 61
cost of sales percentage, p. 64	lender, p. 56	semivariable costs, p. 67
expense timing, p. 65	net earnings, p. 70	variable costs, p. 67

CASE STUDY

"Well, will we get our bonuses this month or not?" asked Marco, the assistant manager at the Waterfalls Grill. He was talking to Kayla, the establishment's manager.

Both Marco and Kayla were paid a monthly salary. However, if their operation achieved monthly financial targets established by the owners, then Kayla and Marco qualified for bonuses. It was one day from the end of the month, and Marco was getting anxious.

"We'll hit our targeted revenue numbers," replied Kayla, "but I'm not sure about our costs. I hope we did well on those, but I just don't know the totals on all of our expenses yet. So I can't tell for sure if we'll hit our profit target."

1. Why do you think owners would tie their managers' compensation to their ability to achieve targeted revenue, expense, and profit goals?

2. How frequently do you think managers should be informed about the financial performance of the operations they are managing? What will happen if they are not informed?

THE IMPORTANCE OF INCOME STATEMENTS

Owners and managers of restaurant and foodservice operations want to regularly assess the financial status of their business. They seek answers to three important questions:

- What is the amount of revenue being achieved?
- What is the level of expense being incurred?
- What is the amount of profit being achieved?

Managers of nonprofit restaurant and foodservice operations such as those in hospitals, nursing homes, schools, and colleges have the same concerns about their own financial performance.

Recall the profit formula from chapter 1:

$$\text{Revenue} - \text{Expense} = \text{Profit}$$

From the profit formula, it is easy to see that managers must be concerned about revenue and expense if they are concerned about their profit.

The **income statement** is the financial report that details an operation's revenue, expense, and profit for a specific time period. The income statement is commonly referred to by several other terms:

- The statement of income
- The statement of income and expense
- The profit and loss (P&L) statement
- The monthly (or annual) summary of income and expense

Of the several alternative terms for an income statement, the **profit and loss (P&L) report** is one of the most popular among nonaccountants. Many accountants prefer to use the terms *statement of income* or *income statement*. Each of these terms will be used in this book to refer to the same report.

The best way to see at a glance how an operation is performing financially is by reading and analyzing its income statement. An income statement provides a snapshot of the operation's financial activity for a specific period of time, such as one month.

Income statements also provide financial data used to create other financial documents. Additionally, managers use income statements to analyze trends and identify areas for improvement. In simple terms, an income statement is a compilation of sales and cost information for a specific period of time. It shows whether an operation has made or lost money during the time period covered by the report. When this information is known, better business decisions can be made by individuals and organizations. The financial

Manager's Memo

It is a mistake to think that nonprofit means there is no concern for revenue and expense levels. Managers of nonprofit facilities such as those in hospitals, schools, and military bases know that revenue must consistently exceed expenses. Otherwise, no money will be available for the replacement of worn-out equipment or the remodeling of kitchen or dining facilities.

Some operations are subsidized by the nonprofit entity managing the foodservice. Because of this, it might appear that managers of these operations do not have to face financial pressures. In fact, because nonprofit restaurant or foodservice operations often work on very tight budgets, controlling expenses and optimizing revenue are especially critical management tasks in these operations.

information presented in income statements is of great interest to four groups:

- Managers
- Owners
- Investors
- Others, including creditors, lenders, and employees

Managers

The best restaurant and foodservice managers are professionals who care very much about the quality of their work. When food is well prepared and properly served (*Exhibit 3.1*), customers are attracted and revenues typically increase. When food-production and service costs are well managed, expenses stay within the estimated levels. When revenues are optimized and costs are managed, profits are generated.

Income statements detail an operation's revenue, expense, and profit. Many managers see these financial statements as a score card for assessing their own managerial performance. The performances of managers, as measured by the financial results contained in the income statements of the operations or establishments they run, are often used to determine pay. In addition, bonuses and other financial incentives are often tied to the financial results of an operation as reported in its income statement.

In many companies, job promotions are based in large part on a manager's performance as measured by the income statement. Income statements are very important in the careers of professional restaurant or foodservice managers. The ability to read and analyze them is an essential skill.

Owners

While the managers of restaurant and foodservice operations are keenly interested in the financial performance of their businesses, the owners of the businesses are usually even more interested. Whether sole proprietors, partners, or corporations, business owners are interested in key pieces of information contained in the income statement:

- Did the business make a profit?
- Did the profits achieved by the business reach the targets that were established for them?
- Are profits increasing when compared to earlier time periods?
- Are profits decreasing when compared to earlier time periods?

Exhibit 3.1

THINK ABOUT IT . . .

Managers who attain superior financial performance typically earn higher pay.

Would you pay more for managers who consistently achieve the financial goals that you set? What would happen if you did not pay them more?

Owners are also interested in the revenue and expense portions of an income statement because these areas directly impact profits. If revenue levels do not reach their targets, it may be difficult or impossible to reach profit goals. Similarly, if expense levels exceed the targets established for costs, it may not be possible for the business to reach targeted profit levels.

Although the owner is the manager in some operations, in many others someone else manages the operation. When that is the case, income statements allow the owner to monitor the manager's performance on a regular basis without actually being in the operation.

Most, if not all, owners purchase and operate businesses with the intent of making a profit. In some cases, a business will not make a profit for a specific month or longer. Then the owners may have to supply additional money to keep the business operating until it is profitable. Income statements help owners estimate the amount of money they may be able to take out of a business from the profit it generates. Income statements can also help owners estimate the amount of money that may be needed by an unprofitable business to pay its bills until it is profitable enough to do so on its own.

Investors

In some restaurant and foodservice operations there are a number of investors. **Investors** supply money to a business. In most cases, investors supply the money to increase their own wealth. They want to receive more money than was initially invested in return for investing. Investors typically receive their money from the profits made by a business. Therefore they are keenly interested in the profits reported on the income statement.

Income statements provide information on profitability and operational efficiency. Investors want to see this information before they make their investments. For this reason many businesses prepare income statements not only annually, but on a monthly basis as well.

Others

Most investors actually invest with the hope that the money they supply to a business will be returned to them along with profits. **Lenders** supply money to a business with the legal requirement that the money, and any interest charged for it, be repaid on an agreed-upon schedule.

Lenders to restaurants and foodservice operations typically include banks, insurance companies, savings and loans, and credit unions. Other sources for borrowing often include friends or relatives. Regardless of the source of money, lenders who consider making a loan to a business will want to know if the loan can be repaid. Because the income statement shows the amount of revenue generated by a business minus the costs, readers of an income statement have a good idea of the remaining funds available for loan repayment.

OPEN FOR BUSINESS

RESTAURANT TECHNOLOGY

Many business owners use their Web sites to attract investors by posting financial information taken from their income statements. This is especially the case with businesses that are owned by corporations, because these organizations issue stock as a way of raising money to fund future growth.

When information taken from income statements is posted for all to see, it is especially important that the information is clear, accurate, and easy to read. The consistent use of GAAP (see chapter 1) is especially critical when using advanced technology communication devices for the posting of important financial information.

If the information on an income statement shows large numbers of dollars available for loan repayment, lenders are more inclined to make loans to the business. If the income statement shows limited dollars available for loan repayment, lenders will be reluctant to make loans to the business.

Before a business has opened, it should develop a complete business plan. Lenders rely on the pro forma information in the operation's pre-opening business plan (see chapter 2) to help estimate the ability of the business to repay its loans on time. For that reason, pro forma forecasts of future income statements estimating revenue, expenses, and profits for a designated time period are an essential part of the financial plan.

In addition to having investors and lenders, most restaurant and foodservice operations will purchase products and services from suppliers that can extend credit to their business. For example, if an operation purchases food from a food supplier, it is common for the establishment to pay the invoice for the food delivered once or twice per month. During the period between when the food is delivered (*Exhibit 3.2*) and the food is paid for, the supplier has extended credit to the business. Before agreeing to extend credit to a business, the supplier will likely want to know a great deal about the ability of the business to pay its bills in a timely way.

Sharing income statements with potential creditors is one way for a business to establish its creditworthiness with its suppliers. When suppliers know a business is profitable, as demonstrated on its income statements, they are more inclined to extend credit. They are also more inclined to make payment terms as favorable as possible. **Payment terms** are the conditions under which a supplier will complete a sale. Typically, these terms specify the time period allowed to a business to pay the amounts due to the supplier.

Payment terms for those businesses that have not established creditworthiness may include payment in advance or payment on delivery. For those businesses that have used their income statements to help establish creditworthiness, the supplier may offer a deferred payment period of 30 days or even more.

Restaurant and foodservice suppliers will, in some cases, even vary the prices they charge managers for products and services. They base prices on their perceptions of a business's ability to pay its bills. For that reason, the income statement can provide valuable information that can actually help lower a business's costs.

While most operations do not share income statement information directly with their employees, they are directly affected by the information. This is because managers and owners make decisions about the amount of money available to pay employees, offer bonus programs, and provide employee benefits based on information contained in a P&L.

THINK ABOUT IT . . .

Would you rather lend money to a business that was already open with a consistent history of profitable operation, or to a yet-to-be-open business with a business plan including forecasts of future profits? Why?

Exhibit 3.2

THE INCOME STATEMENT FORMAT

The income statement is formatted in a manner that exactly follows the profit formula:

$$\text{Revenue} - \text{Expense} = \text{Profit}$$

As a result, an income statement contains three major sections:

- Revenue
- Expense
- Profit

Remembering the order of information presented in an income statement is easy. When accountants prepare an income statement, they first list and add all revenue. They then list and subtract expenses from revenue to calculate profit. Income statements may be very brief or very detailed, but all follow the same basic format. The basic format of an income statement is presented in *Exhibit 3.3*.

Note that *Exhibit 3.3* identifies what will be presented in the income statement. It is incomplete, however, because it does not address the time period from which the information was taken. To create an actual income statement, accountants must first determine the time period that the P&L will address.

Defining the Accounting Period

A P&L can provide summary financial details about an operation. However, the time period to be summarized must first be determined and clearly defined. The development of a P&L begins with the statement of the accounting period it addresses. An **accounting period** is any time period for which financial records are prepared. For example, an accounting period could consist of 12 months. Thus, a manager could create a P&L that summarizes revenue, expense, and profits achieved for the time period January 1 through December 31. The accounting period in this example is 1 year. However, any 12 consecutive months—for example, October 1 through September 30—is also an accounting period of 1 year. In fact, GAAP allows any 52-week consecutive period to be considered 1 year.

ANNUAL P&Ls

In nearly every case a restaurant or foodservice operation will want to prepare a P&L on at least an annual basis. This is because many business taxes are payable annually. Most often, taxes are based on achieved profit levels. As a result, the preparation and payment of personal or business taxes cannot be completed without information from the income statement. In addition to its use in the preparation of taxes, an annual P&L gives the establishment manager a summary of the overall performance in the previous 52 weeks.

Exhibit 3.3	
BASIC INCOME STATEMENT FORMAT	
	REVENUE
Less (minus)	EXPENSE
Equals	PROFIT

To better understand the importance of an annual P&L, consider an establishment that operates in a busy ski resort area. The operation may be extremely busy and profitable during the ski season. In that time period, revenue will be extremely high. When the ski season ends for the year, however, the business may not experience the same revenue levels. By preparing an annual P&L the owners of this operation can assess how their business performed during its busiest and least busy times.

MONTHLY P&Ls

The main reason accountants prepare financial reports is so their readers can use them to make better business decisions. In most cases businesses prepare monthly P&Ls because the information contained in them is of critical importance to timely decision making (see *Exhibit 3.4*).

Knowing about the precise amount of revenue generated in a month helps managers address key operational questions:

- Did monthly revenue levels reach the levels predicted?
- Is revenue increasing when compared to prior accounting periods?
- Is revenue decreasing when compared to prior accounting periods?

In restaurant and foodservice operations serving alcohol, additional questions can be addressed:

- What was the amount of food revenue achieved?
- What was the amount of alcoholic beverage revenue achieved?
- What proportion of total revenue was contributed by food sales?
- What proportion of total revenue was contributed by alcohol sales?

Managers must know about their sales levels, but knowing about the costs of operating a business in a specific month also helps address key operational questions:

- How much was spent for food and beverages during this accounting period?
- How much was spent for labor during the period?
- How much was spent for all other expenses during the accounting period?
- What were the total monthly costs of operating the business?
- Did monthly expenses exceed estimated levels?
  - If so, in what specific areas did expenses exceed estimates?
  - If not, in what specific areas were expenses lower than expected?

Exhibit 3.4

Knowing revenue and expense is important, but knowing the amount of profit, or loss, achieved in an operation helps owners better understand and address key issues:

- What were the profits for this accounting period?
- What percentage of revenue did the profits represent?
- Did profits achieve estimated levels?
- Are profits increasing compared to prior accounting periods?
- Are profits decreasing compared to prior accounting periods?
- Are profits sufficient to allow the business to pay its bills as they come due, or must additional funds be acquired?
- How much, if any, money can be taken from the business for use by the owners of the business?

The answers to questions of these types can be addressed by both monthly and annual P&Ls. Preparing summary financial information on a monthly basis versus only on an annual basis gives owners and managers timelier and more detailed financial facts. In nearly all cases, this helps improve decision making.

Exhibit 3.5		
GAS COSTS (MONTHLY P&L APPROACH)		
Month	**Monthly Cost**	**Daily Cost**
February	$2,800	$100
March	3,100	100
April	3,000	100

P&Ls FOR OTHER ACCOUNTING PERIODS

Increasingly, some operations prefer to create income statements that address a 28-day period. Proponents cite the advantages of having equal four-week time periods from which to make decisions. To better understand the advantages, consider the manager who is concerned about costs related to the usage of natural gas for cooking in the kitchen. See *Exhibit 3.5* to review the manager's findings.

From the monthly expense data it appears the cost of gas fluctuates. The cost of gas increased in March when compared to February costs; but April costs decreased when compared to March. Note that the daily cost of gas, however, did not change. The change in monthly cost reflects the fact that February has 28 days, while March has 31 and April has 30. Using 28-day accounting periods, the gas usage for each period would have been reported as $2,800. This makes it easier to detect real changes in revenue or expenses, rather than changes that occur only because the lengths of months vary.

A second reason for increased popularity of the 28-day accounting period is related to the specific days in the week. Each 28-day accounting period has the same number of weekdays and weekend days, as well as the same number of Mondays, Tuesdays, Wednesdays, and so on. This can be important for those businesses that wish to compare P&L results from two accounting periods, but want to ensure that each has equal numbers of Friday and Saturday nights.

Some restaurant and foodservice managers prepare quarterly (three consecutive months) P&Ls. Others prepare weekly income statements and some even estimate P&L results on a daily basis. In most cases such rapid estimates lack accuracy. This is because they would not include the detailed expense-related information needed to produce a precise P&L using GAAP. They may, however, prove useful in some cases.

Regardless of the accounting period addressed by a P&L, that time period should be clearly stated near the top of the report. This helps the reader easily identify it before the document is reviewed.

Accounting for Revenue

After determining the accounting period to be addressed in an income statement, the revenue generated in that time period is identified. *Exhibit 3.6* is an example of an income statement prepared for Richter's Steak House, an establishment that serves both food and alcoholic beverages. Note that it is a monthly P&L and the time period it addresses is 4/1/2012 to 4/30/2012.

Recall that many reutrant and foodservice professionals may use the terms *income*, *revenue*, and *sales* interchangeably. Some even use the term *sales revenue*.

In *Exhibit 3.6* sales for the period are listed first, and they consist of $80,000 in food sales and $20,000 in beverage sales. These two figures are then added to yield total sales of $100,000.

Sales:	
Food	$ 80,000
Beverage	20,000
Total sales	**$100,000**

In this operation two revenue sources are shown. A **revenue source** is a distinct area, for example a bar or dining room, in which sales are generated. A revenue source can also be the sales generated by a specific product, for example food or gift cards. In general, the more revenue sources identified on an income statement, the greater the detail provided about the business's sales production.

Exhibit 3.6

RICHTER'S STEAK HOUSE P&L FOR THE PERIOD: 4/1/12 TO 4/30/12

SALES	
Food	$ 80,000
Beverage	20,000
Total Sales	**$100,000**
COST OF SALES	
Food	$ 32,000
Beverage	5,000
Total Cost of Sales	**$ 37,000**
LABOR	
Management	6,000
Staff	20,000
Employee benefits	4,000
Total Labor	**$ 30,000**
Prime Cost	**$ 67,000**
Other Controllable Expenses:	
Legal/accounting	500
Music and entertainment	5,000
Marketing	250
Utility services	2,000
General and administrative	4,050
Repairs and maintenance	2,000
Total Other Controllable Expenses	**$ 13,800**
Controllable Income	**$ 19,200**
Noncontrollable Expenses:	
Rent	$ 5,700
Depreciation	3,500
Licenses/permits	100
Leases	2,000
Total Noncontrollable Expenses	**$ 11,300**
Operating Income	**$ 7,900**
Interest expense	800
Other (income) expense	200
Income Before Income Taxes	**$ 6,900**

In the restaurant and foodservice industry there are many commonly identified sales areas and revenue sources:

- Distinct dining areas (in operations with more than one dining area)
- Banquets
- Catering
- Drive-through
- Carryout
- Delivery
- Lounge or bar (*Exhibit 3.7*)
- Bakery
- Gift shop
- Gift certificates and gift cards
- Merchandise, such as T-shirts, caps, and souvenirs

The Uniform System of Accounts for Restaurants (USAR) provides a list of suggested revenue sources for use by managers preparing income statements. Those preparing income statements must list all of the revenue generated by each revenue source during the accounting period addressed by the P&L. They must also include all revenue sources.

PERCENTAGES

Some income statements list the percentage of revenue generated by each revenue source in addition to the source's monetary contribution. *Exhibit 3.8* shows the percentage of revenue generated by food sales and by beverage sales for the Richter's Steak House P&L.

To calculate the sales percentage of a revenue source the following formula is used:

$$\frac{\text{Sales contributed}}{\text{by revenue source}} \div \frac{\text{Total}}{\text{sales}} = \frac{\text{Sales}}{\text{percentage}}$$

For *Exhibit 3.8* the calculations are:

$$\underset{\text{Food sales}}{\$80{,}000} \div \underset{\text{Total sales}}{\$100{,}000} = \underset{\text{Sales percentage}}{80\%}$$

And

$$\underset{\text{Beverage sales}}{\$20{,}000} \div \underset{\text{Total sales}}{\$100{,}000} = \underset{\text{Sales percentage}}{20\%}$$

Exhibit 3.8

DETAIL FROM RICHTER'S STEAK HOUSE P&L FOR THE PERIOD: 4/1/12 TO 4/30/12

Sales		Sales Percentage
Food	$ 80,000	80%
Beverage	20,000	20
Total Sales	**$100,000**	**100%**

Note that the sum of the sales percentages for all revenue sources will always equal 100%. In this example:

$$80\% + 20\% = 100\%$$

Food sales   Beverage sales   Total sales

Managers are often interested in sales percentage figures because it helps them better understand the popularity of various sources from which their revenue is generated.

To illustrate, consider the manager whose operation offers delivery service. As a result, Delivered Meals is designated as a revenue source when the operation's income statement is prepared. In the first months of offering the service, the sales percentage for Delivered Meals was very low; less than 5 percent. However, it has increased each month. As the manager continually monitors the sales percentage for Delivered Meals he or she will have a better understanding of the proportion of sales that can be attributed directly to this new service.

Accounting for Expenses

Cost of sales is the industry term for the food and beverage product expense incurred in the generation of sales. For example, if an operation generated $5,000 in food revenue and the amount of food products required to generate those sales was $1,000, then the *cost* of the sales for food would be $1,000.

As can be seen back in *Exhibit 3.6*, total cost of sales consists of the costs incurred for food ($32,000) and for beverages ($5,000). Total cost of sales is $32,000 + $5,000, or $37,000.

Most managers are interested in knowing their food cost percentage and their beverage cost percentage, as well as their overall cost of sales percentage. *Exhibit 3.9* shows how the income statement would be prepared to provide such information.

Exhibit 3.9		

DETAIL FROM RICHTER'S STEAK HOUSE P&L FOR THE PERIOD: 4/1/12 TO 4/30/12

Sales		Sales Percentage
Food	$ 80,000	80%
Beverage	20,000	20
Total Sales	**$100,000**	**100%**
Cost of Sales		**Cost of Sales Percentage**
Food	$ 32,000	40%
Beverage	5,000	25
Total Cost of Sales	**$ 37,000**	**37%**

A **food cost percentage** is the proportion of food sales spent for food expense.

The formula for a food cost percentage is:

Cost of sales (food) ÷ Food sales = Food cost percentage

In this example:

$$\$32,000 \div \$80,000 = 40\%$$

Cost of sales (food)	Food sales	Food cost percentage

A **beverage cost percentage** is the proportion of beverage sales spent for beverage expense.

The formula for a beverage cost percentage is:

Cost of sales (beverage) ÷ Beverage sales = Beverage cost percentage

In this example:

$$\$5,000 \div \$20,000 = 25\%$$

Cost of sales (beverages)	Beverage sales	Beverage cost percentage

A **cost of sales percentage** is the proportion of total sales spent for the products used to create the sales.

The formula for a cost of sales percentage is:

Total cost of sales ÷ Total sales = Cost of sales percentage

In this example:

$$\$37,000 \div \$100,000 = 37\%$$

Total cost of sales	Total sales	Cost of sales percentage

Managers are interested in various cost of sales percentages. Cost of sales percentages help them better understand the efficiency with which products purchased generate sales. To illustrate, consider the manager whose operation has established a target food cost percentage of 35 percent. When the income statement is prepared, the manager discovers the food cost percentage actually achieved was 40 percent. In this situation the manager would want to determine why the operation's actual food cost percentage exceeds the cost target.

Some managers also list gross profit on the P&Ls they prepare. **Gross profit** is the amount of revenue remaining after the costs of food and beverages have been subtracted from sales. Using the numbers in *Exhibit 3.9*, gross profit from food would be $48,000:

$$\$80,000 - \$32,000 = \$48,000$$

Food sales	Cost of sales (food)	Gross profit

THINK ABOUT IT . . .

Most managers calculate their food and beverage cost percentages separately. Why do you think they do so?

What information would they be lacking if they did not calculate these two cost percentages separately?

Gross profit from beverages would be $15,000:

$$\underset{\substack{\text{Beverage} \\ \text{sales}}}{\$20,000} - \underset{\substack{\text{Cost of sales} \\ \text{(beverages)}}}{\$5,000} = \underset{\substack{\text{Gross} \\ \text{profit}}}{\$15,000}$$

Total gross profit would be $63,000:

$$\underset{\substack{\text{Total} \\ \text{sales}}}{\$100,000} - \underset{\substack{\text{Total cost} \\ \text{of sales}}}{\$37,000} = \underset{\substack{\text{Gross} \\ \text{profit}}}{\$63,000}$$

Of course, restaurant and foodservice operations incur a large number of expenses in addition to food and beverage expenses. These are listed on the income statement after cost of sales.

Because labor costs are a very large expense in most operations, they are usually listed immediately after costs of sales. Management costs are listed first, followed by staff costs, then employee benefits. As shown previously in *Exhibit 3.6*, these labor costs are then summed to arrive at total labor costs.

Prime cost is the sum of food costs and labor costs. The USAR recommends that prime costs in an operation be listed as indicated in *Exhibit 3.6*.

On the Richter's Steak House P&L prime cost is calculated as:

$$\underset{\substack{\text{Total cost} \\ \text{of sales}}}{\$37,000} + \underset{\substack{\text{Total} \\ \text{labor}}}{\$30,000} = \underset{\substack{\text{Prime} \\ \text{cost}}}{\$67,000}$$

EXPENSE TIMING

To be accurate an income statement must list all of an operation's expenses. **Expense timing** refers to the proper method of reporting those expenses. Those managers using the cash accounting method (see chapter 1) recognize and record business expenses as they are paid. But when using the accrual accounting method, expenses are matched with the revenues they have generated rather than with the time when the expenses are paid.

Expense timing is an important issue for most managers because most restaurants and foodservice operations use the accrual method of accounting. When using accrual accounting, some of an accountant's decisions about how to best record the time of expenses are easy. For example, if a case of lettuce is purchased and used in the same month, it is easy to see that the cost of the lettuce is an expense that should be recorded as paid in the month the lettuce was purchased and used. Similarly, costs such as salaries paid to managers in a specific month should be reported on that same month's income statement.

OPEN FOR BUSINESS

MANAGER'S MATH

A manager prepared the sales and the food and beverage expense portions of an income statement for last month.

Last Month

Sales		Sales Percentage
Food	$ 60,000	75%
Beverage	20,000	25
Total Sales	**$80,000**	**100%**

Cost of Sales		Cost of Sales Percentage
Food	$ 20,000	%
Beverage	4,000	%
Total Cost of Sales	**$**	**%**

1. What was the total cost of sales for this month?

2. What was the food cost percentage for this month?

3. What was the beverage cost percentage for this month?

4. What was total cost of sales percentage for this month?

(Answers: 1. $24,000. 2. 33.3%. 3. 20.0%. 4. 30.0%)

In other cases, decisions about how to best record the time of expenses are complex. For example, assume that a manager receives an operation's utility bill on May 15 for the prior month of service. Should the bill be recorded as a utility expense for May or for April? To be most accurate, the bill might be recorded as an April expense because that is when the cost was actually incurred. Taking that approach, however, would delay the preparation of the operation's April income statement until the bill was received in May. The accuracy gained by such an approach would likely be more than offset by the disadvantages of waiting several weeks to receive the utility bill and prepare the P&L.

In this example, GAAP allow the manager to charge the April utility bill to May expense. Similarly, in April, the operation's March utility bill would be timed as an April expense. In all cases, those preparing income statements seek to time expenses as closely as possible to the period in which they generated revenue.

EXPENSE CLASSIFICATION

Costs can be categorized, or classified, in several different ways. Expense classification is used when preparing budgets (see chapter 4) and when preparing income statements. The foodservice industry classifies expenses as controllable, noncontrollable, fixed, variable, and semivariable costs.

One main reason for classifying costs is to differentiate between those costs that management can control and those over which management has little or no control. Identifying and understanding these different types of costs help managers better interpret cost-related information and make better financial decisions.

One of the most common methods of classifying expenses is to categorize them as either controllable costs or noncontrollable costs. These are exactly what their names imply. **Controllable costs** are those costs that management can directly control. **Noncontrollable costs** are those costs over which management has little or no control.

Food cost is an example of a controllable cost. Management can use standardized recipes or exercise standard procedures for portion sizes, and for pricing. For example, if the cost of chicken increases and no action is taken, the operation's food cost will increase. At this point, management can raise the selling price of all chicken entrées, reduce portion sizes, or eliminate chicken from the menu. By taking action, management seeks to exercise some *control* over the effect of the increased cost of chicken.

Another example of a controllable cost is labor cost. By changing the number of hours worked by employees and thus the amount they are paid, a manager can affect labor costs (see *Exhibit 3.10*). For example, suppose an establishment's sales decline and no action is taken to reduce the amount spent for workers. Then worker-related cost as a percentage of sales will increase. By reducing the number of hours worked by employees, this percentage could be brought back to targeted levels.

It should be pointed out, however, that in exercising these options, management must always think about the impact on customers. If the selling price of chicken entrées is increased too much, or if too many server hours are removed from a work schedule, customers may respond negatively to the higher prices or the reduced service levels.

Exhibit 3.10

Rent is an example of a noncontrollable cost. Once a lease has been negotiated, and the monthly payment amount for it has been determined, management has no control over the cost of rent. Another example is license fees. Management has no control over the rate charged for liquor or other licenses.

In addition to being classified as either controllable or noncontrollable, costs can also be expressed as fixed, variable, or semivariable. This group of expense classifications is based on each cost's relationship to sales volume. In other words, does a cost increase or decrease as revenue increases or decreases?

Fixed costs remain the same regardless of sales volume. Insurance is an example of a fixed cost. After insurance policies have been negotiated, the cost remains the same throughout the term of the policy. For example, if the cost of insuring the business is $1,000 per month, it will remain at $1,000 every month. If the establishment has sales of $10,000 one month, $20,000 the next month, and $15,000 the following month, then the insurance cost remains the same. It does not change when sales levels change.

Variable costs are those costs that go up and down as sales fluctuate, and do so in direct proportion. An example of a variable cost is food cost. As sales go up, more food is purchased to replenish supplies and as sales go down, less food is purchased. If adequate controls are in place and there is little waste or theft, the amount of food used is in direct proportion to sales.

Semivariable costs go up and down as sales fluctuate, but not in direct proportion. Semivariable costs are made up of both fixed costs and variable costs. An example of a semivariable cost is labor. Labor is composed of both management and staff costs.

MANAGER'S MATH

Managers calculate product cost percentages based on the revenue the products generate. Remember, for example, that a food cost percentage is calculated as follows:

Cost of sales: Food ÷ Food sales = Food cost percentage

Non-food and beverage product cost percentages are calculated based on *total* sales. These expense percentages are calculated as follows:

Expense ÷ Total sales = Expense percentage

Some managers list expense percentages on their income statements as well as the actual amount of the expense. Calculate the expense percentage for each cost listed. Then answer the questions that follow.

	Sales Amount	Expense	Expense Percentage
Food sales	$15,000		
Beverage sales	5,000		
Total sales			
Cost of sales food		$4,000	_____ %
Cost of sales beverages		1,375	_____
Marketing		150	_____
Rent		1,750	_____
Salaries and wages		3,500	_____
Utility services		300	_____
Insurance		125	_____

1. What was the operation's food cost percentage?
2. What was the operation's beverage cost percentage?
3. What was the highest cost controllable expense?
4. What was the highest cost fixed expense?
5. What was the highest percentage non-food or beverage controllable cost?

(Answers: 1. 26.7%; 2. 27.5%; 3. Cost of sales food; 4. Rent; 5. Salaries and wages)

Exhibit 3.11

AREAS OF OPERATING EXPENSE FROM RICHTER'S STEAK HOUSE P&L

Total cost of sales	$37,000
Total labor	30,000
Total other controllable expenses	13,800
Total noncontrollable expenses	11,300
Interest expense	800
Other (income) expenses	200

Managers are normally paid a salary. Their salary remains the same regardless of the operation's sales volume. If the general manager, assistant manager, and chef are collectively paid $200,000 in salaries per year, they will receive that amount regardless of whether the establishment brings in $1,000,000 or $1,300,000 in revenue per year. Thus, management's salary in this example is a fixed cost.

In most cases, however, staff members such as servers are paid an hourly wage. The workers are scheduled according to anticipated sales. As a result, the cost of hourly employees most often goes up as sales go up and goes down as sales go down. If proper scheduling is used, the cost will go up and down in direct proportion to sales levels. Overall labor cost is considered a semivariable cost because there is a fixed cost component, the management's salary, as well as a variable cost component, the hourly workers' wages.

In some cases managers can experience crossover when classifying costs. Variable and semivariable costs are usually controllable costs. Fixed costs are typically noncontrollable costs. For example, if an operation has a monthly lease payment that is negotiated at $3,000 per month, the cost is fixed. It does not vary according to sales, neither increasing as sales go up nor decreasing as sales go down. It will always remain at $3,000.

If, on the other hand, the lease is negotiated at 6 percent of sales, then rent is a variable cost. The dollar amount will go up as sales go up and down as sales go down. In yet other cases, a lease may call for a monthly payment of $1,000 plus 3 percent of sales. Then rent is a semivariable cost. The $1,000 is paid regardless of sales volume, making it a fixed cost. The variable part of the cost comes from the 3 percent of sales, which increases or decreases as sales go up or down.

GAAP allow accountants some flexibility in the expense classifications used to report information on an income statement. The P&L for Richter's Steak House shown earlier in the chapter (see *Exhibit 3.6*) classifies operating costs in six main areas, as detailed in *Exhibit 3.11*.

Recall from the P&L that the total sales were $100,000. As shown in *Exhibit 3.11*, the sum of all reported expenses was $93,100:

$37,000 +	$30,000 +	$13,800 +	$11,300 +	$800 +	$200 =	$93,100
Total cost of sales	Total labor	Total other controllable expenses	Total noncontrollable expenses	Interest expense	Other (income) expenses	Total expenses

As a result, the income before income taxes was $6,900:

$100,000 −	$93,100 =	$6,900
Total sales	Total expenses	Income before income taxes

The Richter's Steak House P&L follows the USAR suggested format for income statements. Managers and owners can choose to use this format or other formats they find most helpful. In all cases, however, it is of the utmost importance that managers list all of the sales achieved, and all of the operating expenses incurred in their businesses for the accounting period indicated on the income statement.

Accounting for Profits

Managers also calculate their income before income taxes on the P&L. This amount, located at the bottom of the income statement, is also commonly referred to by managers as "profit" or "the bottom line."

If sales are higher than operating costs, then the operation will have a positive income before income taxes. Conversely, if the total costs of operating the business for the accounting period were higher than total sales, then the business operated at a loss and will have a negative income before income taxes. This condition is also known as operating "in the red." This terminology is due to the fact that accountants often print losses in red, or use some other special identifying technique, such as minus signs or brackets, to report the amount of negative income before income taxes, or loss, on an income statement. Profits earned in most businesses are subject to income and other taxes (see *Exhibit 3.12*).

Exhibit 3.12

TYPES OF TAXES

Taxes Due from the Operation

- **Income taxes.** These can be federal, state, or local.

- **Property taxes.** Real property taxes can be a major expense and may be imposed by state or local jurisdictions. They are based on the assessed value of the property.

- **Personal property taxes.** This could include such categories as kitchen equipment and improvements; small wares such as china, glassware, and dining room equipment; and construction in progress.

Taxes Collected by the Operation on Behalf of the Government

- **Sales taxes.** Most states have some sort of sales and use tax. Although it is paid by customers, it is collected by sellers.

- **Payroll taxes.** These can be considered in two categories. One is tax money withheld from employees' paychecks and then paid to the government by the employer. These taxes are also paid by the employee. The other payroll taxes include federal unemployment insurance, workers' compensation, and unemployment compensation.

When all business taxes due have been subtracted from an operation's income before income taxes the resulting amount is referred to as net earnings. **Net earnings** are the amount of after tax income earned by a business during an accounting period.

READING THE INCOME STATEMENT

Managers collect profit and loss data for their operations for a purpose. Investors, owners, and managers look carefully at these reports to determine the profitability of their operations. The reports are often used to judge the efficiency of an operation, to determine where costs have gotten out of line, and to make other key management decisions.

When reading income statements, managers typically analyze the reported sales, expense, and profit data using three important sources of information:

- Budgets
- Standards
- Historical performance

Budgets

Profit and loss reports are useful when comparing what is actually occurring to what was planned. The next chapter in this book addresses how managers prepare **budgets**: the financial plans for operating a facility during a future time period. When such plans have been previously developed, managers can compare their actual operating results against planned or targeted results. When reviewing income statement results against planned results, managers can find the answers to many important operational questions:

- Did total sales meet the planned revenue target?
- For which revenue sources did sales meet the plan?
- For which revenue sources did sales fail to meet the plan?
- Did total costs exceed planned expenses?
- In which specific expense categories did costs exceed planned expense?
- Did the operation reach its profit goals?

Any variation between actual results and planned results indicates that something unexpected has occurred. For instance, actual sales amounts might not be as high as were expected due to bad weather conditions or emergency road repairs. It is easy to see how unforeseen conditions could affect sales.

Unexpected expenses, such as repairs to equipment, may cause costs to be higher than anticipated (*Exhibit 3.13*). Other causes of increased expense may not be so easily identified, and will have to be carefully investigated by the manager. In all cases, managers will want to know what caused the variation between expected and actual results. Then they can take the managerial actions needed to correct the problems and to improve the future operational performance of their businesses.

Standards

An operation may be part of a large company operating many similar restaurant or foodservice operations. Such an operation will likely have company standards against which the operation's financial performance can be compared.

Company standards are used as a guide for how an operation can and should be run. Standards often include goals for percentages of revenue coming from various revenue sources and costs of food and beverages. The amounts spent on controllable and fixed expenses can be addressed by company standards as well.

In some cases, industry-wide standards can be used to assess an operation's financial performance. These standards reflect accepted ranges for certain costs within the restaurant and foodservice industry. Such standards are not an exact measurement. It is important to make sure the values being compared actually fit the nature of an operation. For example, a fine-dining restaurant will have a higher percentage of labor costs than a takeout restaurant.

A fine-dining operation is one that offers guests the highest-quality food and full table service. If the fine-dining manager's goal is to have better service than any other establishment in the area, then that operation should expect to have labor costs that are higher than the industry standard.

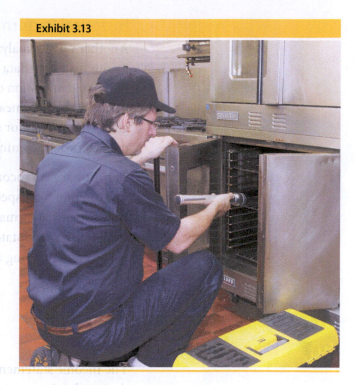
Exhibit 3.13

Historical Performance

Another way to analyze the information on an income statement is to compare it with historical data from the same operation. This can be done for an individual operation or across multiple operations. Using historical performance as a means of evaluating an operation's financial performance is a good way to monitor seasonal revenue changes. It can also be used to remind managers of upcoming local events that had an effect on a previous year's sales.

In summary, an income statement is a compilation of sales and cost information for a specific period of time. The format of the statement may vary somewhat as may the terms used to describe its main parts. In all cases, a complete income statement accurately reports on three areas of financial performance during a specific time period:

1. Revenue

2. Expense

3. Profits

The income statement shows whether an operation made or lost money during the time period covered by the report. As a result, it is an incredibly important management tool. It helps managers gauge an operation's profitability and compare actual results to expected goals. Managers should carefully and periodically monitor the information contained in the income statement. Doing so will help managers identify areas where action must be taken to bring business operations in line with financial targets.

SUMMARY

1. **Explain the purpose of an income statement.**

   Managers, owners, investors, and others have an interest in knowing about the revenue achieved, expenses incurred, and profits generated by a business during a designated period of time. The time period may be 28 days, a month, a year, or any other period that helps communicate the financial performance of a business. The income statement's purpose is to provide this key financial information to these groups so they can analyze it and, by doing so, make better business decisions.

2. **Identify the three major types of financial information included in an income statement.**

   The three major categories of information listed on an income statement, also called a P&L, are sales (revenue), expenses (costs), and income before income taxes (profits). Sales may be reported as a single total or by revenue source. Expenses for food and beverage products sold are listed as are all other controllable and fixed expenses. Finally, pre-tax income achieved by the operation is listed.

3. **Identify operating costs as controllable, noncontrollable, fixed, variable, or semivariable.**

   Controllable costs are those operating expenses that management can directly control. They are different from noncontrollable costs: those expenses over which management has little or no control. Food cost is an example of a controllable cost. Labor is another example of a controllable cost. For example, by varying the number of workers scheduled, a manager can directly affect, or control, the amount spent for labor. Noncontrollable costs are those which management has little ability to change. Rent is a noncontrollable cost because, after a lease is signed, the amount to be paid for rent cannot normally be changed during the period of the lease.

   A fixed cost is an expense that remains the same regardless of sales volume. Insurance is an example of a fixed cost because that expense does not change when sales levels change. Additional examples of fixed expenses can include loan payments, license fees, and rent. Variable expenses change as volume levels change. Food is a variable expense because, as an operation's food sales increase, the amount spent by the operation for food will also increase. Semivariable costs change as sales volume changes, but not in direct proportion.

4. **Explain how managers read and analyze an income statement.**

   Managers analyze an income statement by carefully reading the financial information provided in each of its revenue, expense, and profit sections. This information can then be analyzed by comparing it to three different sources of available data. One comparison that is most often made is an operation's actual performance to its planned or budgeted performance. Differences can be investigated to determine the managerial actions that must be taken to bring actual performance back in line with planned performance. Additional comparisons can be made to company standards, or to industry-wide data that can be used as a standard or goal. Managers can also compare current P&L performance to historical P&L performance of the same operation. They do so to identify seasonal trends and to monitor improvements or declines in their establishments' operating performances.

APPLICATION EXERCISE

The manager of Randy's Restaurant has just received an income statement report comparing the establishment's financial performance this year to last year's performance. After reviewing the report on the following page, answer the questions that follow to help the manager better understand the operation and its financial performance.

RANDY'S RESTAURANT

SALES	This Year	Last Year
Food	$ 750,000	$ 690,000
Beverage	300,000	310,000
Total Sales	**$1,050,000**	**$1,000,000**
COST OF SALES		
Food	$250,000	$225,000
Beverage	80,000	83,000
Total Cost of Sales	**$330,000**	**$308,000**
LABOR		
Management	$ 55,000	$ 52,000
Staff	225,000	221,500
Employee benefits	85,000	83,500
Total Labor	**$365,000**	**$357,000**
Prime Cost	**$695,000**	**$665,000**
Other Controllable Expenses:		
Legal/accounting	$ 1,750	$ 1,690
Music and entertainment	12,000	11,500
Marketing	12,400	12,000
Utility services	18,000	17,500
General and administrative	12,500	12,000
Repairs and maintenance	15,000	13,500
Total Other Controllable Expenses	**$71,650**	**$68,190**
Controllable Income	**$283,350**	**$266,810**
Noncontrollable Expenses:		
Rent	$95,000	$95,000
Depreciation	6,000	6,000
Licenses/permits	500	450
Leases	2,500	2,500
Total Noncontrollable Expenses	**$104,000**	**$103,950**
Operating Income	**$179,350**	**$162,860**
Interest expense	18,000	19,000
Other (income) expense	500	500
Income Before Income Taxes	**$160,850**	**$143,360**

1. What was the difference between the operation's food sales this year from the previous year? Does this mark an improvement or a decline?

2. What was the difference between the operation's beverage sales this year from the previous year? Does this mark an improvement or a decline?

3. What was the difference between the operation's total sales this year from the previous year? Does this mark an improvement or a decline?

4. Did the operation spend more or less for food when comparing this year's expense to last year's expense? By how much?

5. Did the operation spend more or less for beverages when comparing this year's expense to last year's expense? By how much?

6. What was the amount of increase in management costs this year compared to last year?

7. What was the amount of increase in staff costs this year compared to last year?

8. What was the amount of increase in total labor costs this year compared to last year?

9. In what area or areas were this year's expense less than last year's expense?

10. What was the amount of profit made in the establishment this year? What was the amount of profit made last year?

11. Why do you think the operation's cost of sales food this year is higher than last year?

12. Why do you think the operation's cost of sales beverage this year is lower than last year?

REVIEW YOUR LEARNING

Select the best answer for each question.

1. An income statement is also commonly referred to as a(n)
   A. P&L.
   B. budget.
   C. cash flow.
   D. expense classification.

2. An operation's year-end income statement shows before tax profits of $210,000. Revenues for the year were $1,850,000. What were this operation's expenses for the year?
   A. $1,430,000
   B. $1,640,000
   C. $2,060,000
   D. $2,300,000

3. An operation's income statement shows total expenses of $45,500 for a specific month. Before tax profits for the month were $3,250. What was this operation's revenue for the month?
   A. $42,250
   B. $46,750
   C. $48,750
   D. $52,250

4. Why are a business's vendors interested in information contained in that business's income statement?
   A. So they can arrange for the best time to make deliveries
   B. To help the vendor secure future orders from the business
   C. To assist in determining which products should be sold to the business
   D. So they can make decisions about payment terms that should be offered

5. A manager's total revenue for an accounting period is $150,000. Revenue from one of the operation's three revenue sources is $30,000. What was the sales percentage of that revenue source?

   A. 10%

   B. 20%

   C. 30%

   D. 40%

6. What is an example of a controllable cost?

   A. Rent

   B. Insurance

   C. Marketing

   D. Loan payments

7. What is an example of a fixed cost?

   A. Utility services

   B. Salaries and wages

   C. Licenses and permits

   D. Repairs and maintenance

8. What is the formula for prime cost?

   A. Total cost of sales − Total labor = Prime cost

   B. Total cost of sales + Total labor = Prime cost

   C. Total cost of sales − Controllable income = Prime cost

   D. Total cost of sales + Controllable income = Prime cost

9. A manager's operation had an income before income taxes of $2,000 in a month. Total expenses were $18,000 in that month. What was the operation's total sales amount in that month?

   A. $20,000

   B. $25,000

   C. $30,000

   D. $35,000

10. A manager compares the revenue results for a 28-day P&L period to the results of the 28-day P&L report from the previous 28-day period. What source of information is the manager using to analyze the revenue portion of the current P&L statement?

    A. Budget

    B. Chain standard

    C. Industry standard

    D. Historical performance

FIELD PROJECT

Visit a local restaurant or foodservice operation to talk with the manager about the operation's income statement. During your visit ask the manager the following questions:

1. What is the name the operation uses for its income statement (e.g., income statement, P&L, or other name)?

2. Who prepares the report?

3. How often is the report prepared?

4. What is the term the operation uses to identify its revenue (e.g., revenue, sales, or income)?

5. How many different revenue sources are identified on the report?

6. What are the names of the major expense categories used to prepare the report (e.g., controllable, noncontrollable, variable, fixed, or some other classification)?

7. Are revenue and expenses also expressed as their percentage of sales?

8. What is the term used on the report to identify the operation's profits?

9. Who receives copies of the report?

10. Who is responsible for analyzing the data in the report?

Ask the manager to describe examples of how he or she uses information in the report to make operational decisions.

4

Budgeting

INSIDE THIS CHAPTER

- **The Purpose of Budgets**
- **Budgets Overview**
- **Revenue Forecasting**
- **Budgeting Expenses**
- **Budgeting for Profits**

CHAPTER LEARNING OBJECTIVES

After completing this chapter, you should be able to:

- Explain the purpose of an operating budget.

- Identify and describe the major types of budgets used in restaurant and foodservice operations.

- Summarize the method used to forecast an operation's revenue.

- Summarize the method used to forecast an operation's expenses.

- State the importance of accurately budgeting for profits.

KEY TERMS

amortization, p. 97

annual budget, p. 81

capital, p. 83

capital budget, p. 83

capital expenditure, p. 83

contracted expense, p. 96

covers per server, p. 92

day part, p. 88

depreciation, p. 97

labor standard, p. 90

long-range budget, p. 83

moving average, p. 85

occupancy cost, p. 96

operating budget, p. 80

overhead, p. 89

profit per guest served, p. 99

short-range budget, p. 83

CASE STUDY

"It's broken again," said Larry.

"Not again!" replied Peggy, the manager of Schafer's German Haus restaurant.

Larry was talking about the dishwasher at Schafer's German Haus. The machine had been installed nearly 20 years ago when the restaurant had just opened. Because the restaurant had been a big success since the day it opened, the machine had gotten a lot of use.

Now, it broke down frequently and that caused major problems getting enough clean glasses and dishware to the service and cook staff when the restaurant was full, as on this day.

"I'll call the repair company," sighed Peggy.

"I think you should call a dishwasher salesperson," said Larry.

1. Some restaurant and foodservice equipment expenses are so large they cannot be entirely paid for from only one month's operating profits. In addition to items such as a dishwasher replacement, what examples of other costs should owners and managers plan for well in advance?

2. What will happen to an operation if its owners and managers do not plan ahead for these kinds of repair or replacement expenses?

THE PURPOSE OF BUDGETS

When it comes to finances, it is often easy to spend more than intended. A business may also require funds for special purposes, but not have them available when needed. Having a budget helps managers plan the financial activities related to their daily operations. An **operating budget** is a projected financial plan for a specific period of time. Its purpose is to list the anticipated sales revenue and projected expenses of an operation. It also provides an estimate of the profit or loss expected for the budget period.

A budget serves as a guide for making spending decisions in the short and long terms. While a budget can be a valuable tool, it is only as accurate as the care and detail that go into its preparation. Operating budgets are often prepared monthly, though they can be prepared for shorter or longer periods depending on the structure of the organization. Operating budgets serve many purposes in the management of a restaurant or foodservice operation:

- Analyze needs, such as for food, beverages, staffing, and supplies

- Outline operating goals and managers' performance responsibilities

- Measure actual performance against anticipated performance

- Provide guidance for needed corrective actions

An operating budget is a necessary tool for managers. However, preparing one is not a simple process. Putting together a useful and accurate budget requires time and care. With a well-prepared budget, managers are better able to address key management tasks:

- Estimate revenue

- Control expense

- Manage cash

In most cases, managers prepare an operating budget for presentation to an operation's owners. This process takes several steps:

1. Gather prior period budget information.

2. Determine the new budget period.

3. Gather needed operating information.

4. Determine the budget format.

5. Analyze the budget's impact.

6. Present the budget.

Step 1: Gather Prior Period Budget Information

The first step in the development of an operating budget is to obtain any existing budget information. This step includes collecting information about an operation's past budget performance. Budgets are typically kept on file from year to year, and actual financial performance will be found on an operation's income statements from previous accounting periods (see chapter 3).

Step 2: Determine the New Budget Period

Budgets can be prepared for a variety of time periods. An **annual budget** that addresses estimated financial performance of an operation for 52 consecutive weeks is very common. However, budgets may be prepared for a variety of time periods based on the needs of the operation and the wishes of its owners:

- Week
- 28-day period
- Month
- Year
- Multiple years

Managers determine the format and time frame for their budgets to make them most useful to themselves and to the owners of the operation.

Step 3: Gather Needed Operating Information

To prepare a budget, managers need information about an operation's past and current performance. Operating information found on income statements can be helpful. In addition, some additional information will not be listed on the income statement but can be very helpful in estimating future costs. For instance, a manager might want to know the amount currently being paid for the ingredients used to prepare very popular menu items. To obtain as much relevant revenue and expense-related information as possible, managers review data from a variety of sources:

- Daily sales records
- Weekly sales records
- Records of food purchases
- Records of beverage purchases
- Supply purchase records
- Employee schedules and payroll records
- Variable expense records
- Fixed expense records

Exhibit 4.1

Exhibit 4.1

Step 4: Determine the Budget Format

The information to be included in a budget must be presented in an easily readable and easily understandable format. In some cases, only the manager of an operation will review budgets and their format. In other cases, information in the budget may be shared with kitchen managers, chefs, beverage managers, and others whose input in the budget preparation process is valuable (*Exhibit 4.1*). Many managers use the USAR (see chapter 1) for a list of expense categories they can use in budget preparations.

Step 5: Analyze the Budget's Impact

One of a manager's most critical budget-related tasks is to analyze the impact of the budget on the operation's profitability. When a budget is presented to an operation's owner, the manager is likely to be asked important questions about the impact of the budget:

- What level of revenue is forecast?
- Is the revenue estimate readily achievable?
- Are budgeted expenses in line with established standards or targets?
- Are forecasted profits in line with established profit targets?

Step 6: Present the Budget

The final step in the process of preparing a budget for an operation's owners is the actual presentation of the budget. During the presentation, managers must be prepared to explain how the budget was prepared. They must also explain any operating assumptions made by the manager in the budget's preparation. Examples of assumptions include increasing or decreasing menu prices, changes in employee wages, or a change in operating hours. In all cases, a manager should be able to explain and defend any assumptions used in the preparation of the budget.

BUDGETS OVERVIEW

Managers can best understand budgets by comparing them to the income statements described in chapter 3. The income statements report the actual revenue, expenses, and profits or losses resulting from the operation of a business. The operating budget predicts or estimates these same values for a future time period.

Because budgets are estimates of future financial performance, they can vary in length and in purpose. There are three very common types of budgets used in restaurant and foodservice operations:

- Short-range budgets
- Long-range budgets
- Capital budgets

Short-Range Budgets

A **short-range budget** is one that is typically prepared for an accounting period in the near future. It often addresses financial performance for one year or less. If a 12-month period is included in the short-range budget, the period may consist of a calendar year or a fiscal year.

In many cases, managers create monthly operating budgets then sum the information in each monthly budget to create an annual budget. Similarly, managers may prepare weekly budgets that are then summed to create monthly budgets. In each of these cases, short-range budgets are created to provide operating guidance to managers. Because they address relatively brief time periods, short-range budgets can be reasonably accurate.

Short-range budgets provide managers with the most up-to-date budget data possible. Because of their detailed information, short-range budgets can be used, for example, to estimate the number of labor hours needed next week or the next two weeks. When these types of data are known, worker schedules can be prepared that agree with the amounts budgeted for worker pay.

Long-Range Budgets

A **long-range budget** is one that usually addresses accounting periods of two to five years. As the name implies, a long-range budget provides a long-term view of an operation's financial performance. Long-range budgets forecast the financial performance of an operation far into its future. Long-range budgets are also helpful for those owners and organizations that are rapidly expanding their businesses. These business owners may plan to open one or more new establishments each year for the next several years. In such a case, a long-range budget would be essential for understanding the revenue to be generated with the additional operations. It would also be needed for estimating the expenses to be incurred when operating a rapidly expanding number of restaurant or foodservice operations.

Capital Budgets

Some expenses incurred by a business are not recorded on the P&L. These include expenses related to the use of land, property, equipment, and other business assets involving a business's capital. **Capital** is the money, property, and other valuables that collectively represent the wealth of an individual or business.

In the restaurant and foodservice industry, **capital expenditures** generally refer to the purchase of items that cost a specified amount such as $5,000 or more. The items have a useful life of more than one year. A **capital budget** is one that addresses a business's capital expenditures for a specific period of time. For example, a five-year capital budget would include detail about

Manager's Memo

In some cases a short-range annual budget does not address 12 months of operating results. This is the case, for example, in seasonal resorts that are open only during a portion of a year. In these operations, revenue may be achieved only in specific months of the year, while expenses such as rent, utilities, insurance, and the like may be incurred for 12 months.

There are many examples of such seasonal operations:

- Golf courses
- Ski resorts
- Sports facilities and complexes
- Beach resorts

In each of these cases, a manager may be called on to create a short-range budget that addresses a *season*, rather than a 12-month year. The principles of budget preparation, however, remain the same in either case.

capital purchases to be made within the next five years. Because capital expenditures often involve the use of significant funds, they must be planned for carefully. Planning for capital expenditures is so essential to an owner's long-term profit goals that the use of capital budgets will be addressed in detail in chapter 10 of this book.

REVENUE FORECASTING

In most operations the budgeting process begins with a forecast of revenue. This figure will affect many other items to be included in the budget. As discussed in the previous chapter, some costs change as sales levels fluctuate. That is why it is especially important to start with a solid sales forecast before calculating any other figures used in the operating budget.

To prepare revenue forecasts, managers first establish the time frame for the forecast, such as a week, month, quarter, or year. They then collect information, assess trends, and review any marketing activities planned for the period that could significantly impact sales. When those tasks have been completed well, an accurate revenue forecast can be created.

Managers consider data from several sources when preparing their revenue forecasts:

- Historical data
- Current data
- Future data

Historical Data

In many operations, what has happened in the past is a good indicator of what may happen in the future. In most cases, managers who have information about historical revenues, or the number of guests served in the past, can make better predictions about future sales.

In general, the more extensive the historical data available to managers, the better their forecasts will be. For example, if managers have historical records indicating the revenue achieved by their operations on the past 20 Sundays, they are more likely to be better able to forecast this coming Sunday's business than if they have data for only the last 2 Sundays.

Effective managers record their revenues carefully and refer to these records when preparing their revenue forecasts (see *Exhibit 4.2*). They review prior period sales, including the number of guests served, the amount spent per guest, and what items guests ordered from the menu.

Exhibit 4.2

There are several types of historical data that managers may find valuable when forecasting future revenue:

- Prior day's sales
- Average achieved sales for the prior five same days, such as the previous five Saturdays or Mondays
- Prior week's average daily sales
- Prior two weeks' average daily sales
- Prior month's average weekly sales
- Prior two months' average weekly sales
- Same date sales from prior year

It is important to recognize that merely assuming that what happened last week will happen this week is not usually a good idea. An operation can have good sales weeks followed by bad sales weeks due to factors beyond management's control. Changes in an area's economic conditions, severe weather, road construction, or other events can drastically affect sales levels. It is wrong to assume that a period's sales forecast will be exactly the same as the previous period's actual sales.

One way to forecast in spite of such fluctuations is to use the **moving average** technique. Using this technique, sales information for two or three recent and same length periods is averaged together. The average can produce a forecast that is more likely to be accurate, since it is not based solely on one period that might have had unique circumstances.

Current Data

When preparing their revenue forecasts, managers should consider historical data at the same time they assess their operation's most recent sales information. Managers must do this to incorporate their operation's most recent revenue performance. To illustrate, consider the manager whose operating revenue has, on average, increased 10 percent each month from the same month the previous year.

Suppose, however, that in the last two months the increase has been closer to 5 percent. This may mean that the 10-percent increase trend has slowed significantly or may have even stopped. In this case, a revenue forecast for next month reflecting a 5-percent increase may be more accurate than a forecast predicting a 10-percent revenue increase. To improve their forecast accuracy, effective managers should always consider historical sales trends. At the same time, they must assess the most recent sales trends.

UNDERSTAND THE BIG PICTURE

As general manager of a hotel property (my first big responsibility), I was developing my first budget. I didn't have a very strong accounting team, so I was leading most of the process. We spent weeks developing the budget, but I spent all of my time on the income statement, focusing only on GAAP EBITDA. I remember vividly the day I pronounced the budget "complete" for the following year and started communicating the details to the entire staff. While the GAAP EBITDA looked good and was an improvement from the previous year, I hadn't run the cash flow analysis until *after* I had started telling everyone the numbers.

Once the cash flow statement was developed for my "first great budget," it showed that we were in a negative cash position four times throughout the year and that we did not have a revolving credit line to use during these situations. I was able to fix it by changing the budget and strategy (when we would be purchasing certain items, who and when we would hire staff, etc.). This *substantially* changed the budget. I had to go back and explain to the staff that the budget numbers I had given them—that they had bought into—were incorrect. I then had to explain a whole new set of numbers to them. So, I learned a key lesson about the importance of understanding the *entire* picture and *all* of the financial statements.

Future Data

Evaluating future market conditions is often a good way to increase the accuracy of revenue forecasts. This is because local events and activities can have a significant impact on an operation's sales levels. For example, consider the manager who learns a competitor will be opening a new establishment nearby in the next six months. Such an event will likely impact the sales of the manager's operation and, as a result, the manager's revenue forecast. Similarly, assume the manager of a hospital foodservice operation learns that the staff cafeteria will be closed next year for three weeks as it undergoes remodeling. In this case, the revenue for this operation will be reduced or even eliminated during the remodeling period.

Managers also carefully evaluate the likely impact of planned advertising and promotion programs included in their marketing plans. The impact of these planned activities can and should be considered when estimating future revenue levels.

In many cases, local events such as concerts, fairs, festivals, and sporting events may directly impact a manager's revenue forecast. Local newspapers, radio, and trade or business associations can be good sources of information about upcoming local events. These events can affect an operation's future sales volume.

A variety of methods are used to forecast restaurant and foodservice sales and costs, and most of them rely directly on having accurate historical, current, and future data. When the actual revenue forecast is produced, managers almost always base it on the number of customers to be served and the average sale per customer. The most common restaurant and foodservice revenue forecasting techniques are based on the following calculation:

$$\begin{array}{ccc} \textbf{Number of} & & \textbf{Average sale} & & \textbf{Sales} \\ \textbf{customers} & \times & \textbf{per customer} & = & \textbf{forecast} \end{array}$$

For example, if a manager estimated that 20,000 customers would be served in an upcoming accounting period and that each customer would spend $12, the manager's revenue forecast would be:

$$\begin{array}{ccc} \textbf{20,000} & & \textbf{\$12} & & \textbf{\$240,000} \\ \textbf{Customers} & \times & \textbf{Average sale} & = & \textbf{Revenue} \\ & & \textbf{per customer} & & \textbf{forecast} \end{array}$$

Managers may use operational records such as sales histories and production sheets that indicate the number of menu items sold to provide valuable historical information. See *Exhibit 4.3*. They may also generate similar records from their POS systems. These records, when carefully analyzed, can be used to calculate what has happened in the past, what is happening now, and what is likely to happen in the future. This includes trends related to the popularity of various menu items.

Exhibit 4.3

SAMPLE PRODUCTION SHEET

RESTAURANT TECHNOLOGY

Day and Date: Tuesday, July 1
Weather: Sunny
Total Meals Served: 200

Meal: Dinner _____

Item	Forecasted	Prepared	Number Sold	Waste
Salmon	45	45	40	5
Beef Filet	30	25	22	3
Baked Ham	10	10	61	9
Lasagna	80	15	61	8
Lamb Chop	5	10	10	0
	230	225	200	25

There are several software products available to calculate sales forecasts. Most operations can run historical sales and production reports from their point-of-sale (POS) systems. The information on these reports is then used to anticipate what is likely to occur moving forward.

Managers can also use spreadsheet software to help them do the calculations required for preparing a sales forecast. It is important to recognize that forecasts are not precise facts. Forecasts are based on assumptions. Managers who review their forecasts every month can fine-tune them against what really happens. As a result, in most cases, with practice and help from easy-to-use advanced technology tools, managers can constantly improve their forecasts.

Forecasting by Revenue Source

Many restaurant and foodservice operations record revenue on the income statement based on its source. For example, an establishment with a bar will separately record its restaurant and bar income on its P&L. When that is the case, managers may choose to create their revenue forecasts based on these same revenue sources.

Forecasting by revenue source is especially helpful when, for example, the revenue generated by one source is staying constant or declining, while revenue from another source is increasing.

OPEN FOR BUSINESS

MANAGER'S MATH

Don is preparing a revenue forecast for next month. His operation includes three revenue sources. Create the revenue forecast for Don and answer the questions that follow.

Revenue Source	Estimated Number of Customers	Average Sale per Customer	Next Month's Revenue Forecast	This Month's Actual Revenue
Restaurant	4,500	$22.50		$ 98,500
Lounge	1,000	14.30		13,500
Banquet room	250	18.50		10,250
Total/ Average	**5,750**			**$122,250**

1. Is Don forecasting an increase or decrease in total revenue for next month when compared to this month?

2. In which revenue source(s) is Don predicting an increase in sales?

3. In which revenue source(s) is Don predicting a decrease in sales?

4. What is Don's average sale per customer estimate for next month?

5. What suggestions would you have for Don about actions that he might take in the future to improve his operation's revenue?

(Answers: 1. Decrease. 2. Restaurant and lounge; 3. Banquet room; 4. $20.90; 5. Answers will vary.)

THINK ABOUT IT . . .

Some managers believe they can increase sales by opening earlier or closing later.

What could be some disadvantages of extending operating hours as a way to increase revenue?

Forecasting by Day Part

Some managers find it helpful to create their revenue forecasts based on individual day parts. A **day part** is a specific segment of the day. For example, some operations have traditionally served breakfast, lunch, and dinner at different times of the day, and these form distinct day parts. Other operations may serve only lunch and dinner and thus may consider their sales to come from only two day parts. Still other operations may wish to identify more than three day parts.

When managers use day parts for the creation of forecasts, it is important to remember that sales must be recorded at the end of each day part. That is, if an operation seeks to create separate revenue budgets based on day parts, revenue for each day part must be carefully reported when the day part is concluded and before the next day part begins. When historical day part records exist they can help managers create forecasts for future day part sales.

BUDGETING EXPENSES

After there is a reliable forecast of sales revenue, managers can move forward and forecast costs for the budget period. Because past history is a key to accurate cost forecasting, managers should use all applicable records and tools available to them as they analyze their historical cost data. High volume is no guarantee of high profitability. Managers must also know and control their operating expenses. When they have carefully reviewed their past expenditures they are ready to create forecasts of future operating expenses.

In general, there are three major categories of costs for a restaurant or foodservice operation:

- Food cost
- Labor cost
- Other costs

Food cost and labor cost (*Exhibit 4.4* on next page) each have components that are directly related to sales levels and are therefore considered to be either variable or semivariable costs. Because of this relationship, it is easy to see why accurate sales information is needed prior to creating expense forecasts. Additionally, there are other expenses to consider. These include items such as utilities, marketing, equipment maintenance, services such as trash removal and snowplowing, and costs associated with occupying a building. These kinds of costs are often referred to as overhead.

Exhibit 4.4

Food Cost

In chapter 3, *cost of sales* was defined as the industry term for the food and beverage product expense incurred in the generation of sales. Food cost is the actual dollar amount of food used during an accounting period. The key to forecasting food cost is to know an operation's desired, or target, food cost percentage. Food cost percentage is a measurement of the relationship between food sales, or revenue, and the money spent on food to generate those sales.

The formula for food cost percentage is as follows:

$$\textbf{Cost of food} \div \textbf{Food revenue} = \textbf{Food cost percentage}$$

An operation's food cost is forecast using the following formula:

$$\begin{matrix} \textbf{Sales} \\ \textbf{forecast} \end{matrix} \times \begin{matrix} \textbf{Food cost} \\ \textbf{percentage} \end{matrix} = \begin{matrix} \textbf{Food cost} \\ \textbf{forecast} \end{matrix}$$

For example, if an operation's forecasted sales are $14,500 for a period, and the targeted food cost percentage for the operation is 27 percent, then the forecasted food cost is $3,915:

$$\begin{matrix} \textbf{\$14,500} \\ \textbf{Sales forecast} \end{matrix} \times \begin{matrix} \textbf{0.27} \\ \textbf{Food cost percentage} \end{matrix} = \begin{matrix} \textbf{\$3,915} \\ \textbf{Food cost forecast} \end{matrix}$$

As long as management has an accurate sales forecast and a target food cost percentage, the calculation of the food cost forecast is very straightforward. The same is true of beverage costs. The method managers use to initially establish their target food and beverage costs, however, are important and must be well understood by managers.

To establish a target food cost percentage, managers first review recipes and prices to determine the food cost percentage that should be obtainable. Sometimes referred to as a theoretical food cost, it would be the food cost obtainable if 100 percent of all food purchased were converted to sales.

Realistically, operations rarely achieve this theoretical target. That is because some food items will be lost through spoilage, errors in preparation, and even employee theft. Managers can, however, assess the difference between their theoretical food costs and their actual historical food costs on a monthly basis. If the differences are significant, managers can implement procedures to address these unfavorable differences.

Managers should establish the food cost percentage most likely to result from their improvement efforts. Then they can identify a realistic target food cost percentage to be used in the preparation of the budget. This percentage is then applied to the budget's revenue forecast to determine the anticipated food cost, as well as its impact on profits. If profits are too low, the revenue or food cost target must be reassessed. The methods used to properly manage and reduce food and beverage costs will be explored in detail in chapter 7.

Labor Costs

The calculations required to prepare a labor cost budget can be complex. This is true because labor costs include managers' salaries, which are a fixed expense, employees' hourly wages, which are a variable expense, and employee benefit costs.

Labor costs and food costs, when added together, make up an operation's prime costs (see chapter 3). Prime costs can account for 50 percent or more of an operation's total costs. Labor is one of every food operation's largest expenses, so budgeting them accurately is important. Fortunately, there is a step-by-step process that managers can follow to forecast these critical costs.

Step 1: Calculate Total Available Labor Dollars

Calculating the amount that can be spent on labor is often related to a labor standard. A **labor standard** is a measure that indicates what a labor cost should be. Labor standards are determined by management and are designed so an operation can achieve a profit.

Like food cost, labor cost is usually expressed as a monetary amount and as a percentage. The formula used to calculate a budgeted labor cost percentage is as follows:

$$\frac{\textbf{Budgeted}}{\textbf{cost of labor}} \div \frac{\textbf{Revenue}}{\textbf{forecast}} = \frac{\textbf{Budgeted labor}}{\textbf{cost percentage}}$$

To determine the total available labor dollars for a period, the operation's standard or targeted labor cost percentage is multiplied by the sales forecast for the period. The result is the amount available to spend for labor.

For example, in an operation with an established 30 percent labor cost standard and an $800,000 sales forecast, the amount to be budgeted for labor would be $240,000.

$$\textbf{Sales forecast} \times \frac{\textbf{Standard labor}}{\textbf{cost percentage}} = \frac{\textbf{Dollars available}}{\textbf{for labor}}$$

In this example the calculation would be:

$$\underset{\text{Sales forecast}}{\$800{,}000} \times \underset{\substack{\text{Standard labor}\\\text{cost percentage}}}{0.30} = \underset{\substack{\text{Dollars available}\\\text{for labor}}}{\$240{,}000}$$

To illustrate the preparation of a labor cost forecast for one week, assume the manager of the Tiki Hut restaurant is preparing a weekly operating budget. If the standard budgeted labor cost percentage for all wages, salaries, payroll taxes, and employee benefits is 28 percent, and the sales forecast for next week is $17,000, the amount of money available for labor for that week is $4,760.

$$\underset{\text{Sales forecast}}{\$17{,}000} \times \underset{\substack{\text{Standard labor}\\\text{cost percentage}}}{0.28} = \underset{\substack{\text{Dollars available}\\\text{for labor}}}{\$4{,}760}$$

Step 2: Subtract Costs of Benefits and Deductions

Now that there is a forecasted amount of money available for labor, the next step is to subtract the cost of benefits and deductions. These amounts must be accounted for and subtracted from the total dollars available for labor wages.

Assume the Tiki Hut expects to spend $1,748 on employee-related taxes and benefits during the upcoming one-week period. The manager of the Tiki Hut would determine this information based on mandatory tax rates and contributions to be paid by the business as well as the cost of any benefits given to employees. These benefits may include the cost of items such as employee meals, reserves for paid vacation or sick leave, and health insurance contributions. The dollars available for payroll would now look like this:

$$\underset{\substack{\text{Available}\\\text{for labor}}}{\$4{,}760} - \underset{\substack{\text{Benefits and}\\\text{deductions}}}{\$1{,}748} = \underset{\substack{\text{Payroll}\\\text{available}}}{\$3{,}012}$$

Step 3: Subtract Fixed Labor Costs

Now that the dollar amount available for scheduling employees has been calculated, the next step is to calculate how much of payroll is a fixed cost for management salaries and how much is variable for hourly employees, like kitchen staff (*Exhibit 4.5*). This is important for creating a work schedule because, for the most part, only the variable-cost employees are listed on a work schedule.

To calculate the number of dollars available for scheduling hourly employees, managers subtract the

THINK ABOUT IT . . .

Inaccurate sales forecasts could cause either too many or too few employees to be scheduled. If too many workers are scheduled, profits can suffer. What would be the impact if too few workers were scheduled?

Exhibit 4.5

total of fixed cost management salaries from the payroll dollars available.

$$\begin{matrix} \textbf{Payroll dollars} \\ \textbf{available} \end{matrix} - \begin{matrix} \textbf{Fixed cost} \\ \textbf{salaries} \end{matrix} = \begin{matrix} \textbf{Dollars available for} \\ \textbf{employees receiving wages} \end{matrix}$$

Assume that management salaries at the Tiki Hut total $1,350 per week. The labor dollars available for hourly (waged) employees are then $1,662:

$$\begin{matrix} \textbf{\$3,012} \\ \textbf{Payroll dollars} \\ \textbf{available} \end{matrix} - \begin{matrix} \textbf{\$1,350} \\ \textbf{Fixed cost} \\ \textbf{salaries} \end{matrix} = \begin{matrix} \textbf{\$1,662} \\ \textbf{Dollars available for} \\ \textbf{employees receiving wages} \end{matrix}$$

Step 4: Distribute Remaining Labor Dollars Among Hourly Positions

After the amount that can be spent on hourly-paid employees is known, it must be broken down between the front-of-the-house (FOH) and back-of-the-house (BOH) positions. The reason for this is the difference

Exhibit 4.6

in hourly wages paid to these employees. Servers generally receive tips and are therefore paid less per hour by an establishment than job classifications that do not receive tips.

Managers can determine the number of hourly staff needed by using productivity standards. One very popular method of scheduling service staff is by using a labor productivity standard known as covers, or guests, per server. **Covers per server** is the number of customer meals that a waitstaff member can serve in an hour (*Exhibit 4.6*). Each operation should have a standard figure for covers per server that is based on past customer counts and productivity levels. This standard is then measured against the sales forecast to determine the number of servers to schedule.

At the Tiki Hut, the production standard is 20 covers per server per hour. The forecast for a daily lunch rush assumes a four-hour period. The forecast predicts 300 guests, or 300 covers. Using this information, 3.75 servers must be scheduled.

$$\begin{matrix} 300 \\ \textbf{Covers} \end{matrix} \div \begin{matrix} 4 \\ \textbf{Hours} \end{matrix} = \begin{matrix} 75 \\ \textbf{Covers per hour} \end{matrix}$$

$$\begin{matrix} 75 \\ \textbf{Covers} \\ \textbf{per hour} \end{matrix} \div \begin{matrix} 20 \\ \textbf{Covers} \\ \textbf{per server} \end{matrix} = \begin{matrix} 3.75 \\ \textbf{Servers} \end{matrix}$$

The number of servers to schedule is rarely even. The question then becomes: round up or round down? There is no consistent answer as it depends on the employees involved. If the staff is relatively new and not fully trained, it would be wise to round up and add another person. On the other hand, if the staff is experienced with a high productivity ratio, it would probably be best to round down. The service schedule should then be further refined, as not all of the guests are going to arrive in an orderly fashion of 75 guests per hour. In the example shown in *Exhibit 4.7*, during the hour of 12:00 p.m. to 1:00 p.m., a spike of 90 covers is expected. This is 10 covers more than the standard for the four servers.

Exhibit 4.7						
STANDARD SERVICE SCHEDULE FOR THE TIKI HUT						
Position	**10:00**	**11:00**	**12:00**	**1:00**	**2:00**	**Total**
Number of covers	15	75	80	90	40	**300**
Server A	X	X	X	X	X	5 hours
Server B		X	X	X	X	4 hours
Server C		X	X	X		3 hours
Server D		X	X	X		3 hours
Total hours						**15 hours**

During this time period, the waitstaff will be working at a maximum rate with four servers. Consequently, the schedule may call for one server to be ready to serve guests when the operation opens, and then more servers can be added as the customer counts increase over the meal period.

Because the number of server hours is known (15 in this example) the wages paid to servers can be calculated. Assume wages per hour for servers in this operation are $5.50 excluding tips. The total server wages would be $ 82.50 per day:

15.00	×	$5.50	=	$82.50
Server hours		**Wage**		**Server wages per day**

If the establishment is open six days per week, the weekly payroll for servers would be $495.00 per week:

$82.50	×	6	=	$495.00
Server wages per day		**Days per week**		**Server wages per week**

Once the servers are scheduled, the number of hours available for the rest of the positions needs to be determined. How does management know what amount of labor dollars remains? Determining the remaining payroll dollars available is calculated using the following formula:

$$
\begin{array}{ccccccc}
\textbf{Payroll} & & \textbf{Fixed} & & \textbf{Server} & & \textbf{Dollars available} \\
\textbf{dollars} & - & \textbf{payroll} & - & \textbf{payroll} & = & \textbf{for employees} \\
\textbf{available} & & \textbf{dollars} & & \textbf{dollars} & & \textbf{receiving wages}
\end{array}
$$

In this example the calculation is:

$$
\begin{array}{ccccccc}
\$3,012 & - & \$1,350 & - & \$495 & = & \$1,167 \\
\textbf{Payroll} & & \textbf{Fixed} & & \textbf{Server} & & \textbf{Dollars available} \\
\textbf{dollars} & & \textbf{payroll} & & \textbf{payroll} & & \textbf{for employees} \\
\textbf{available} & & \textbf{dollars} & & \textbf{dollars} & & \textbf{receiving wages}
\end{array}
$$

At this point, the remaining $1,167 in available payroll dollars are divided by the average wages per hour of needed workers to determine the number of hours available to schedule. This includes bus staff, cooks, ware washers, cashiers, and all other remaining positions.

In most cases, workers in nonserver positions will be paid a variety of different wage rates. Assume, however, that the *average* nonserver wage rate paid at the Tiki Hut was $9.00 per hour. In this example, with $1,167 of available wages, the manager would be able to schedule 130 additional worker hours per week while still staying within the targeted labor cost standard:

$$
\begin{array}{ccccc}
\$1,167 & \div & \$9.00 & = & \textbf{129.7 which rounds up to 130} \\
\textbf{Available wages} & & \textbf{Per hour} & & \textbf{Work hours}
\end{array}
$$

If the number of hours available for scheduling these workers is insufficient to complete all required work, managers must then reassess each of the key labor cost–related variables:

- Sales forecasts
- Salaries to be paid
- Hourly wages to be paid
- Productivity standards

Other Expenses

While food and labor in most cases make up the largest expenses for most restaurant and foodservice operations, operations also incur a variety of other expenses. These include items such as the cost of utilities, marketing, and

RESTAURANT TECHNOLOGY

While the task of assembling a schedule can seem daunting, there are a number of software programs available to assist managers. Some are stand-alone scheduling programs, and some are integrated into complete restaurant or foodservice accounting programs. Most will analyze the payroll and sales records, figure the covers per server and the average wage, and show the breakdown of fixed and variable labor.

While the programs perform most of the calculations automatically, it is still management's responsibility to ensure that the correct numbers of staff are scheduled to meet the forecasted sales volume.

equipment repairs and maintenance. All expenses classified as "other expense" are identified on the income statement and may be listed under a variety of headings:

- Controllable
- Noncontrollable
- Variable
- Fixed
- Contracted
- Occupancy

GAAP rules allow owners some flexibility in how they list their other expenses on the income statement, but all must be listed. In most cases managers create budgets that address their other expenses in the same way they are listed on the P&L. In all cases, however, managers follow a basic procedure when forecasting their other expense amounts:

- Identify all operating expenses except cost of goods, labor, and costs related to occupying the operation's physical space.
- Obtain historical revenue and other expense records.
- Obtain copies of contracts for services to be provided to the operation during the budget period (e.g., trash removal, snow plowing, window washing, and the like).
- Review historical equipment repair costs.

When the appropriate historical and current records have been collected and reviewed, managers can begin to estimate their future operating costs in each of the other expense categories. For budgeting purposes, other expenses are first assessed based on being either variable or fixed.

Variable Other Expenses

Variable costs (see chapter 3) are those that change in relationship to revenue. As revenue increases, these costs increase. As revenue declines, these costs decline as well. When a manager has historical records of variable expenses, and a forecast of future revenue, it is easy to forecast the amount of a future other expense. This is especially the case when managers establish the amount of an expense based on the revenues forecast. For example, if a manager

---

MANAGER'S MATH

Dawn is preparing a budget for her operation. She has forecasted revenue of $1,200,000 for the budget period and now wants to complete the variable expense portion of her forecast. Dawn reviewed her historical cost percentage records. She then established her target variable cost percentages for several variable cost categories. Use Dawn's target cost percentages to complete her variable expense forecast and then answer the questions that follow.

Revenue Forecast: $1,200,000

Variable Expense Cost	Historical Expense Percentage	Target Expense Percentage	Variable Expense Forecast
Marketing	2.8%	3.0%	
Glassware	0.25	0.15	
Paper products	0.25	0.25	
Linens	1.0	0.75	
Flowers and decorations	0.50	0.25	
Kitchen utensils	0.25	0.25	

1. What is the amount Dawn will budget for marketing?
2. What is the amount Dawn will budget for linens?
3. What is the amount Dawn will budget for kitchen utensils?
4. What would be the impact on marketing costs if Dawn sets that expense at 3 percent of revenue and then exceeds her forecasted revenue amount?

(Answers: 1. $36,000; 2. $9,000; 3. $3,000; 4. More dollars will be available for marketing activities.)

determines that the target for marketing costs will be 3 percent of revenue, the amount to be spent on marketing would be calculated as shown:

$$\text{Sales forecast} \times 0.03 = \text{Marketing cost forecast}$$

When any other expense is variable, managers simply identify their historical or targeted percentage cost. They then multiply that percentage times their revenue forecast to arrive at the forecasted other expense amount.

Fixed Other Expenses

Fixed other expenses do not vary with sales volume. For example, if a manager incurs Web site hosting charges of $100 per month, this cost will stay the same regardless of the number of customers served by the operation. Because fixed costs do not vary with sales volume, managers can enter these costs directly into their budgets based on the known amount of expense to be incurred during the budget period. In addition to variable and fixed expenses, managers can calculate their contracted expenses and the costs of occupying the space that houses their businesses.

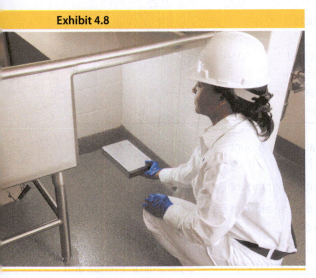

Exhibit 4.8

Contracted Expenses

A contracted expense is one in which a manager uses an outside vendor to perform a needed task or provide a needed service. Depending on the operation, managers may incur a number of contracted expenses:

- Pest control (*Exhibit 4.8*)
- Background music
- Lawn care services
- Musicians
- Ventilation system cleaning
- Draft beer line cleaning

In most cases, historical records and copies of current contracts will give managers the information they need to accurately forecast these expenses. The specific terms of these contracts should be carefully reviewed so managers are very familiar with the services they will be provided and the amount they will pay for them.

Occupancy Expense

An occupancy cost is one related to the expense of occupying a building that houses a restaurant or foodservice operation. Examples of occupancy costs include rent, insurance, and property taxes. In many cases, accountants preparing an operation's income statement will list these as noncontrollable expenses. Managers preparing budgets, however, must be sure to include all applicable occupancy costs. This is because these expenses directly affect the amount of profit that will be indicated in the budget.

Many of the occupancy costs incurred by an operation, such as rent or insurance, are fixed costs that will not change from month to month. In some cases, rent may have a fixed component and an amount due that is directly tied to sales volume. In addition, there are costs related to depreciation and taxes that are figured based on specific formulae. These formulae consider the value of the equipment, furniture, and fixtures owned by the operation and included in occupancy costs. Because the value of these owned items will vary from one operation to the next, these calculations will also vary by operation and, at times, can be fairly complicated.

Depreciation is a method of calculating and recording the reduction in value of a tangible, or physical, asset over its useful lifetime. These GAAPs let businesses make an expensive investment without showing a big loss at the time the investment is purchased. Amortization is similar to deprecation. **Amortization** is the reduction in value of an intangible asset such as the right to use a franchise trademark. Depreciation and amortization are important ways that businesses manage the amount of taxes they owe, since taxes are based on a business's profit or loss in any given year.

Depreciation and amortization amounts are a noncash expense included on an operation's income statement. There are guidelines that must be followed for calculating depreciation and determining useful life estimates for items such as equipment and vehicles. These guidelines are established by the Internal Revenue Service (IRS) and GAAP.

Most often, managers will not be involved in calculating depreciation for assets purchased by their operations or in preparing amortization schedules. In most cases, they should consult with a qualified accountant to ensure that depreciation and amortization amounts to be included on their income statements are calculated according to the law and to GAAP.

To complete the occupancy expense portion of their budgets, managers take specific steps:

1. Identify all occupancy expenses.
2. Obtain historical occupancy expense and sales history.
3. Summarize relevant financial terms of rent contracts.
4. Prepare rent summary to include monthly cash rent, common area maintenance (CAM) charges, and percentage rent calculation, if applicable.
5. Prepare a monthly budget of rent and occupancy costs.
6. Identify depreciation and/or amortization schedules.
7. Assess occupancy costs, applicable taxes, and depreciation amounts on profitability.

Manager's Memo

Consider the establishment owner who buys a new stove for $10,000. If the cost of the stove could not be depreciated, it would have to be recorded as an expense in the year it was purchased. As a result, the accounting records would show a significant drop in the operation's profits for that year, whereas following years might show profits above normal.

Because the stove continues to contribute to the establishment's sales throughout its useful life, which is five years, its cost is depreciated gradually, and the expense is spread evenly over the useful life of the stove.

If the establishment couldn't depreciate the stove, its taxes would be low the first year and much higher in the following years. With depreciation, the tax advantage of the stove's expense is also spread over the useful life of the stove.

When all food, beverage, labor, and other expenses have been entered into the budget, managers are ready to assess the profit levels they have forecast for the time period addressed in their budgets. If the profits estimated to be achieved do not meet the owner of the operation's requirements or standards, managers must work with them to adjust occupancy expenses or revise profit goals.

BUDGETING FOR PROFITS

Now that management has determined what sales and costs are expected to be, they can estimate the expected profit or loss for the budget period. To better understand profits and the budgeting process, it is helpful to recall the profit formula presented in chapter 1:

$$\text{Revenue} - \text{Expense} = \text{Profit}$$

Businesses operate to make a profit. Even nonprofit organizations operating restaurant or foodservice facilities must keep expenses at targeted levels. Accurately predicting profits helps managers evaluate the cost standards and benchmarks used in budget preparation. Owners, investors, lenders, and others are very interested in the profitability of a business. Therefore, accurately forecasting profits is one of a manager's most important tasks.

Actually, managers who have forecasted their revenue and identified their expenses will have already created a profit forecast. The expected profit or loss of an operation is simply the difference between the budgeted revenue and the budgeted expense. Typically, the profit amount is expressed as a monetary amount such as $10,000, and as a percentage of sales, such as 10 percent.

Profit Evaluation

Managers use two sets of data to assess the amount of profit projected in a budget: historical data and current data.

HISTORICAL DATA: Based on an operation's past profit performance, historical data are often a good indicator of future performance. One of the first assessments managers should make about budgeted profit levels is how the profit compares to previous periods:

- Are profits projected to increase from previous periods?
- Are profits projected to decline from previous periods?
- Are profits as a percentage of sales projected to increase?
- Are profits as a percentage of sales projected to decrease?
- Are changes in profits due to changes in sales?
- Are changes in profits due to changes in expenses?

CURRENT DATA: In addition to comparing the budget to historical data, managers should compare profits estimated by the budget to the most recent performance data available. Comparisons should be made based on the monetary amount of profit forecasted and by profit as a percentage of sales. This is done using the forecasted profit as a percentage of sales formula:

$$\text{Profit forecast} \div \text{Revenue forecast} = \text{Profit percentage forecast}$$

Benchmarking

Benchmarks help managers determine if the profits they have forecast meet established standards or targets. For example, if a manager operates a business and knows that other similar businesses typically average a profit of 10 percent, then the manager may consider that information as he or she establishes his or her own benchmarks for operational performance. Benchmarks or standards of expected performance may also be established by an operation's owner or by the person who supervises the manager of an operation.

Profit per Guest Served

In some cases it is helpful for managers to calculate the profits their operations will achieve based on the number of guests served. **Profit per guest served** is calculated as:

$$\text{Profit} \div \text{Number of guests served} = \text{Profit per guest served}$$

For example, if a manager served 500 guests in a week and achieved profits of $800, the profit per guest served would be:

$$
\begin{array}{ccccc}
\$800 & \div & 500 & = & \$1.60 \\
\textbf{Profit} & & \textbf{Number of} & & \textbf{Profit per} \\
& & \textbf{guests served} & & \textbf{guest served}
\end{array}
$$

When managers create a revenue budget they begin by forecasting the number of guests that will be served in the budget period. When forecasted profits are calculated managers can compute their forecasted profit per guest served using the formula:

$$
\frac{\textbf{Forecasted}}{\textbf{profit}} \div \frac{\textbf{Forecasted number}}{\textbf{of guests served}} = \frac{\textbf{Forecasted profit}}{\textbf{per guest served}}
$$

When they have forecasted revenue, expenses, and profits, managers have completed the budgeting process. *Exhibit 4.9* on the following pages illustrates a completed operating budget for BeBe's Courtyard Bistro. It is similar, but not identical, to the format used for an operation's income statement (see chapter 3).

Note that, like many establishments, the sales volume of BeBe's varies based on the time of year. Thus, some months are profitable and other months show a loss (in red). Calculated amounts for revenues, expenses, profits, and/or losses using the procedures presented in this chapter are included in the budget and can be seen at a glance.

Exhibit 4.9

BEBE'S COURTYARD BISTRO—OPERATING BUDGET

	January	February	March	April	May	June
Sales						
Food	$ 16,500	$ 24,750	$ 33,000	$ 41,250	$ 49,500	$ 66,000
Beverage	5,525	8,290	11,050	13,815	16,575	22,100
Total:	**$22,025**	**$33,040**	**$44,050**	**$55,065**	**$66,075**	**$88,100**
Cost of Sales						
Food	$ 6,600	$ 9,900	$ 13,200	$ 16,500	$ 19,800	$ 26,400
Beverage	1,660	2,485	3,315	4,145	4,975	6,630
Total:	**$ 8,260**	**$12,385**	**$16,515**	**$20,645**	**$24,775**	**$33,030**
Gross profit						
Total:	**$13,765**	**$20,655**	**$27,535**	**$34,420**	**$41,300**	**$55,070**

Gross profit = Total sales − Total cost of sales

	January	February	March	April	May	June
Controllable Expenses						
Salaries and wages	$ 7,050	$ 9,910	$ 13,215	$ 16,520	$ 18,500	$ 24,670
Employee benefits	1,320	1,980	2,645	3,305	3,965	5,285
Utilities	1,250	1,250	1,250	1,250	1,250	1,250
Marketing	500	500	500	500	500	500
Administrative	1,000	1,000	1,000	1,000	1,000	1,000
Repairs and maintenance	1,000	1,000	1,000	1,000	1,000	1,000
Total:	**$12,120**	**$15,640**	**$19,610**	**$23,575**	**$26,215**	**$33,705**
Noncontrollable Expenses						
Occupation expenses	$ 2,500	$ 2,500	$ 2,500	$ 2,500	$ 2,500	$ 2,500
Interest expenses	160	215	270	270	270	270
Total:	**$ 2,660**	**$ 2,715**	**$ 2,770**	**$ 2,770**	**$ 2,770**	**$ 2,770**
Total expenses						
Total:	**$14,780**	**$18,355**	**$22,380**	**$26,345**	**$28,985**	**$36,475**

Total expenses = Controllable expenses + Noncontrollable expenses

	January	February	March	April	May	June
Operating profit						
Total:	**($ 1,015)**	**$ 2,300**	**$ 5,155**	**$ 8,075**	**$12,315**	**$18,595**

Operating profit = Gross profit − Total expenses

	January	February	March	April	May	June
Adjustments						
Depreciation	$ 1,800	$ 1,800	$ 2,250	$ 2,250	$ 2,250	$ 2,250
Amortization	1,000	1,000	1,000	1,000	1,000	1,000
Total:	**$ 2,800**	**$ 2,800**	**$ 3,250**	**$ 3,250**	**$ 3,250**	**$ 3,250**
Income before income taxes	**($ 3,815)**	**($ 500)**	**$ 1,905**	**$ 4,825**	**$ 9,065**	**$ 15,345**

Income before income taxes = Operating profit − [Depreciation + Amortization]

July	August	September	October	November	December	Annual Total
$102,300	$102,300	$69,300	$33,000	$16,500	$13,200	$567,600
34,255	34,255	23,205	11,050	5,525	4,420	190,065
136,555	136,555	92,505	44,050	22,025	17,620	757,665
40,920	40,920	27,720	13,200	6,600	5,280	227,040
10,275	10,275	6,960	3,315	1,660	1,325	57,020
51,195	51,195	34,680	16,515	8,260	6,605	284,060
85,360	85,360	57,825	27,535	13,765	11,015	473,605
38,235	38,235	25,900	13,215	7,050	5,640	218,140
8,195	8,195	5,550	2,645	1,320	1,055	45,460
1,250	1,250	1,250	1,250	1,250	1,250	15,000
500	500	500	500	500	500	6,000
1,000	1,000	1,000	1,000	1,000	1,000	12,000
1,000	1,000	1,000	1,000	1,000	1,000	12,000
50,180	50,180	35,200	19,610	12,120	10,445	308,600
2,500	2,500	2,500	2,500	2,500	2,500	30,000
270	270	255	245	230	220	2,945
2,770	2,770	2,755	2,745	2,730	2,720	32,945
52,950	52,950	37,955	22,355	14,850	13,165	341,545
32,410	32,410	19,870	5,180	(1,085)	(2,150)	132,060
2,250	2,250	2,250	2,250	2,250	2,250	26,100
1,000	1,000	1,000	1,000	1,000	1,000	12,000
3,250	3,250	3,250	3,250	3,250	3,250	38,100
$ 29,160	$ 29,160	$16,620	$ 1,930	($ 4,335)	($ 5,400)	$ 93,960

SUMMARY

1. **Explain the purpose of an operating budget.**

   An operating budget is prepared to help managers plan for the financial activity taking place in their facility. An operating budget is a projected financial plan that addresses a very specific time period. Its main purpose is to list the anticipated sales revenue and projected expenses of an operation and to give an estimate of the profit or loss expected for the period. Because it is a plan for financial success, a budget also serves as a guide for making good spending decisions and for taking appropriate corrective actions if forecasted performance is not achieved.

2. **Identify and describe the major types of budgets used in restaurant and foodservice operations.**

   The three major types of budgets used in restaurant and foodservice operations are the short-range budget, the long-range budget, and the capital budget. A short-range budget is typically prepared for an accounting period in the near future and addresses financial performance for one year or less. A long-range budget usually addresses accounting periods of two to five years. Capital is the money, property, and other valuables that collectively represent the wealth of an individual or business. A capital budget identifies the timing of future capital expenditures of items that cost, for example, $5,000 or more and have a useful life of more than one year.

3. **Summarize the method used to forecast an operation's revenue.**

   The two basic pieces of information required to develop a revenue budget are the number of customers to be served and the average sale per guest. Managers establish their revenue forecast by multiplying the number of guests to be served by the average sale per guest. Managers can better estimate both the number of guests to be served and average sale per guest by relying on historical, current, and future sales-related data.

4. **Summarize the method used to forecast an operation's expenses.**

   In general, there are three major categories of costs for a restaurant or foodservice operation. These are food (and beverage) costs, labor costs, and other operating costs. Food costs and variable labor costs are directly related to sales levels. They can be forecast by multiplying their targeted variable expense percentage by the amount of forecasted sales. Fixed and semivariable costs are forecast based on current expense levels. Additional sources of fixed and semivariable cost information include contracts written for services provided to an operation, known occupancy costs, and/or historical cost records from previous accounting periods as reported on income statements.

5. **State the importance of accurately budgeting for profits.**

   Most businesses operate to make a profit. Even nonprofit organizations that operate foodservice facilities must control expenses and generate income in excess of expenses, or at least keep expenses at targeted levels. Accurately predicting profits helps managers evaluate the standards they are using for expenses and helps owners assess the quality of their investments. Because many interested parties are concerned about an operation's profit levels, accurately forecasting profits is one of a manager's most important tasks.

APPLICATION EXERCISE

You have been recently hired as general manager of Lucky's. It is September 1, and you must prepare the operating budget of this establishment for the first quarter of the upcoming calendar year, and submit it to the corporate office. Since you have been at the operation for only a month or so, you must rely solely on historical data. You gather sales reports and records for the months of January through August of the current year.

Using the data and the budget worksheet provided, prepare the operating budget for Lucky's for the months of January through March of the upcoming year. Here is the information you determined from the most recent sales and costs records:

- Sales are 10 percent higher than those of the same month during the previous year.

- Food cost percentage is steady at 32 percent.
- Fixed labor costs are steady at $9,000 per month.
- Variable labor costs are 15 percent of sales.
- Occupancy costs will remain steady at $2,000 per month.
- Other controllable costs are expected to be $10,000 per month.
- Marketing costs have been fixed at $1,000 per month.
- For January, February, and March of last year, Lucky's sales revenues were as follows:
  - January: $60,000
  - February: $50,000
  - March: $55,000

	January	February	March
Sales			
Food			
Total sales			
Cost of Sales			
Food			
Total cost of sales			
Gross profit			
Controllable Expenses			
Salaries and wages			
Marketing			
Other controllable expenses			
Total controllable expenses			
Noncontrollable Expenses			
Occupancy costs			
Total noncontrollable expenses			
Operating Profit and Income Before Depreciation and Taxes			

REVIEW YOUR LEARNING

Select the best answer for each question.

1. A capital budget is prepared to address the
   A. quantity of food to purchase.
   B. expenses for food, labor, and occupancy.
   C. purchase of land, buildings, and equipment.
   D. optimal product inventory levels for an operation.

2. How many years are typically addressed in a long-range budget?
   A. 1–2
   B. 2–5
   C. 6–7
   D. 8–10

3. What is the name of the financial report whose format most closely resembles that of a budget?
   A. Balance sheet
   B. Income statement
   C. Debt service summary
   D. Statement of cash flows

4. What is the first item to be calculated when preparing an operating budget?
   A. Total sales
   B. Labor costs
   C. Food expense
   D. Occupancy costs

5. The formula used to forecast an operation's revenue is
   A. Number of customers × Average sales per customer.
   B. Number of customers ÷ Average sales per customer.
   C. Number of customers + Average sales per customer.
   D. Number of customers − Average sales per customer.

6. A manager budgets food sales of $80,000. The operation's target food cost percentage is 30%. What is the forecasted amount to be spent for food?
   A. $2,400
   B. $24,000
   C. $26,500
   D. $37,500

7. What is the formula for determining the amount of money available for variable labor costs?
   A. Payroll dollars available − Fixed cost salaries
   B. Payroll dollars available + Fixed cost salaries
   C. Revenue dollars × Forecasted labor cost percentage
   D. Revenue dollars ÷ Forecasted labor cost percentage

8. A manager scheduled six servers to work. The total number of hours worked by all six servers was 15 hours. The six servers waited on a total of 900 guests. What was the number of covers served per hour?

A. 30

B. 60

C. 90

D. 120

9. What is an example of an occupancy cost?

A. Income taxes

B. Property taxes

C. Food sales taxes

D. Liquor sales taxes

10. A manager budgeted revenues of $60,000 for a future time period. Profits for the period are forecast at 15% of revenue. What is the manager's profit forecast?

A. $400

B. $900

C. $4,000

D. $9,000

5

Managing Cash and Accounts Receivable

INSIDE THIS CHAPTER

- Cash Management
- Petty Cash Fund Management
- Accounts Receivable (AR) Administration

CHAPTER LEARNING OBJECTIVES

After completing this chapter, you should be able to:

- Explain the importance of safeguarding cash in a restaurant or foodservice operation.

- Describe the steps required to process guest checks for payment.

- Explain the procedures used to complete a bank deposit.

- State the importance of effectively managing a petty cash fund.

- Explain the methods used to manage an operation's accounts receivable (AR).

KEY TERMS

accounts receivable (AR), p. 122

aging schedule, p. 124

bleeding, p. 116

cash, p. 108

credit terms, p. 124

gratuity, p. 110

guest check, p. 109

house account, p. 123

opening cash bank, p. 116

over, p. 117

payment card, p. 114

petty cash, p. 119

petty cash voucher, p. 121

point-of-sale (POS) system, p. 108

reconciliation, p. 116

secret shopper, p. 109

service charge, p. 111

short, p. 118

subtotal, p. 110

tendered, p. 112

variance, p. 118

CASE STUDY

"This is the second time this week," said Kathy.

"I know," replied Jodi, "but I really don't know what's going on."

Kathy was the supervisor at the Banks restaurant. Jodi was a server who, along with Kathy, ran the cash register and processed guest payments.

For the second time in a week, the amount of money in the cash drawer at the end of Jodi's shift was off. It was less than the sales records kept in the machine indicated.

"It was only you and I that had access to the cash," said Kathy, "and the cash register says we are $20 short."

"Maybe the machine made a mistake?" asked Jodi.

1. What are some reasons there could be a difference between the amount of money a restaurant or foodservice operation *should* have collected, and what it *actually* collected from guest sales?

2. What do you think will happen in an establishment if its manager cannot adequately protect all of the sales revenue?

107

CASH MANAGEMENT

Managers prepare budgets, in part, to estimate the amount of income their operations will achieve in a specific accounting period. The effective management of income actually earned in an operation requires managers to carefully monitor three important areas:

- Cash management
- Petty cash
- Accounts receivable

Each of these critical finance-related areas will be addressed in this chapter.

To properly manage an establishment, there must be guidelines in place to ensure responsible handling of cash and other guest payments. **Cash** is most often considered to be only the currency and coins guests use to pay their bills. Increasingly, however, noncash payments are made by guests in a variety of forms. These include personal checks, gift cards, coupons, and electronic fund transfers that result from guests' use of credit and debit cards. Managing cash is a critical accounting activity. All cash collected must be secured if it is to be available to pay the operation's bills and provide the profits forecasted in its budget.

Cash management begins with the collection of payments from guests for all items purchased (*Exhibit 5.1*). Basic math skills and attention to detail are important for calculating what guests owe and when operating the business's **point-of-sale (POS) system**. This is a machine that records guest purchases as well as other important operating data. Sometimes referred to as a cash register or cash drawer, the POS system also records payments from guests and makes change during transactions.

Regardless of the system in use, cash must be well managed. The guidelines for managing cash listed in this chapter are a good starting point for any operation. Many operations already have their own procedures in place as well.

It is a manager's job to ensure that any procedures related to handling cash are properly communicated and enforced. There are three common ways to monitor how employees handle cash:

1. **Manage by walking around:** It is always a good idea for managers to allow their employees to see them and know that they are around, both to help them and to coach them. If a manager sees an employee not following an approved cash handling procedure, the manager can point out the problem to the employee and explain how to correct the problem. The visible presence of managers can also help serve as a deterrent to employee theft.

Exhibit 5.1

2. **Monitor with a surveillance system:** Use of closed-circuit cameras is a way to detect improper cash handling, including theft. If there is a dispute about the denomination of a bill that a customer gives an employee, managers may be able to quickly play back the surveillance tape and correct the situation with visual proof. Just having video cameras visible can also be a deterrent for employees to be careless or to consider stealing. In most cases managers prefer not to have video cameras visible to guests. If cameras or alarm systems are used, it is important to note that a video camera security system is intended to permanently record any activities. In all cases, managers who record employees should check to ensure they are following appropriate laws. They must do so because an owner's right to unlimited monitoring and surveillance, even on his or her own property, is not absolute and is subject to governmental restrictions.

3. **Hire secret shoppers:** **Secret shoppers** are companies that send hired customers into an establishment to check the service level of employees. These customers then give a thorough report about every interaction that occurred during their visits. This is a good way to monitor employees without changing their behavior, as they might when a manager is present.

Exhibit 5.2

Regardless of the combination of methods used to monitor employees, managers focus on key activities:

- Ensuring the security of cash at all times
- Verifying the exchange of cash between employees
- Auditing and reviewing cash handling procedures
- Reconciling cash on hand with POS records (*Exhibit 5.2*)
- Preparing bank deposits
- Verifying bank deposits

These key activities must be controlled if managers are to ensure that all money finds its way to the operation's bank account. If it does not, profits are reduced, and employee theft may increase. Then managers risk being accused of carelessness in the management of their operations' money.

Cash Control

In many respects, the control of cash begins with an operation's sales to its customers. In most restaurant or foodservice operations, a guest's purchases are recorded on a guest check. A **guest check** is simply a record listing the food and beverages purchased. It may also be used to indicate the total amount a guest will be charged for the purchases. *Exhibit 5.3* is an example of a paper guest check used in this manner.

In today's high-tech restaurant and foodservice industry, most guest check calculations are automated and computerized. It is rare to see a noncomputerized cash register in a modern restaurant. As a result, managers will seldom need to calculate guest checks by hand. Exceptions include a POS equipment malfunction, or working in a remote or low-tech location. When faced with such realities, however, and to better understand POS systems operations, it is helpful for managers to understand what goes into the accurate calculation of guest checks.

Guest Checks

When calculating a guest check, all of a guest's purchased items are listed and their costs are added together, resulting in a **subtotal** of the check. In many cases, the purchases will first be separated into different categories, for example, by food or beverage. This might be done to obtain information for sales records or for sales tax purposes.

In some states, alcoholic drinks are taxed at a higher percentage than non-alcoholic drinks. In other states, the selling price of alcoholic drinks already includes the tax. Thus these amounts should be separated on the guest check to ensure that the guest is not taxed twice for the same purchase.

Sales tax, if applicable, is then added to the subtotal. To calculate the sales tax, a POS system automatically multiplies the subtotal by the percentage of sales tax required by state and local law. The tax rate has been programmed into the machine. Managers must ensure all applicable laws are considered when calculating sales tax to ensure that the correct amounts are charged.

In the sample guest check in *Exhibit 5.3* the sales tax is 6 percent. This means that the subtotal of $17.50 is multiplied by 0.06 to calculate the sales tax. Then the sales tax of $1.05 is added to the subtotal to create the total the customer must pay.

The total amount collected from a guest includes payment for purchases, sales taxes that will vary based on state and local law, and a **gratuity**. In most cases, the amount of gratuity,

Exhibit 5.3

Guest Check

Table No. 15	No. Persons 2	Server No. 1	Check No. 0801	
1	Roast beef sandwich		6	00
1	Large Cola		1	50
1	Cheeseburger		5	50
1	Extra Mayo			50
1	Small Milk		1	25
1	Apple Pie		2	15
	Food Total		14	15
	Beverage Total		2	75
	Subtotal		17	50
	+ Tax (6%)		1	05
	Total		$18	55
	For Your Convenience 15%		$2	63
	20%		$3	50
	Thank You - Call Again			

Guest Receipt			
No. Persons	Date	Check No. 0801	Amount

commonly known as a tip, is left to the customer's discretion. In the United States, it is customary to tip a server an amount equal to 15 to 20 percent of the check subtotal. There are circumstances, however, where the gratuity is included in the check total. Some establishments automatically add a **service charge**. This is a service-related fee assessed by the operation and retained by the operation. Payment of a service charge is mandatory, and is often assessed to larger dining parties, such as six or more people. In most cases, guests do not expect to leave an additional amount as a tip if they have been assessed a service charge. Local tax and state rules and regulations will prevail as to whether or not any gratuity or service charge is susceptible to taxation.

In the sample guest check in *Exhibit 5.3*, tip calculations for both 15 and 20 percent are provided at the bottom of the check. This provides the customer with a recommended tip range. Some people also carry wallet-sized charts, or tip tables, to help them quickly determine an appropriate tip. An example of a tip table is shown in *Exhibit 5.4*.

OPEN FOR BUSINESS

MANAGER'S MATH

Managers are sometimes forced to operate without POS systems. Common causes can include equipment failure, power surges, and machine damage caused by careless employees or managers. When a manager or employee is forced to operate without a working POS system, he or she must then calculate guest purchases by hand. Calculate the tax amounts due for each of the following guest checks. Create a table like the one shown.

Purchase Amount per Guest Check	Taxes Due at 6% Tax Rate	Taxes Due at 7% Tax Rate	Taxes Due at 8.5% Tax Rate
$ 28.50	$_____	$_____	$_____
$ 32.95	$_____	$_____	$_____
$ 65.90	$_____	$_____	$_____
$225.85	$_____	$_____	$_____

Do you think most servers can accurately calculate, by hand, the taxes due on food and beverage sales? Explain your answer.

(Answer: Answers will vary.)

Exhibit 5.4

TIP TABLE

Check Subtotal	15%	18%	20%
$ 5.00	$ 0.75	$ 0.90	$ 1.00
10.00	1.50	1.80	2.00
15.00	2.25	2.70	3.00
20.00	3.00	3.60	4.00
25.00	3.75	4.50	5.00
30.00	4.50	5.40	6.00
35.00	5.25	6.30	7.00
40.00	6.00	7.20	8.00
45.00	6.75	8.10	9.00
50.00	7.50	9.00	10.00
60.00	9.00	10.80	12.00
70.00	10.50	12.60	14.00
80.00	12.00	14.40	16.00
90.00	13.50	16.20	18.00
100.00	15.00	18.00	20.00

RESTAURANT TECHNOLOGY

Increasingly, guests rely on smartphone apps to help them with a variety of daily tasks. One such task is calculating the amount of tip they wish to leave.

Many tip calculation apps not only calculate a tip but also have a bill split feature. This allows the user to quickly tabulate the individual bills of multiple diners in a group. The bill split feature allows the user to identify the precise amount each diner is to pay. These tip-related apps are inexpensive or free to obtain and fun to use.

Satisfied guests pay for their dining experiences through a variety of transactions, including both cash and noncash payment options. Depending on the operation, guests might also pay their checks through interaction with different employees, including servers, cashiers, and bartenders. Guest payment of bills usually takes place without incident. At the same time, it is important for all employees to understand the best practices for processing guest checks.

Processing Guest Checks

Cash is still a popular form of guest payment. However, handling actual currency comes with its own set of concerns. Being familiar with the different bills and coins that make up U.S. currency will go a long way toward processing cash payments accurately.

INSPECTING THE AUTHENTICITY OF BILLS

Each bill of U.S. currency has different security features that make the bill difficult to counterfeit. These features also provide ways to determine if bills are authentic. When a customer presents cash, it is important to check the authenticity of the bills, especially when large denominations are used. Counterfeiters do not often go to great lengths to recreate bills that have little value, such as $1 bills. Also, accepting a large bill that might be counterfeit puts the operation at risk of losing a significant amount of money.

All U.S. currency has a portrait of a historical U.S. figure on the face of the bill. The universal seal to the left of each portrait represents the entire Federal Reserve System. Each bill also has a unique serial number, made up of letters and numbers, printed twice on the front of the note.

A letter and number beneath the left serial number identify the issuing Federal Reserve Bank. In addition, features such as watermarks, colored threads, and color-changing ink that reacts to different types of light can make a fake bill lacking these traits easy to spot. Additional information on spotting counterfeit bills is available from the website of the United States Secret Service at www.secretservice.gov.

Counting Back Change

The amount of cash tendered, or given by guests, and received by employees for bill payment often exceeds the amount of the guest's bill. Due to the busy pace and sometimes crowded payment areas, restaurant and foodservice employees can easily become distracted when making required change. Some con artists, known as "quick-change artists," try to use this to their advantage by claiming they presented a bill of a higher denomination than they actually did. So how does an operation protect itself from such a scam? When making change, it is important for cashiers and others receiving payments to follow specific steps:

1. **Announce the total owed by the guest:** This should always be done before accepting the customer's payment. For example, say, "That will be six dollars and eleven cents, please."

2. **When the guest tenders the money for payment, place it in a visible spot:** Possible locations include the counter, to the side of the register, or on top of the register.

3. **Announce the value of the payment presented:** For example, say, "From twenty dollars . . . ."

4. **Verbally count the change upward, from the smallest coin to the largest denomination:** In this example, the cashier would begin making change with four pennies, stating "4 cents makes 6.15." Cashiers then continue to state each coin and bill denomination and value, adding up to the original amount presented for payment.

5. **Place the change directly into the guest's hand:** Change should be placed in the customer's hand, not left on the counter to be picked up.

6. **After the guest has acknowledged the change, the original payment is placed into the cash register:** This avoids any confusion on the part of the employee or guest over how much cash the guest presented.

Change should always be given in the largest denominations possible. For example, it is better to give one dime than two nickels, one quarter instead of two dimes and one nickel, or one five-dollar bill instead of five singles. This can save time and improve accuracy, reducing the likelihood of counting errors.

Noncash Payments

Many times a customer will pay with something other than cash. Forms of noncash payment include traveler's checks, personal checks, credit cards, debit cards, coupons, and gift certificates or gift cards. Not all operations accept all these forms of payment.

TRAVELER'S CHECKS

Traveler's checks are considered the same as cash, and are therefore the target of counterfeiters. Change for a traveler's check is given in actual currency and coin. Traveler's checks come in similar denominations as cash and have security features similar to those found on paper currency. These features include watermarks, raised textures or engraving, and holographic threads.

The most important security feature on traveler's checks is the actual witnessing of the countersigning process itself. When accepting a traveler's check, the owner of the check countersigns the check in the presence of the cashier accepting the check. Then, the signature is compared to the original signature placed on the check at the time of issue. In cases where the check is already countersigned, the presenter should be asked to sign it again on the reverse side and also to present photo identification. The identification should then be compared against the information and signatures on the check.

There are certain indications that a traveler's check has been stolen or had the original signature removed by chemical means, called *washing*. These include a brownish signature area or missing or smudged background printing. If there are any questions or doubts about accepting a traveler's check, the issuer's customer service department should be contacted for verification of the check.

PERSONAL CHECKS

Personal checks are still a popular method of payment in the United States. However, many operations do not accept personal checks because of the risks involved. Check fraud is the largest reported fraud in the United States, involving billions of dollars. For check payments, it is standard to ask the customer for proof of identification. Acceptable identification is a valid driver's license or passport.

PAYMENT CARDS

Payment cards include bank or other financial institution–issued credit cards and debit cards. Payment card processing procedures can vary, but the basic procedures are fairly standard.

To begin, payment cards are swiped through a machine to obtain authorization from a databank. Then, an authorization response is displayed on the credit card machine. If the card is not authorized for use, a "declined" message will appear.

When debit cards are used, guests will key in their pin numbers to initiate payment authorization. Once a credit card has been authorized and the slip has printed out, the customer will total and sign the slip while the cashier keeps the card in his or her possession.

Before returning the credit card to the customer, the signature on the payment card should be compared with the signature on the credit card slip. This is one way to verify the customer's identity. If the signatures are different, servers should politely ask the customer to provide additional identification. Acceptable forms of identification include a valid driver's license or passport.

Typically, credit card payments do not require additional identification unless fraud is suspected, or the back of the card has not been signed. One way to detect fraud is to compare the embossed number on the card against the four digits of the account number displayed on the terminal. After confirming the customer's identity via signature or other identification, it is then time to return the card to the customer along with a copy of the card's receipt.

PROCESSING THE PAYMENT TABLESIDE

The procedure for processing payment as part of table service is very similar to how it is processed at the register. There are four simple steps to process a payment when serving customers tableside:

1. Present the check at the table.

2. Collect payment from the customer.

3. Process the payment.

4. Return change or payment card receipt and payment card.

For credit card payments, the card and credit card receipt are brought to the table together. It is helpful for servers to explain to customers which copy they should sign and which one they should take. After it is signed (*Exhibit 5.5*), the operation's copy of the receipt should be collected and immediately put in a secure place.

When processing a cash payment, servers do not need to count out the change to the customer and repeat the totals. Rather, they simply make the change away from the table and then return the change to the customer.

Cash Security

Managers who have implemented control systems designed to properly collect all guest payments still face two significant cash security–related challenges:

- Maintaining security of on-premise cash
- Preparation and verification of bank deposits

On-Premise Cash

Experienced managers know that cash loss or theft can happen in the blink of an eye. Once payments have been accepted, receipts must be stored securely. *Exhibit 5.6* on the following page outlines standard procedures for ensuring the secure storage of cash and noncash receipts in a restaurant or foodservice operation.

Exhibit 5.5

OPEN FOR BUSINESS

RESTAURANT TECHNOLOGY

Increasingly, restaurant and foodservice managers are purchasing the advanced technology equipment needed to collect guest payments tableside, without the server or cashier ever leaving the table. Managers cite several advantages to such a system:

1. Customers maintain visual sight of their cards, allowing them to enjoy a higher level of personal security and reduced potential for fraud.

2. Faster, friendlier checkout increases the speed of table turnover, bringing more business through the operation in the same amount of time.

3. Tableside payment technology reduces transaction time by allowing the customer to enter the gratuity in a single transaction, eliminating the need for preauthorization.

Exhibit 5.6
SAFEGUARDING CASH, CHECKS, AND RECEIPTS

1. During hours of operation, restrict access to coins, currency, checks, and payment card receipts. Each cashier should be assigned his or her own cash drawer. If possible, only one person should have access to a register.
2. All payments should be secured in the register, which should be closed at all times and also locked when unattended.
3. Large bills should immediately be stored in a secure location, such as under the register drawer or in a drop safe near the register.
4. Cash, checks, payment card receipts, and other payment forms such as coupons or gift certificates should be relocated to a safe or other locked secure place at regular intervals determined by the management, or when business is slow. Access to the safe should be limited to a minimum number of people. If multiple managers are on during a shift, only one should have access to the safe.
5. When servers end their shifts, the manager should count the money and immediately secure any payment card receipts.
6. Money in the safe should be stored in counted-out register drawers or in durable pouches. The zippered pouches keep money and coins secure and are easy to transfer when making deposits.

Bleeding a cash register refers to the process of removing cash from the register during the hours of operation to secure the cash in a safe. Bleeding is a security-related cash activity. A manager usually bleeds a register at set times or after a busy sales period. The register is counted and all of the money, except for a specified amount, is removed. Cashiers just remove an amount, give it to the manager, and have the manager sign a document to be placed in the drawer stating that the manager received that exact amount. There may be no time during a busy shift to count what is in the register. The removed money is then immediately put into a pouch and placed in a secure location or safe. A signed slip of paper that reports how much money was taken out is put into the register. Sometimes a manager will quickly bleed only large bills, such as $50s and $100s, putting them into a more secure location for safekeeping.

At the end of the day or designated shift, managers reconcile the amount of cash that should be on hand with the amount of cash that is actually on hand. **Reconciliation** means to check one against another for accuracy. When performing a cash register or POS system reconciliation, a comparison is made to confirm that the money, checks, and credit card receipts in the cash drawer are equal to the recorded sales for a particular time period, less the amount of the opening cash bank. The **opening cash bank** is the amount of money initially placed in the drawer. It is the amount used to make change for guests during an operating shift. The size of the bank will be determined by the amount of money the manager estimates will be needed during the shift.

The opening cash bank amount must be subtracted from the total cash in the drawer to determine the actual amount of cash collected during the shift.

If a manager is not actually conducting the reconciliation, he or she should certainly be overseeing it. Once the money has been turned over to the manager, he or she should always recount it.

The completion of a cash reconciliation is a three-step process:

1. Run a sales report.
2. Count the receipts.
3. Address variances, if any.

RUN A SALES REPORT

The first step to performing a cash register reconciliation is to produce a sales report. Depending on the operation, sales reports should be based on either an individual employee or a specific cash register. In a counter-service operation, it is common to run sales reports by register. When that is done it is best to allow only one employee access to that register during a shift. That way, if there is a discrepancy, managers can address it with the individual assigned to that cash drawer. Modern POS systems have many security options that prevent anyone, except the approved and logged-in user, from having access to the cash drawer.

Many operations have servers manage their own money during a shift and then print out a sales report at the end of the shift. In this case, a sales report must be run for each server because each one has individual sales records.

COUNT THE RECEIPTS

After the sales report is printed, managers count the money in the cash drawer. When counting a cash register drawer, it is helpful to have a worksheet with a blank table to complete, which separately counts each denomination of bill or coin and has an area for check, payment cards, and any other payment forms, such as gift certificates or coupons that the operation accepts. It is important to make sure all credit card tips have been entered correctly, and that a signed receipt from each individual credit card transaction is accounted for.

It is a good policy to always have two people count the contents of the register drawer in each other's presence and/or in view of the video surveillance camera (*Exhibit 5.7*). Once they have agreed to the counted amount, both employees then sign a slip so there is a record of the reconciliation.

ADDRESS VARIANCES, IF ANY

After the register contents have been totaled, the amounts must be compared to the figures on the sales report. Ideally, the content of the register is the same as the figures on the sales report. If more money is on hand than is indicated by the sales report, the cash drawer is said to be **over**. If less money

Exhibit 5.7

is on hand than is indicated by the sales report, the cash drawer is said to be **short**. If there are overages or shortages, this difference between the report and the actual cash count is called the **variance**. It is imperative that managers identify how the variance might have occurred.

The solution could simply be that two bills or credit card receipts have stuck together, causing one to go uncounted in the total. Unfortunately, sometimes the answer is that an employee is stealing from the drawer, or is not able to handle cash properly. Theft or the mishandling of cash, either by employees or by customers, is a very real risk in the restaurant and foodservice industry. Recording variances is a good way to look for patterns over time. If an employee's drawer is frequently short, he or she should be closely observed and coached.

Overages in a drawer can also be a problem. While they might seem like extra income for the establishment, they are usually a sign of carelessness or dishonesty. An employee might be overcharging customers and then pocketing the "extra" money. Frequent overages should signal closer observation just as much as frequent shortages should. Any overages should be recorded and the money retained by the establishment.

Employees should be aware of what will happen if their drawers are over or short at the time of reconciliation. Depending on the operation and applicable state laws, employees might be responsible for all shortages. An advantage of such an approach is that employees will be vigilant in their cash handling procedures. Alternatively, this approach can sometimes decrease employee morale. Another practice is to set a certain dollar value that the drawer can be over or short. Whatever over–short policy is implemented, employees should be fully aware of the policy, and it should be consistently enforced. At the time of reconciliation, all paperwork should be completed promptly. Tax and tip records should be entered into the appropriate reports. Variances and any actions taken to address them should also be recorded.

Verification of Bank Deposits

Preparing a bank deposit is the final action taken by managers before removing money from the operation. Bank deposits should be made on a daily basis, and sometimes even more than once per day, depending on sales volume. It is not safe, for workers and the business, to keep large amounts of cash in the operation for any length of time.

The preparation and final verification of bank deposits is also a four-step process:

1. Count the deposit.
2. Prepare the deposit slip.
3. Secure and transport the deposit.
4. Record the actual deposit.

COUNT THE DEPOSIT

The first step to preparing a bank deposit is to count the cash, personal checks, and traveler's check receipts to determine the amount to be deposited. Every time the contents of the operation's safe are counted, there should be a signed record of how much was removed. Two different people should verify these amounts. The only money left in the safe after a deposit has been made should be petty cash and any money reserved for use in cash banks. **Petty cash** is used in case of an emergency and for small-dollar purchases. The size of a petty cash fund will vary per establishment, and methods for its control are addressed in this chapter.

PREPARE THE DEPOSIT SLIP

Once the total deposit has been counted and confirmed by two people, a deposit slip needs to be prepared. Most banks provide preprinted slips for the convenience of their customers. An example of a bank deposit slip is shown in *Exhibit 5.8*.

RESTAURANT TECHNOLOGY

Banks employ humans, and humans can make mistakes. Managers need to follow up and ensure the amounts of money deposited in their operations' bank accounts are the same amounts properly credited to their accounts. Online banking makes it easy for managers to do so. In most cases it is a good idea to use an online banking system to verify that bank deposit slips and actual bank records do, in fact, match. If possible, this should be done within 48 hours of the time the deposit is made.

Exhibit 5.8

FIRST WORLD BANK			
545 MAIN STREET			
ANYTOWN, USA 54321			

THE BURGER STOP
30 Third Avenue
Anytown, USA 54321

ACCOUNT: 54976 3154 02

NAME: John Smith
SIGNATURE: John Smith
DATE: 06/29/12
VERIFIED BY: Betty Ross   DATE 6-29

CASH	AMOUNT	CHECKS	AMOUNT
PENNIES	1.12	(List individually)	
NICKELS	2.00	1	56.25
DIMES	2.30	2	61.75
QUARTERS	5.25	3	43.13
		4	105.62
ONE	26	5	7.33
FIVE	35	6	
TEN	40	7	
TWENTY	120	8	
FIFTY		9	
HUNDRED	100	10	
CASH TOTAL		CHECK TOTAL	
	331.67		274.08
TOTAL DEPOSIT			
	605.75		

DEPOSIT TICKET

The amount of individual bills and coins should be recorded in the appropriate spaces on the slip. In addition, each check should be listed by its check number and amount. The deposit slip should then be totaled and checked by a second person.

KEEPING IT SAFE

Managers responsible for making bank deposits should take great care for their personal safety as well as the security of their operations' cash deposits. To enhance personal safety when making bank deposits, managers can take specific steps:

- Vary the time at which bank deposits are made.

- Do not advertise the fact that cash is being carried when transporting money to the bank.

- Do not establish a routine for cash movements; if possible, vary the route taken when making bank deposits.

- Carry a personal alarm when transporting money to the bank or carry a mobile phone in case help is needed.

- In situations where the amount of money to be deposited is extremely large, the deposit must be made very late at night, or where the location of the bank causes legitimate concern for the personal safety of the individual making the deposit, the use of an armored car service to pick up and make all of an operation's bank deposits should be considered.

SECURE AND TRANSPORT THE DEPOSIT

Before going to the bank, managers should secure the cash for the deposit in a sturdy and locked pouch. The deposit should then be transported directly to the bank, and the manager should make sure he or she receives a deposit receipt confirming that the deposit was made.

RECORD THE ACTUAL DEPOSIT

In the final step of deposit verification, the manager should record the actual amount of the deposit in the establishment's internal financial records system.

PETTY CASH FUND MANAGEMENT

In most cases, managers should seek to minimize the use of cash when buying any item for their operations. Payment by check allows for better control of expenses and is easier to analyze when internal or external audits of an operation are performed (see chapter 1). There are, however, two reasons managers hold cash on premise:

- Opening cash banks
- Minor purchases

Managers should keep funds for opening cash banks separate from those used for minor purchases. Funds for minor purchases are kept in a petty cash fund. A petty cash fund may also be referred to as a petty cash account. It is used for small purchases that are best paid for in cash. This is because it is more practical or less expensive to do so. Examples of minor expenses include miscellaneous hardware and some office supplies, or emergency food and beverage purchases from grocery stores.

Employees can misuse a petty cash fund. Therefore, managers must carefully monitor the money held in these accounts.

Petty cash funds must be kept in a secure location such as a locked manager's office or safe. Managers must develop and ensure the consistent use of policies and procedures detailing who is allowed access to petty cash funds and in what circumstances the funds can be used.

Managers responsible for the security of petty cash funds implement specific control procedures:

- The amount of money established for the petty cash fund should be no more than what is needed for a defined period of time, such as two or four weeks.

- A check is written from the operation's bank account payable to "petty cash" and is cashed. The amount of the check is used to create the petty cash fund.

- As minor purchases are made, cash is removed from the petty cash bank as needed to pay for the purchases. A record is made of the amount removed.

- After the purchase, the change from the purchase and the receipt documenting the purchase are returned to the petty cash fund. At this time, managers must confirm that the amount of the receipt plus the amount of change returned is equal to the amount of money previously removed for the purchase.

- Change from the purchase and the accompanying receipt are placed in the secured petty cash fund. In some operations a **petty cash voucher** is attached to the receipt. A petty cash voucher is used to document information about the petty cash purchase:

  - Date of the purchase
  - Individual authorizing the purchase
  - Amount of money removed from the fund
  - Individual removing the money
  - Individual receiving the money
  - Purpose of the purchase
  - Date the receipt and change are returned to the fund

- When the petty cash fund is near depletion, another check is written to petty cash, for the amount of paid receipts in the petty cash fund. This amount should bring the petty cash fund back to its original management-approved amount.

- At all times, the petty cash fund should contain cash in the bank and paid receipts for all purchases that will equal the established amount for the petty cash fund.

Only one individual should be responsible for managing an operation's petty cash fund. Specific policies regarding what may be purchased and the maximum purchase amount permitted should be documented and consistently enforced.

There are other important procedures related to the management of petty cash funds:

- All purchases must be preapproved by management.
- A receipt must accompany all purchases.
- The petty cash fund must be kept in a secure, locked area at all times.
- Petty cash funds should not be mixed together with cash register funds.
- All funds used to replenish the petty cash fund should be charged to a petty cash expense account.

THINK ABOUT IT . . .

Assume that the ink on your guest check printer has run out during a busy meal period.

Would you send an employee to buy a replacement ink cartridge? Would you use a petty cash fund? Explain.

121

- There should be no "borrowing" of money from a petty cash fund.

- Petty cash funds should be spot-checked on a routine but random basis.

- At all times, the amount in the fund, including cash, petty cash vouchers, and paid receipts, should equal the authorized amount of the petty cash fund.

ACCOUNTS RECEIVABLE (AR) ADMINISTRATION

Accounts receivable (AR) are those amounts due to the operation from others, usually customers and clients. In a restaurant or foodservice operation, accounts receivable will typically be of three types:

- Prepaid sales
- Payment card sales
- House accounts

Prepaid Sales

Prepaid sales include those sales of items such as gift certificates and gift cards. These types of gifts are very popular during holidays and special occasions. In this case, the customer immediately pays for products or services but does not receive them at the time of purchase. The accounting for gift card sales presents a dilemma for managers. To understand why, consider the operation that sells a $100 gift card to a customer on the first day of the month. If the sale is reported on that day, it would appear that revenue of $100 was achieved, yet no product cost was incurred. Recall that GAAP require income to be reported at the time it is produced. However, if the gift card was actually used on the first day of the *next* month, cost would be incurred in that month, but no revenue would be reported. Similarly, if the gift card was lost and thus never redeemed, no product expense would ever be incurred for its sale, despite the fact that legitimate revenue was received.

Variation exists in how operations account for gift card sales. In most cases it is best to record the sale at the time the card is used, not at the time it is sold. Managers should understand their own operation's prepaid purchases reporting policies. They must carefully explain their own correct procedures for reporting gift certificate and gift card sales to all employees who process guest payments.

Payment Card Sales

Payment cards include debit cards, credit cards, and travel cards that are presented at the time a sale is made. The sale is recorded at the time of the guest's purchase. The actual money to pay for the guests' charges will be sent to the operation by the company or banking entity issuing the payment card.

Therefore it is important that managers forward requests for payment accurately and in a timely manner. The procedures for payment used by each card company vary somewhat. However, in all cases managers perform specific tasks to submit payment requests:

- Confirm appropriate supporting documentation has been secured, typically a signed document or PIN pad entry.
- Total the batch of card charges.
- Confirm payment card charge amounts with POS records.
- Submit (electronically) the card charges.
- Verify the amount transmitted.
- Verify the date of the transmittal.

When these steps have been followed, managers can help ensure all monies legitimately owed to the operation can be properly credited to its bank account.

House Accounts

A **house account** is an arrangement whereby a customer is allowed to buy products and services on credit. One example of this can be found in a country club where members simply sign for their food and beverage purchases as they are made, and are then billed monthly for the amount due.

In addition to individuals, some businesses use house accounts to keep a record of their employee's food and beverage expense. For example, a software company's sales staff may use a specific establishment to entertain clients. In this situation, the software company employee entertaining the client simply signs his or her guest check at the end of the meal, and the restaurant adds a pre-agreed-upon gratuity. In this example, the business with the house account would be billed monthly by the establishment for purchases made by the business's sales staff when they entertained their clients. *Exhibit 5.9* illustrates some differences between a prepaid sale, a payment card sale, and a house account.

Exhibit 5.9

ACCOUNTS RECEIVABLE SALES

	Prepaid Sale	Payment Card Sale	House Account
Payment	Made prior to receiving products and services	Made when receiving products and services	Made after receiving products and services
Revenue recorded	At time of product consumption	At time of product consumption	At time of product consumption
Money received	At time of purchase	Upon funds transfer	Upon guest payment

Before a manager allows someone to establish a house account at the operation, there should first be a thorough explanation of the credit terms extended. **Credit terms** are the payment rules established for the account. These include such terms as how much credit is to be extended, or the credit limit, and when and how often payment is to be received. It can also include any fees or penalties for a late payment. If a payment is late, management needs to stick to the agreed-upon credit terms to prevent further late payments. These terms can help prevent huge losses from an individual account.

Managers need to follow a reliable process to effectively manage house accounts. House accounts receivable systems should include four steps:

1. **Record the AR accurately:** Any time an item or service has been delivered, it should be immediately recorded. This will ensure accurate billing and minimize the likelihood of forgetting the details of who owes what.

2. **Generate bills and invoices promptly:** The sooner a bill is generated and delivered to the client, the sooner the clock starts ticking on the window of time for payment. Usually, bills are due 30 days after the date of the invoice. These terms might vary based on the customer, his or her history with the operation, volume of business, and other factors.

3. **Collect delinquent accounts effectively:** Money that has not been received after the service has been completed is not earning a return for the operation. This causes a greater loss than just the amount of the unpaid bill itself. The longer the bill remains uncollected, the more money is lost. Collection procedures typically begin with a series of reminder phone calls (*Exhibit 5.10*). Handled delicately and professionally, many receivables are paid after such contact. Any such contact should be documented. In extreme cases, delinquent accounts might be sent to a lawyer or collection agency for further action.

It is helpful for managers to look at an operation's accounts receivable to determine how old the receivables are (i.e., how long they have remained unpaid). Most operation's credit terms state that receivables more than a certain number of days old are considered past due.

A tool for reviewing such information is called an aging schedule. An **aging schedule** is a chart that shows the age of all receivables not yet paid. The schedule reflects the totals for an operation's outstanding

Exhibit 5.10

accounts receivable, broken down in 30-day increments. Percentages are assigned to each age category as well. *Exhibit 5.11* shows a sample aging schedule for an operation.

Exhibit 5.11

SAMPLE AGING SCHEDULE

Age	January 31, 2012		February 29, 2012	
0–30 days	$4,000	74.7%	$3,000	50.9%
31–60 days	1,000	18.7	2,000	33.9
61–90 days	250	4.7	750	12.7
Over 90 days	100	1.9	150	2.5
Total	**$5,350**	**100.0%**	**$5,900**	**100.0%**

According to the information in *Exhibit 5.11*, at the end of January, about 75 percent of the total outstanding receivables was less than 30 days old. At the end of February, only about 51 percent was that young. Though this might appear positive at first, it is clear that $1,000 moved from the 0 to 30 days category into the 31 to 60 days category during that one-month period. When the February receivables older than 30 days are added together, you can see that the amount is about 49 percent of the total outstanding receivables. In January, only about 25 percent of the total receivables were older than 30 days.

Based on this example, it is evident that this operation did not accrue many new accounts receivable during the month of February. However, the accounts receivable from prior months are getting older and still have not been paid. This is a good indication that the operation needs to focus more attention on collecting past-due receivables. Depending on the credit terms for the accounts, late fees might be charged to these accounts as well.

4. **Record, store, and deposit payments:** House account payments that have been received should be recorded, stored securely, and deposited as soon as possible. This ensures that accurate credit for payment has been given to guests, and that the operation's house account AR records are continuously updated.

THINK ABOUT IT . . .

Why does it matter if clients pay their bills on time or not, as long as the operation eventually gets the money it is owed?

SUMMARY

1. **Explain the importance of safeguarding cash in a restaurant or foodservice operation.**

   Managers responsible for an operation's cash must address the key tasks of ensuring the security of that cash at all times, and verifying the exchange of cash between employees and guests. They also must also ensure that cash is protected until it is deposited in the bank. These key activities must be controlled if managers are to ensure that all money collected by an operation finds its way to the operation's bank account. If it does not, profits are reduced and employee theft may increase. Then managers risk being accused of carelessness in the management of their operation's money.

2. **Describe the steps required to process guest checks for payment.**

   The processing of guest payments begins with the subtotaling of guest purchases on a guest check. The appropriate tax is then applied to the subtotal amount. Tips or service charges are then added to the guest's total bill. If cash is used to pay the bill, the currency used should be verified as authentic, and change due to guests is counted back to them. If payment cards or other non-cash forms of payment are used, these must be processed appropriately. If payment is collected tableside, the guest's change or signed payment card receipt is returned to the guest after payment has been processed.

3. **Explain the procedures used to complete a bank deposit.**

   The preparation and final verification of bank deposits is a four-step process. The first step is to count the cash and traveler's check receipts to determine the amount to be deposited. Once the total deposit has been counted and confirmed by two people, a deposit slip is prepared. The deposit slip amount should be checked by a second person. Before going to the bank, the deposit should be placed in a sturdy and locked pouch. The deposit should then be safely transported directly to the bank. The manager should make sure he or she receives a deposit receipt confirming that the deposit was made and is properly recorded and verified. Finally, the manager should record the actual amount of the deposit in the restaurant's internal financial records system.

4. **State the importance of effectively managing a petty cash fund.**

   Funds for very small purchases are kept in a petty cash fund. A petty cash fund, or account, is used because smaller purchases are sometimes best paid for in cash. This is because it is more practical or can even be less expensive to do so. Examples of minor expenses include miscellaneous small quantities of office supplies, or emergency food purchases from grocery stores. A petty cash fund can be misused or stolen by employees. As a result, managers must carefully monitor the receipts and the money held in these accounts.

5. **Explain the methods used to manage an operation's accounts receivable (AR).**

Accounts receivable exist when a sale is made at a time different from when money is collected for the sale. When an AR is the result of customers being granted credit through the use of a house account, managers must carefully monitor those accounts. They can do so by regularly assessing both the amount of money owed and the length of time the money has been owed. An aging schedule shows the amount of money owed to the operation, as well as the length of time the money has been owed. If the length of time the money has been owed becomes excessive, managers must take steps to collect these outstanding amounts.

APPLICATION EXERCISE

Damon is the manager of a buffet-style, salad-bar restaurant called Green Garden. One of his regular customers is Mr. Abbott, who owns an import business across the street. For years, Mr. Abbott has been bringing his business clients to Green Garden for its buffet lunch. It is convenient, and he always knows it will cost $12.95 per client. Mr. Abbott has been a customer since before Damon was even hired.

When Damon reviews the accounts receivable for Green Garden, he notices that Mr. Abbott 's account is more

than 90 days past due, which is very out of character. Mr. Abbott is still bringing his clients to lunch at least twice a week, but he has not made a payment in over three months. Every visit is still recorded in Mr. Abbott's house account and added to his running total. Damon searches, but cannot find a written record of the credit terms of Mr. Abbott's house account. Given this information, answer the following:

1. How should Damon approach Mr. Abbott about his past-due house account?

_____

_____

_____

2. What are some possible short- or long-term credit terms that Damon might want to establish for Mr. Abbott's account?

_____

_____

_____

REVIEW YOUR LEARNING

Select the best answer for each question.

1. **A guest's bill is $80. The tax rate to be paid on the bill is 6%. By what number should the guest's bill be multiplied to determine the amount of tax due?**
   A. 6
   B. 0.6
   C. 0.06
   D. 0.006

2. **How do secret shoppers help evaluate how well cash-handling practices are followed in an operation?**
   A. They attempt to use "quick-change" techniques to short the cashier.
   B. They observe employees' actions and report their findings back to management.
   C. They approach other customers, asking them about their experiences at the operation.
   D. They try to leave the operation without paying their bill to see if they will be stopped by an employee.

3. **The most critical part of accepting a traveler's check for payment is**
   A. witnessing the countersigning of the traveler's check.
   B. verifying the validity of the traveler's check with its issuer.
   C. holding up the traveler's check to the light to look at the watermark.
   D. asking for valid identification from the person presenting the check.

4. **What does it mean to "bleed" the register?**
   A. To exchange one person's cash drawer with another's
   B. To prepare the cash for the register reconciliation process
   C. To allow more than one cashier access to the same register
   D. To remove excess cash and large bills to a more secure location.

5. **What is the final action taken by managers before removing money from the operation?**
   A. Petty cash verification
   B. Bank deposit preparation
   C. Cashier drawer reconciliation
   D. Evaluation of large currency for counterfeits

6. **Who determines the amount of service charge to be paid by restaurant or foodservice customers?**
   A. Servers
   B. Customers
   C. Large party hosts
   D. Owners or managers

7. **What is the amount that should be in a petty cash fund at all times?**
   A. The established starting amount in cash
   B. Cash + Receipts that total the established starting amount
   C. Cash – Receipts that total the established starting amount
   D. The established starting amount and the value of all purchase receipts

8. **How is a petty cash fund initially created?**
   A. A check is written to "petty cash."
   B. Money is taken from the cash drawer.
   C. A check is written to the manager who then cashes it to fund the account.
   D. An amount of revenue equal to the established fund amount is taken from a bank deposit.

9. **When is the proper time to record the sale of a gift card as revenue?**
   A. When the card expires
   B. When the card is purchased
   C. When the card is given to its intended user
   D. When the card is used to pay for products and services

10. **The main purpose of an accounts aging schedule is to**
    A. increase AR sales.
    B. decrease AR sales.
    C. determine paid ARs.
    D. determine past-due ARs.

FIELD PROJECT

Visit a local restaurant or foodservice operation to talk with the manager about cash security in his or her operation. In the meeting, ask the manager the following questions:

1. What is the process for recording sales in the operation (e.g., cash register, POS, or other system)?

2. What is the process for reconciling the amount of cash in cash drawers with sales as they have been recorded by the system used in the operation?

3. How frequently is the amount of cash in cash drawers reconciled with reported sales?

4. What management action is taken if a cash drawer is found to be short in the reconciliation process?

5. What management action is taken if a cash drawer is found to be over in the reconciliation process?

6. What is the procedure used to process credit card and debit card charges?

7. How are any employee tips that are charged to payment cards distributed to employees?

8. Does the business operate with a petty cash find? If so, what types of purchases are permitted from that fund? What is the process used to replenish the fund?

9. Does the operation allow its customers to have house accounts? If so, what information is obtained from customers before credit is granted to them?

10. Based on your personal experience, how can I ensure the security of cash in a restaurant or foodservice operation I may someday operate?

6

Managing Accounts Payable

CHAPTER LEARNING OBJECTIVES

After completing this chapter, you should be able to:

- List and describe the five steps in the management of an operation's accounts payable (AP).

- Discuss the importance of verification in the invoice payment process.

- Identify common causes of invoice payment disputes.

- Describe the reasons for coding and recording invoice payments.

- Explain the difference between a random and a targeted accounts payable audit.

CASE STUDY

"Do you want me to pay this month's bill from Charlie's Tap Service for his weekly cleaning of our beer lines?" asked Flory, the bookkeeper at the Blackwood Pub. Flory was talking to Jack, the beverage manager at the Blackwood.

"Isn't it for the same amount as last month?" asked Jack. "Four trips, at $200 for each cleaning trip. That's what he always charges."

"Yes, it is," replied Flory. "The bill is for $800."

"Well, what's the problem?" asked Jack.

"Well, maybe nothing . . . but you know how Charlie always lists the dates he cleaned our lines? And then puts those dates on the invoice?" said Flory.

"Right, he always does that. He has for years. So what?" replied Jack.

"Well, for last month he listed himself as being here on the 15th," Flory said. "But that was the day we were closed when the power was out all over the city because of that big storm we had."

"So he couldn't have cleaned the lines that day," said Jack, slowly.

"Not unless he had a key and worked in the dark," joked Flory.

1. What could be some reasonable explanations for the apparent mixup in this invoice for beer line cleaning services?

2. Based on the information in the case, do you think this business is prepared to address any intentional efforts on the part of vendors to defraud the operation? Why or why not?

ACCOUNTS PAYABLE (AP) ADMINISTRATION

As a constant part of business, money is always flowing. Money and goods flow among suppliers and vendors to buyers and customers. A restaurant or foodservice operation can be both a buyer and a seller on any given day. For example, a manager might order fruit from a produce supplier in order to sell a fruit salad to a guest. In this example, the manager will owe the produce company for the ordered product. This is because, with the exception of alcoholic beverages, payments for ordered food, supplies, and services are *not* usually made at the time the products are delivered or the service is provided.

Suppose a bread vendor delivers fresh bread daily to an operation. It would be cumbersome to pay that vendor each day for the bread products delivered. Typically, a vendor such as this would establish the creditworthiness of the operation. Then it can send a bill for delivered bread on a weekly, biweekly, or monthly basis.

An **invoice** is a formal, detailed, and written request for payment. An invoice is also commonly called a bill. An invoice should include a variety of important payment-related information:

- Name of the company to be paid
- Address of the company to be paid
- Invoice date
- Reason the payment is due (i.e., the products or services provided)
- The amount to be paid including any applicable taxes
- The payment's due date
- Special payment terms, if applicable

An invoice may also include the account number of the business paying the invoice, and detailed information about the products or services sold. For products, this includes their prices, delivery time and description, purchase unit size, price per purchase unit, and total amount for the individual items. In the case of services, an invoice typically includes a brief description of the scope of work performed, and the amount charged for individual items or supplies used.

In some cases the bill may include the name of the person initially authorizing the purchase, and the supplier's contact information. If multiple invoices are due and payable, the total balance owed by the business to the vendor is included. *Exhibit 6.1* shows many of the product and service categories for which invoices are typically received by restaurant or foodservice operations.

Exhibit 6.1

PRODUCT AND SERVICE CATEGORIES

Food and Beverage Products: These are the items operations prepare for customers. Examples include the following:

Food Items
- Meat
- Poultry
- Eggs
- Processed food products
- Fish and other seafood
- Dairy
- Produce
- Dry, frozen, and canned products

Alcoholic Beverages
- Spirits
- Beer
- Wine

Nonalcoholic Beverages
- Soft drinks
- Coffee and tea
- Juices
- Bottled waters

Nonfood Items: These items are directly related to the sale of food and beverages. For example, linens, candles, and flowers are used for tabletops, and paper bags are used for takeout orders. Other examples include the following:

- Uniforms
- China and glassware
- Silverware
- Bar supplies
- Paper products
- Cleaning supplies
- Menus and beverage lists
- Music
- Kitchen utensils and supplies

Furniture, Fixtures, and Equipment (FF&E): Items in this category may be purchased or leased. Examples include dishwashing machines, dining-room tables and booths, and beverage dispensing equipment. These relatively expensive items typically require maintenance and repair. Other examples of FF&E include the following:

- Chairs and barstools
- Lighting fixtures
- Bars
- Cooking equipment
- Refrigeration
- Plumbing fixtures

Business Supplies and Services: These services and supplies are required for the management or marketing of the operation:

- Office supplies and equipment
- Point-of-sale (POS) systems
- Computers
- Cell phones
- Credit card processing equipment
- Financial and legal services
- Insurance
- Marketing and advertising

Support Services: These services are tied to the actual operation of the business:

- Linen and uniform rental
- Waste removal
- Flower services
- Music services
- Pest control services
- Parking and valet services

Maintenance Services: Maintenance services are required for the upkeep of the facility. These may include the following:

- Cleaning services
- Plumbing and heating
- Groundskeeping
- Painting and carpentry
- Equipment repair and maintenance

Utilities: This category includes charges for utilities required to operate the business:

- Gas
- Oil heating
- Electricity
- Water and sewage
- Telephone service
- Internet access

Legitimate invoices should, of course, be paid in a timely manner and in accordance with all agreed-upon terms. The total of all invoices that are due and payable in an operation at any point in time are referred to as the operation's **accounts payable (AP)**.

AP needs to be closely managed and monitored through the use of a carefully established process. Unintentional oversights or theft can easily occur if these accounts are mismanaged.

From an accounting perspective, the effective management of AP requires attention to each of the five key AP management–related steps:

1. Invoice approval
2. Confirmation of invoice amount
3. Invoice coding
4. Invoice payment
5. Recording of invoice payments

Invoice Approval

Every operation should have a system in place to ensure that bills are paid in an accurate and consistent manner. The process begins with invoice approval. When a shipment is delivered to an establishment, a **delivery invoice** that indicates products, including quantities and prices, is typically included. Vendors may also mail invoices. Many suppliers send bills on a regular basis, such as monthly or weekly.

Exhibit 6.2

Regardless of how they are received, there should be a designated place to put invoices as they are received at the operation (*Exhibit 6.2*). A clipboard or a simple in-box or file folder clearly labeled for invoices only will help keep invoices from being lost, misplaced, or overlooked. It is important to manage AP invoices carefully because if a vendor is not paid on time, it can affect the operation's access to credit in the future. This can make even simple transactions such as ordering food or supplies quite complicated.

One of the most critical management tasks in AP administration is ensuring that payment is made to vendors only for products and services actually received. For example, a lawn service invoice may be received by the manager that includes charges for lawn mowing, edging, and chemical weed treatment. Certainly the bill should be paid if the services have been performed. However, payment should be withheld if all services have not been performed, or if the services were not completed at the agreed-upon quality level. Managers should process invoices for payment submitted only by those vendors who have delivered the operation's authorized products and services at the authorized price. The quality of the products and manner of delivery must be those agreed upon by both the business and vendor.

Invoice approval in the restaurant and foodservice industry most often requires managers to be diligent in two areas: product verification and service verification.

PRODUCT VERIFICATION

The task of paying the bills for products that were purchased involves much more than writing a check. Much of the revenue generated by an operation is spent on food and beverage products required to generate that revenue. All vendors must be paid what they are owed. However, it is equally important to ensure that they are not paid more than they are owed.

The responsibility for making correct payments begins when initial product purchase decisions are made. It continues as they are received, and ends when payments are made. How does the person paying vendors for products actually know that the products were ordered and received by the business? How does the manager know the agreed-upon price that should be paid for the products? The answers are found in the documents that are needed to process vendor invoices or statements for payment. The task of paying vendors' invoices requires communication, information, and coordination between an operation's purchasing, receiving, and accounting personnel prior to bill payment.

In some large operations, several individuals may be involved in bill payment. In smaller operations, the owner or manager may perform the majority of bill payment tasks. In both cases, when an invoice is received the first step of the invoice payment process is basically the same, regardless of whether a manual or electronic system is used.

Exhibit 6.3 shows the basic types of documents that contain information useful to verify the amounts owed vendors for product purchases. Each becomes increasingly important as the dollar value of purchases increases.

Exhibit 6.3

PURCHASING-RELATED DOCUMENTS

Document	Purpose
Purchase requisition	Used by storeroom or production employees to alert buyers that additional quantities of products are required to restock inventory levels.
Request for proposal	Used by purchasing personnel to request prices from approved vendors for products of specified quality.
Purchase order	Used by purchasing personnel in some operations to formally order products from vendors.
Delivery invoice	Used by vendors to indicate products, including quantities and prices, that are delivered to the restaurant or foodservice operation. Purchasers pay the amount specified on the delivery invoice after it is signed by the person receiving products for the establishment.
Vendor statement	Used by vendors to summarize delivery invoice charges during a specific time period. Agreements with managers, for example, may allow payment of all invoices for two weeks according to a summary statement that includes delivery invoice numbers, dates, and amounts owed.

There are some common methods used to route the important purchasing-related documents through the operation:

- **Small-volume establishment with owner-manager present:** Products are ordered and may be received by the manager. A copy of the purchase order (PO), a document authorizing a purchase (see *Exhibit 6.4*), may or may not be used, and the applicable delivery invoice is used by the owner-manager for payment purposes. In this case, the owner may pay the bills or transfer the documentation to a designated bookkeeper for eventual payment.

- **Small-volume establishment with absentee owner:** In this situation, a manager is employed by the owner. Purchasing and receiving activities may be undertaken by the manager and his or her staff, with documentation routed to a bookkeeper for payment. However, the vendor may be requested to send a separate copy of each delivery invoice directly to the absentee owner or bookkeeper. This permits comparison of both copies of delivery invoices and helps ensure that managers are not submitting falsified invoices.

- **Large hospitality operation with separate purchasing and accounting departments:** A copy of the purchase order that authorized the purchase commitments is sent from purchasing staff to receiving and storage personnel. Incoming orders are checked against the purchase order. The purchase order and signed delivery invoice are then routed to the purchasing department. They will be matched up before being routed to the accounting department as authorization for payment.

In some large establishments, purchase orders and applicable delivery invoices move from receiving personnel to the chef or manager who, in turn, forwards them to purchasing personnel. These staff members have significant knowledge about the needs of the organization, and they can review this documentation.

They may ask several types of questions:

- Do we normally purchase all of these items and in these quantities?

- Do the prices seem reasonable and in line with other recent purchases?

- Is the delivery invoice from one of our approved vendors?

- Did an employee sign a delivery invoice at the time of delivery verifying that products listed on the vendor's bill were indeed received by the business?

Exhibit 6.4

SAMPLE MULTIPART FORM PURCHASE ORDER

Operation's name: _____

Operation's address: _____

Purchase order number: _____ (Show this number on all orders)

Order date: _____

Transportation requirements: _____

_____

Send order by date: _____

Quantity Ordered	Size of Unit	Item Description	Unit Price	Total Price
			Subtotal	
			Tax	
			Shipping	
			Total	

If you cannot comply with these directives, please immediately notify the person below.

Returns policy: _____

For Use by Receiving Clerk

Received by: _____

Date received: _____

Condition of goods: _____

Other remarks: _____

Ordering party contact information: _____

Authorized signature: _____

ORIGINAL

VENDOR

RECEIVING

ACCOUNTING

Exhibit 6.5

SERVICE VERIFICATION

In a large number of cases, verifying that the services were actually performed for an invoice is easy. If, for example, carpet was to be cleaned, it will be easy to determine if the work was done. Similarly, if an invoice for the repair of a piece of equipment is received, it is a simple matter to determine if the equipment is currently functioning properly. In many cases, the work of a service provider is assessed at the time the work is completed. In some cases, however, the verification of services performed and the quality level at which they were performed can be challenging.

Consider, for example, the vendor that cleans the exhaust hoods in an operation. In this case, it may not be easy for the manager to determine if the work completed was performed properly and thoroughly. In such cases, the good reputation of the entity supplying the service is essential. In all cases, it is the job of the manager to ensure that services for which invoices have been received were, in fact, delivered at the agreed-upon quality level (see *Exhibit 6.5*).

In addition to invoices that require product or service verification, managers will encounter invoices for a variety of other expenses that must be verified and paid:

- Annual property tax bills
- Sales tax bills
- Phone bills
- Utility bills
- Franchise fees
- Insurance costs
- Equipment and supplies

In the case of invoices sent for product and service purchases, as well as all other legitimate business expenses, managers must carefully verify that the invoice submitted does, indeed, reflect an actual operating cost.

Confirmation of Invoice Amount

Delivery invoices indicate the services, products, and quantities of items for which suppliers make payment requests. They must be carefully studied for accuracy. Managers must ensure that there are no quantity or price differences between the items ordered and the items received. They must also

Manager's Memo

False invoices for products or services that an operation never ordered or received cause millions of dollars of business overpayments every year. In many cases, phony invoices are created to look genuine.

The success of the fraudulent invoice sender relies on the fact that, in some organizations, the systems in place to detect fraudulent invoices are poor or even nonexistent.

Some sophisticated tricksters even make sales calls to restaurant or foodservice operations to get the name of managers whom they can then include on the fraudulent invoices. This is to make them appear more legitimate. Managers must be diligent and should never pay an invoice unless it can be verified as authentic and legitimate.

ensure that all arithmetic **extensions** on the delivery invoice are correct. Extensions are arithmetic calculations made on delivery invoices. For example, the item quantity must be multiplied by the purchase unit price for each product delivered to determine the total cost for each product. This total cost must be added for all products to confirm that the total amount of the invoice is correct.

There are typically only two reasons why payment amounts listed on invoices should not be paid: legitimate invoice corrections and illegitimate invoices and scams.

LEGITIMATE INVOICE CORRECTIONS

In many cases, the person managing an operation's AP will not be the same person who ordered or received the products indicated on invoices that are to be paid. In such cases, the person responsible for AP might have the appropriate individual, with knowledge of the purchase terms and product delivery, sign or initial a document to authorize payment of the invoice.

When the items ordered match perfectly with the items delivered (*Exhibit 6.6*), delivery invoices should match perfectly with the bills sent to an operation for payment. Well-trained and knowledgeable receiving personnel, however, may sometimes identify problems during delivery that must be corrected with a **credit memo**. This is a written record of a proposed adjustment to a delivery invoice. Credit memos can be created for a variety of legitimate reasons:

- **Incorrect price charged:** For example, the purchase order price is $6.07 per pound; the delivery invoice states the price is $6.87 per pound.

- **Back order:** Product was not available and could not be delivered, but was included on the delivery invoice.

- **Short weight or count:** For example, 10 cases were ordered per the purchase order and included on the delivery invoice, but only 4 cases were delivered and received.

- **Items rejected because they were unacceptable:** For instance, items did not meet product specification requirements and were rejected upon attempted delivery, but were listed on the delivery invoice.

It is critical that product delivery problems, if any, be noted at the time of delivery. Those responsible for AP must be informed of any problems, because a credit memo reduces the amount that an operation owes a vendor for a delivered order. *Exhibit 6.7* on the following page shows a sample credit memo.

Exhibit 6.6

Exhibit 6.7

SAMPLE CREDIT MEMO

Date: _____   Credit memo no.: _____

Vendor: _____

_____

_____

_____

_____

Issued to: _____

_____

_____

_____

Account no.: _____

For invoice no.: _____

Item	Purchase Unit	Number of Purchase Units	Price per Purchase Unit	Total Price

				Total	$

Reason for credit (check):

☐ Back order   ☐ Incorrect quality   ☐ Incorrect item

☐ Short start count/weight   ☐ Incorrect price   ☐ Not ordered

☐ Other:

_____

_____

Authorized signatures:

_____   _____

Vendor's representative   Purchaser's representative

In most cases the credit memo is issued to the establishment purchasing the product by the vendor's representative. This is typically the delivery person, and the memo applies to a specific invoice. Items to be deducted from the amount owed to the vendor are listed, with the reason the credit is being granted. The signature of the vendor's representative confirms that the products noted in the credit memo were *not* received or accepted, and that their value should be deducted from the amount owed to the vendor. The receiving employee should also sign the credit memo to confirm that a copy was received. Duplicate copies of credit memos are required. One copy is for the vendor, and the other copy is for the person responsible for the operation's AP administration.

Credit memos are most typically issued at the time of delivery. Credit memos should be treated like cash. They represent a reduction of the amount otherwise owed to the vendor based on the delivery invoice. They must be carefully routed to the person responsible for AP in a way that best ensures that they will not be lost, discarded, or ignored. Most frequently, they are attached to the applicable delivery invoice and routed to accounting personnel for their use in adjusting invoice amounts and subsequent payments.

Special procedures are required when credit memos are the basis of invoice adjustments:

- The person responsible for AP may contact the vendor from whom a credit memo has been issued to confirm that it was received.
- When the delivery invoice is received in the accounting department and filed for future payment, the credit memo can be attached to the original delivery invoice.
- An internal record-keeping system is put in place to ensure that the operation does not pay invoices until they have been adjusted by any applicable credit memos.

ILLEGITIMATE INVOICES AND SCAMS

There is no question that managers should pay all legitimate invoices. However, it is just as certain that they must not pay illegitimate invoices or fall victim to invoice scams. An **invoice scam** is a bill for goods and services the operation did not order or did not receive. Businesses are common targets for invoice scams. Typically the scam involves products routinely ordered by a business:

- Copy paper
- Ink and office supplies
- Light bulbs
- Equipment maintenance contracts
- Ads and advertising

Managers can help protect their operations from invoice scams by consistently following key fraud prevention principles:

- **Understanding the right not to pay:** If a vendor sends an invoice for a product that was not ordered, there is no legal obligation to pay the invoice. Even if unordered products are, in fact, delivered to the operation, there is still no obligation to pay. The law treats these unrequested deliveries as gifts to the operation. Those initiating the invoice scams may state in writing or by phone that the operation is obligated to pay for any delivered items, but the operation is not legally required to pay.

Exhibit 6.8

- **Matching invoices to purchase orders:** Some, but not all, restaurant or foodservice operations require the use of purchase orders before products and services are requested by staff. When a purchase order system is in place, all invoices should be matched against the original purchase order authorizing the purchase. If no purchase order exists for the invoice, it should not be paid. In operations that do not use a purchase order system, invoices should not be paid unless payment has been authorized by the person responsible for buying the products or services addressed in the invoice.

- **Providing AP-related training:** In many cases, invoice scammers will maintain that the products or services listed on their bills were in fact ordered by the operation. This can happen, for example, when a scammer calls the operation. The scammer may convince the employee that the product or service being offered is such a good deal that it should be purchased immediately over the phone. For that reason, managers should teach everyone in the operation that when taking a call from a telemarketer, they should state: "I am not authorized to make purchase decisions of this type." The employee should then refer the caller to the operation's manager (*Exhibit 6.8*).

Invoice Coding

It is not only important for a manager to pay the operation's bills, but it is equally important to know about the nature of the expenses incurred. For example, a manager may want to know exactly how much money is being spent on equipment repairs for a given month or year. Obviously, then, the manager must keep a record of how much money is being spent for parts and labor to repair the operation's equipment. To do so, managers use a system of coding to assign actual costs listed on invoices to predetermined cost areas.

Managers code invoices to specific cost categories to report accurately. It also enables them to better analyze their expenses. It is important to categorize payables so that the operation has an accurate, detailed history of its costs of doing business. This cost information aids in the budget planning process and can indicate where spending has fallen below or above what was forecast in the budget.

When preparing invoices for payment, bills should be coded according to the operation's established **chart of accounts** for expenses. A chart of accounts is simply a list of categories used to organize an operation's revenue and cost information.

In the restaurant and foodservice industry, several account categories for costs are commonly used:

• Food

• Beverages

• Supplies (other than food, such as paper products and chemicals)

• Services (exterminator, equipment maintenance, and landscaping)

• Advertising

• Utilities

A unique number, or **account code**, is usually assigned to each of the accounts listed on the chart of accounts for expenses. These codes might be specific to one operation or department, or might be codes determined by a corporate office. Such codes aid in tracking the costs for the operation.

Here is an example: At one hotel, some beverages are ordered separately at the lobby bar, the restaurant, the pool bar, and the banquet departments. The managers for each of these different areas approve invoices for such items that are ordered and received by their departments. The hotel has an established code number of "75" for beverages. When an invoice comes in to the pool bar for piña colada mix, the manager of the pool bar will code it to 75 when approving it for payment. The same is true for champagne received in the banquet area, and so forth. If coding is accurate and consistent, when the general manager of the hotel looks at a report for account code 75, it will reflect a summary of all the beverage expenditures for the entire hotel operation.

Invoice Payment

Despite the diligent efforts of those responsible for AP administration, mistakes can be made in paying invoices. Data entry errors can be commonplace unless the manager has established solid procedures to ensure that legitimate invoices are paid only for the amount actually due.

In a well-managed operation, invoices and payments are checked by at least two individuals. Software developed to match invoice numbers against the operation's check number used to pay the invoice is invaluable in this process.

RESTAURANT TECHNOLOGY

OPEN FOR BUSINESS

A recent invoice scam is the direct result of the increase in managers' use of technology. It is increasingly common because of the widespread creation and use of restaurant and foodservice Web sites. In this scam, a few months before an operation's domain registration is about to expire, it will get a "renewal notice." A domain is the Web address of an operation. Having an up-to-date domain registration is the way an operation maintains control of its own Web address. In this scam, a dishonest person sends an apparently official-looking renewal notice via regular mail or email, warning that if the operation does not pay the invoice, it will lose its domain name and thus its specific Web address.

Often the invoice will indicate that the operation must reregister for a lengthy period, or will suggest adding services. Whatever the scam, these companies always charge inflated prices and, if the operation pays the invoice, it may or may not get a renewed domain registration.

The only legitimate renewal notice will come from the company originally used to register and maintain the operation's domain name. Managers should make a note of their actual domain host and keep it handy to avoid this increasingly common scam.

The intent of this type of software is simply to help ensure that all AP are processed only for the amount of the invoices due, and that each legitimate invoice is paid only one time.

In addition to paying the proper amount, an effective manager knows that there is a proper time to pay each invoice. Some operations gain a reputation with suppliers for paying invoices very promptly and in accordance with all contract terms previously agreed upon. This makes the best vendors eager to do business with them. This can be good, but it is also important to know that the amount of cash maintained in the operation's bank account must be carefully managed. As a result, an effective manager maintains good payment relations with vendors, many of which are likely to be such local businesses as plumbers, electricians, food vendors, and the like.

It is also important to recognize that in nearly every business, including restaurant and foodservice operations, those customers who pay bills long after they are actually due are also likely to be serviced slowly by their vendors. In fact, prompt payment of invoices is so important to many smaller businesses providing goods and services that better purchase prices and delivery terms can often be negotiated. In addition, some vendors will actually offer their customers the choice of paying less than the full invoice if invoices are paid promptly.

In most cases, managers should take advantage, whenever possible, of discounts offered by vendors for prompt payment. Some vendors will give a discount of 1 to 5 percent of the invoice price if a bill is paid within a specific time period. The manager should take advantage of every opportunity to build positive vendor relations and help ensure lowest costs. This is done by managing the accounts payable process and paying the operation's bills in a timely manner. Prompt payment also ensures a good reputation with the supplier. In contrast, once an establishment has a known history of being delinquent, it may be difficult to obtain food, beverages, supplies, or services on anything other than a cash basis. This could be inconvenient and problematic for the manager.

The accounts payable system must include a process by which payment of an invoice is actually approved by someone with the authority to do so. This person should be aware of the overall budget for the operation and the current state of the operation's finances. In most operations, the manager will review all AP-related paperwork to ensure it is accurate, and then sign the invoice as approved to be paid. This authorization process can catch errors and also help prevent theft. After all required steps have been completed, the bill or invoice should be paid. In many operations the person who authorizes the invoice for payment is a different person than the one who issues the check for payment. This separation of duties helps reduce the possibilities of theft and fraud,

MANAGER'S MATH

OPEN FOR BUSINESS

Ira is the manager of Southview CharGrill. He likes to take advantage of early payment discounts when processing his accounts payable. For example, if the manager receives an invoice for $1,000 and a 5 percent discount is allowed for early payment, the manager pays only 95 percent of the invoice: $1,000 × 0.95 = $950.00.

He has received several invoices this week that allow discounts for early payment. Using a chart like this one, fill in the savings amounts and revised invoice amounts for each vendor. Then answer the questions that follow.

Vendor	Discount for Early Payment	Original Invoice Amount	Savings Amount	Revised Invoice Amount
Bartle's Produce	2.0% if paid within 14 days	$1,580.00	_____	_____
Metz & Metz Meats	1.0% if paid within 30 days	3,260.00	_____	_____
Old Tymey Breads	3.5% if paid within 10 days	505.60	_____	_____
Barmen's Ice Cream	1.0% if paid within 30 days	325.00	_____	_____
Barry's Dairy	2.5% if paid within 14 days	910.00	_____	_____
	Total	$_____	$_____	$_____

1. What will be the total amount paid for these invoices if Ira does *not* take advantage of any early payment discounts?

2. What will be the total amount of discount Ira's operation can achieve if all invoices are paid in a manner that allows him to take advantage of the early payment discounts?

3. What will be the total amount paid for these invoices if Ira does take advantage of all the early payment discounts offered?

(Answers: 1. $6,580.60; 2. $107.90; 3. $6,472.70)

which become more probable when one manager or department is responsible for both approving and paying bills.

In most cases, invoices will be paid by individual invoice or as part of a larger account statement.

- **By individual invoice:** After a manager has reviewed and approved invoices, the individual invoices are manually or electronically filed for payment by a specific due date. These bills are paid when due. For example, if an approved invoice must be paid by July 16, it may be pulled on July 10 for final review, signature, and check mailing on July 11 to allow time for mail delivery.

• **By statement:** Processed documentation is filed by name of vendor while the accounting personnel await receipt of a statement of account. A statement of account typically lists multiple invoice amounts due to the vendor. For example, a bakery vendor that delivers daily (*Exhibit 6.9*) may request payment every two weeks.

The vendor submits a statement of account listing multiple delivery invoices applicable to the two-week period for which payment is requested. When the vendor's statement is received, applicable invoices are retrieved. Then all invoices referred to in the statement, less any adjustments required by credit memos, can be paid at the same time. A sample statement of account is shown in *Exhibit 6.10*.

Exhibit 6.10

SAMPLE STATEMENT OF ACCOUNT

Statement 107643

Bellnot Brothers Produce

102 Broadway

Bayside, FL 00000

Telephone: 000-000-0000

Email: 0000@000.000

Fax: 000-000-0000

Account no.: _____1735_____

Delivered to: Deep Sands Bistro

300 Ocean View Lane

Deep Sands, FL 00000

Attention: Jack, Director of Purchasing

Telephone: 000-000-0000

Invoice No.	Delivery Date	Amount Due	Adjustment	Net Amount Due
10711	9/10/12	$173.59		$173.59
10928	9/13/12	310.80	($21.55)*	289.25
12541	9/18/12	190.51		190.51
13401	9/23/12	290.18		290.18
			Total due	$943.53

*Credit Memo #2138

Payment due upon receipt. Please send payment to the above address.

Duplicate: Please return top copy with payment, and retain second copy for your records.

Thank you.

When invoices are to be paid either individually or as part of a statement, a check covering the correct amount of the vendor's bill should be prepared for signing. If a manual system is used, each invoice or statement that is paid should be marked to indicate the date and amount of payment and check number. Marking and processing should be done in a way that it is possible to verify that a payment has been made, and to reduce the chance that an invoice could be paid twice.

Recording of Invoice Payments

While it may seem simple to ensure that each accounts receivable invoice is paid only once, that is not the case. Careful attention to detail is needed to make sure that invoices are paid and their payment is recorded properly. An effective manager creates a system whereby total payments to vendors match vendor billings exactly, with no overpayments or underpayments.

A voucher system is one good way to help keep records of payments made to vendors. When using this system, a manager authorizes payment of an invoice, and then an accounts payable voucher is prepared. Vouchers are numbered forms that have space to record the information about the payment. This information should include the date of the payment, the check number, and the amount and recipient of the check. An example of an accounts payable voucher is shown in *Exhibit 6.11*. If used, the purchase requisition, purchase order, and/or signed delivery invoice can also be attached to the voucher. This shows proof of the actual order and that the order was received.

The accounting function, including that applicable to AP administration, was one of the first areas within the restaurant and foodservice industry to become automated. Today, even the smallest of operations or the accounting/bookkeeping services that they hire can use "off-the-shelf" or other software to develop the organization's financial statements.

Advantages of electronic AP systems include greater accuracy, increased speed of processing, and improved ability to retrieve and manage AP records. Because of their relatively low cost, electronic rather than manual invoice filing systems are increasingly used to carefully record and track supplier payments.

Exhibit 6.11

ACCOUNTS PAYABLE VOUCHER

Voucher #: XB445

Pay to: _____

Address: _____

Date paid: _____

Amount of check: _____

Check #: _____

Prepared by: _____

Approved for payment by: _____

Posted by: _____

Audited by: _____

Date	Description	Amount	Discount amount	Net amount	Account code	Amount

Some restaurant or foodservice managers and their vendors are using electronic funds transfer (EFT) to simplify the invoice payment process and reduce associated payment costs. For example, purchasers can authorize automatic payments to be charged to a business credit card or be withdrawn from a business checking or savings account. The funds that are collected are then directly deposited into the vendor's business account.

One advantage to managers using EFT options is improvement in the documentation of bill payment. One advantage to vendors offering EFT options is the faster receipt of payments that are due to them. Electronic bill payment is just one example of how advancements in technology have improved the efficiency of operations that use it effectively.

ACCOUNTS PAYABLE (AP) AUDITING

It is essential that managers institute security procedures to control an organization's funds as AP payments are made. Security control at the time of bill payment begins with the development of effective policies and procedures that are consistently used. Managers must ensure that basic security controls are in place in the accounting department to minimize opportunities for dishonest staff members to commit embezzlement. **Embezzlement** is the act of stealing financial assets, including cash, from a business.

To protect against potential loss, employees who handle the organization's bill payments can be bonded. The **bonding** of employees is an arrangement with an insurer in which, for a fee, the insurance company guarantees payment to an operation for a financial loss caused by the actions of the specific covered employee.

In all operations, basic AP management procedures should be developed and enforced:

- Banks are notified of personnel authorized to write checks; copies of their signatures are on file at the bank.

- The name of the person or vendor receiving payments must be the same on the check, the check recording system, and the invoice paid.

- After they have been paid, invoices should be filed by supplier name, along with the purchase order and delivery invoice or other authorizing documents, for future reference.

- A system must be put in place that makes it impossible for an invoice to be submitted two or more times for payment.

- All checks written should be made payable to a person or company; no checks should be made payable to cash. Checks written to petty cash may be permitted. Managers should routinely examine the check registry, or list of processed checks, to learn and inquire about new suppliers and one-time transactions.

- Bank records should be carefully examined to confirm that all checks issued have been processed. No checks should be missing. Checks should be used in numerical sequence without skipping.

Additional procedures specifically for the control of noncash or check payments for purchases can be developed and should be followed consistently:

- All checks should be numbered by the printer of the checks, and supplies of blank checks should be kept under lock.

- The person who signs checks should mail them; they should not be returned for mailing to the individual who processed the invoice for payment.

- It is a good idea to require more than one signature by a manager or an owner for checks in excess of a specified amount.

- Invoices and vouchers should be clearly marked as being paid when checks are written.

- Blank checks for emergency or other use are never signed.

- A system to control spoiled, voided, or other unused checks is used. There should be no way that such checks can be fraudulently cashed by dishonest employees.

Regardless of the AP-related policies that have been put in place, these policies must be consistently followed if they are to be effective. In chapter 1, auditing was described as the field of accounting that addresses the independent verification of a business's financial records. The periodic auditing of AP procedures is of great value.

There are several reasons for conducting an AP audit:

- Reviewing operational procedures to ascertain whether results are consistent with established objectives and goals

- Recommending financial, operational, and accounting improvements

- Determining the overall quality of internal controls

- Determining that proper accounting, financial, and control systems and procedures are consistently used

- Ensuring that AP-related accounting activities conform with Generally Accepted Accounting Principles (GAAP), as well as any applicable state or federal laws and regulations, contractual obligations, and standard business practices

- Determining the extent to which the operation's assets are properly safeguarded against losses of all kinds

- Serving as a visible deterrent to employee theft and fraud

A thorough audit will examine several key areas within an AP system:

- Duplicate or erroneous invoice payments

- Invoice pricing and extension errors

- Credit memo processing

- Appropriate use of on-time payment allowances or rebates

- Adherence to purchasing policies and procedures

- Potential for employee fraud or theft

AP-related audits typically consist of two different types: random audits and targeted audits.

Random Audits

Audits can be conducted when no prior notice has been given to an operation's accounting staff. They can also be scheduled in advance. **Random audits** are those in which auditors randomly choose a variety of AP-related financial transactions for close examination (*Exhibit 6.12*).

The rationale behind a random audit is that by choosing financial transactions randomly, audits will have the best opportunity to review a variety of AP payment-related systems and thus assist in fraud and theft detection.

Exhibit 6.12

Targeted Audits

Targeted audits are those that closely examine only a specific type of financial transaction. In this case, a single portion of the entire AP system is thoroughly examined. Like random audits, targeted audits may be scheduled in advance or performed without any prior notice to those who manage an operation's AP system. The purpose of a targeted audit is to very closely examine the financial systems used in one specific area of an operation's AP system. This way, auditors can make specific improvement recommendations for that area.

Audits may be scheduled according to a predetermined time pattern or date. For example, an operation may choose to schedule an audit the first week of each fiscal year, or the first week of every calendar quarter. Unannounced audits may, of course, be undertaken at any time the owners of a business elect to do so.

When conducting an AP audit, the auditors seek to follow an **audit trail**. These are the steps in the payment process that are supported by verifiable documents or other tangible proof. For example, in an operation that uses all of the documents described at the beginning of this chapter in *Exhibit 6.3*, the invoice verification audit trail would appear as shown in *Exhibit 6.13*.

WHAT'S THE FOOTPRINT?

Some managers think green with regard to their kitchens and dining rooms, but think less about going green in areas such as accounting. The office environment actually offers many great opportunities to go green and save:

1. Use recycled paper products throughout the office.

2. When purging files or documents, use a shredder and recycle the shredded paper.

3. Refill or recycle ink and toner cartridges.

4. Use only rechargeable batteries in battery-powered devices.

5. Turn off computer monitors to reduce energy usage by as much as two-thirds.

These are just a few tips. With a bit of innovation and creativity, an accountant's office can implement many ways to conserve resources and save money.

Exhibit 6.13

AUDIT TRAIL FOR INVOICE VERIFICATION

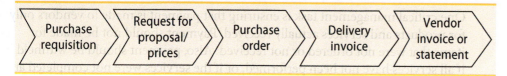

Purchase requisition → Request for proposal/prices → Purchase order → Delivery invoice → Vendor invoice or statement

---

In those operations not using all of the documents in *Exhibit 6.13*, the audit trail would include the documents that are in use. Additional audit trails address other key AP-related areas:

- Invoice approval systems
- Invoice coding systems
- Invoice payment systems
- Recording of invoice payment systems

It is important to note that the primary objective of any audit is not to catch criminals, but rather to keep honest people honest by reducing opportunities for theft. Additionally, a properly performed audit should provide valuable information that can be used to improve operations. This will help ensure the responsible safeguarding of company assets.

Honest managers should never fear financial audits. They should view them as an essential tool for use in the improvement of a restaurant or foodservice operation.

SUMMARY

1. **List and describe the five steps in the management of an operation's accounts payable (AP).**

   The five key steps in the management of accounts payable are (1) invoice approval, (2) confirmation of invoice amount, (3) invoice coding, (4) invoice payment, and (5) recording of invoice payments. Invoice approval is essential because operations want to pay only for those goods and services they have actually ordered and received. Confirmation of amount owed is critical because managers want to pay only the amounts they actually owe, at the prices they were promised. Invoice coding improves managers' understanding of their operation and aids in the budgeting process. Timely payment of invoices is important to maintain creditworthy status with vendors. Finally, careful recording of invoices that have been paid helps prevent double payment of invoices and keeps critical expense records up-to-date.

2. **Discuss the importance of verification in the invoice payment process.**

   One critical management task is ensuring that payment is made to vendors only for products and services actually received. Payment should not be made for items that were not ordered or not received. Also, payment should be withheld if all services have not been performed, or if the services were not completed at the agreed-upon quality level. Managers should process invoices for payment submitted only by those vendors who have delivered the operation's authorized products and services at the authorized price. The product quality and manner of delivery must be agreed upon by both the business and vendor.

3. **Identify common causes of invoice payment disputes.**

   There are primarily two reasons that an invoice for products or services should not be paid, or should be paid for an amount different than the amount stated on the invoice. The first of these is that a legitimate adjustment be made to the invoice due to differences between the stated amount on the invoice and the amount the operation actually owes. Examples include incorrect prices charged, back orders, undelivered product, short weight or counts, or items rejected due to poor quality. In these cases, credit memos must be processed or contact must be made with the vendor to determine the actual amount due and payable.

   The second reason an invoice should not be paid is if the operation is the victim of a fraudulent invoice scam. In this case, the operation must have procedures in place to identify and to refuse payment of these false invoices.

4. **Describe the reasons for coding and recording invoice payments.**

   Managers code invoices to track the amounts, as well as the nature, of the expenses they incur. Managers assign code numbers to different categories of costs to keep a record of how much money is being spent in each category. Managers code invoices to specific cost categories to report expenses accurately, and to enable them to better analyze their operations. When expenses are coded, managers have an accurate and detailed history of the cost of doing business. This cost information can then be used in budgeting and can help managers identify where spending is excessive, or where it has fallen below budget forecasts.

5. **Explain the difference between a random and a targeted accounts payable audit.**

Random audits are those in which auditors choose a few of a wide range of AP-related financial transactions for very close examination. By using the random audit approach, auditors have the best opportunity to review a variety of AP payment–related systems.

In a targeted audit, auditors closely examine only a specific type of financial transaction within a larger group of transactions. In a targeted audit, all of a single portion of the AP system is very closely examined. Like random audits, targeted audits may be scheduled in advance or performed without prior notice to those who manage an operation's AP system. In both cases, the purpose of audits is to make specific accounting improvement recommendations.

APPLICATION EXERCISE

Imagine that you are the manager for an operation that employs a part-time bookkeeper to help manage your accounts payable system. The division of duties is such that you are the final authority for bill payment authorization. The bookkeeper prepares payment checks for your final signature, at which point the checks are mailed by the bookkeeper.

Recently you have found that your operation failed to take advantage of some early invoice payment discounts that were substantial. In addition, your operation incurred some late charge penalties on other invoices that were not paid in a timely manner.

Outline a series of steps you and your bookkeeper can take to ensure that your operation optimizes its ability to take advantage of timely payment discounts, and minimizes its chances of paying charges related to late invoice payments.

Use the steps to write a formal AP policy designed to address the tasks you and the bookkeeper will each perform as you address this important issue.

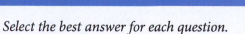

REVIEW YOUR LEARNING

Select the best answer for each question.

1. **What must managers do next after receiving an invoice for payment?**
   A. Approve the invoice for payment
   B. Enter the invoice in the AP system
   C. Pay the amount listed on the invoice
   D. Code the invoice to the proper cost category

2. **The purpose of a credit memo is to**
   A. record vendor payments.
   B. obtain early payment discounts.
   C. detect and prevent invoice scams.
   D. correct the amount due listed on an invoice.

3. If needed, when should credit memos be issued?

    A. When invoices are paid

    B. When invoices are received

    C. When products are ordered

    D. When products are delivered

4. What is the result of AP-related errors made in invoice extensions?

    A. Product inventories will be excessive.

    B. Ordered products may not be received.

    C. Total amounts billed to the operation will be incorrect.

    D. Records of the operation's invoice payment dates will be incorrect.

5. What vendor-supplied document lists multiple invoice amounts due to the vendor?

    A. Purchase order

    B. Chart of accounts

    C. AP check registry

    D. Statement of account

6. What products or services are most likely to be involved in an attempted invoice scam?

    A. Food products

    B. Office supplies

    C. Beverage products

    D. Lawn care services

7. What would be the result of errors made in invoice coding?

    A. Total operating expenses are overestimated.

    B. Total operating expenses are underestimated.

    C. Expenses are assigned to the wrong cost categories.

    D. Expense payments are assigned to the wrong accounting period.

8. At what stage in the bill payment process do managers code invoices?

    A. Prior to invoice approval

    B. Prior to invoice payment

    C. Prior to receiving the invoice

    D. Prior to receiving a statement of account

9. The steps in payment processing that are supported by verifiable documents or other tangible proof are

    A. an audit trail.

    B. a random audit.

    C. a targeted audit.

    D. an independent audit.

10. What type of audit is designed to examine a single area within the entire AP system?

    A. Random audit

    B. Targeted audit

    C. Scheduled audit

    D. Unannounced audit

FIELD PROJECT

Select a local restaurant or foodservice operation. It may be a commercial or a noncommercial operation, and it may be from any segment of the industry. Talk to the manager about the purchasing and accounts payable documentation system in place in the operation. Specifically, obtain the answers to the following questions:

For purchased products:

1. Who is authorized to purchase products in the operation?

2. What documentation is required to initiate a product purchase?

3. What documentation is typically received from vendors upon product delivery?

4. What internal documentation is used to confirm delivery of products?

5. Who is authorized to manage the operation's AP system?

6. What systems are in place to ensure invoices for purchased products are paid only once and for the proper amount?

For purchased services:

1. What services does this operation typically purchase from outside vendors?

2. Who is authorized to obtain vendor services needed in the operation?

3. What documentation is required to initiate a service request?

4. What internal documentation is used to confirm services have been completed as contracted?

5. What systems are in place to ensure that invoices for services are paid only once and for the proper amount?

7 Controlling Foodservice Costs

INSIDE THIS CHAPTER

- Cost Control
- Food Cost Control
- Labor Cost Control
- Other Expense Control

CHAPTER LEARNING OBJECTIVES

After completing this chapter, you should be able to:

- Describe the steps needed to implement a foodservice cost control system.

- List the four key areas related to controlling food costs.

- Describe the methods used to assess variable labor costs.

- Explain the importance of controlling fixed labor costs.

- Describe the different types of costs included in an operation's other operating expenses.

CASE STUDY

"I don't get it," said Gabriel, a line cook at the Starburst diner.

"Don't get what?" asked Ralph, the diner's day manager.

"Well, yesterday afternoon before I left, I pulled two boxes of link sausages out of the freezer for this morning's breakfast. I like to thaw here in the refrigerator overnight."

"That makes sense," said Ralph. "So what's the problem?"

"Well, this morning, there's only one box left. There's no way we sold a box of sausages last night. I mean, we might have gotten a few breakfast requests in the evening, but I can't believe we would have sold more than one or two orders for eggs. And when we do, some people will order a ham slice or bacon."

"So where's the other case of sausages?" asked Ralph.

"That's what I don't get," said Gabriel. "I've looked all over the kitchen. They're just gone."

1. What could be some explanations for the disappearance of this case of sausages?

2. Who in a restaurant or foodservice operation is responsible for ensuring the security of the products and supplies the operation buys? What do you think will happen if the person or persons fail to do it?

157

COST CONTROL

Controlling and reducing operating costs are desirable actions for ensuring the ongoing financial health of restaurant and foodservice operations. Taking steps to control operating costs depends on understanding which costs might be out of line, and how to correct them. At the same time, any operational adjustments must ensure continuation of the operation's required levels of quality, safety, sanitation, and customer service.

With experience, managers learn to quickly spot some cost control concerns in their operations. Other cost control analyses take a more detailed approach to evaluate and correct potential problem areas. Volumes of guidelines and other information are available to help restaurant and foodservice managers in their cost control efforts. Effective cost control begins with the operating budget, which is the financial plan for a restaurant or foodservice operation (see chapter 4).

The budget clearly outlines financial targets related to both sales and costs. If a budget is planned carefully, the future should hold relatively few surprises. To make sure of this, the process of controlling costs begins right where the budgeting process leaves off. To control operating costs, managers must follow specific steps:

1. Collect Accurate Sales and Cost Data

Historical sales information that details how much revenue an operation has generated in the past is just as important to cost control as it is to budgeting and other management functions. The relationship between historic sales and the costs that were incurred to achieve those sales is often proportional. Many foodservice costs change depending on sales volume. In order to know whether costs are within an appropriate range, it is imperative to start with accurate revenue information.

Revenue should be tracked and recorded for different periods. This includes yearly, monthly, weekly, daily, day part or meal period, and even hourly periods:

- Yearly and monthly data are used for budgeting and income statement purposes.
- Weekly and daily sales information is used for purchasing and scheduling.
- Daily and day-part data are also used for employee scheduling as well as for production planning.

Sales information can come from several sources. Yearly and monthly sales information comes from the income statement. Hourly, daily, and weekly figures are usually generated by point-of-sale (POS) system reports. In operations that do not have POS systems, this information comes from tabulating guest checks or periodic cash register readings.

In addition to having accurate sales information, it is also necessary to have accurate cost information. Most cost information can be taken from operational records. Many POS systems track inventory, food waste, and employee work hours. Management can create and maintain control systems that provide detailed information about inventory and food costs, payroll costs, and actual labor hours used.

2. Monitor and Analyze Sales and Costs

Sales and cost figures are monitored and compared to budgeted amounts, operational standards, and historical information to identify any variances. This monitoring should be done on a regular and ongoing basis. This is a good way to check how the operation is running. It can also prevent future problems by identifying them early.

Every item on the budget should be checked, if possible, against actual figures, and the difference should be noted. This is called a **line item review**. When the budget is compared to the actual revenue figures, the numbers for each item should be identical, or at least very close to each other. Any variance between the budget and the actual amounts may be expressed as a dollar amount, as a percentage, or both. A format for comparing budgeted and actual amounts using a line item review is illustrated in *Exhibit 7.1*.

Exhibit 7.1				
SAMPLE LINE ITEM REVIEW				
Budget Item	Budgeted Amount	Actual Amount	Variance	Variance Percentage
Food sales	$100,000	$90,000	$10,000	−10%

All restaurant and foodservice operations have standards or goals. In the case of controlling costs, the standard represents the level at which a cost should be. Standard costs are carefully calculated to ensure that the operation achieves profitability. At the same time, it must maintain quality products and service levels.

Exhibit 7.2

For example, an operation should always be concerned about providing good customer service. This requires the operation to have the appropriate level of labor on site at all times (*Exhibit 7.2*). With this consideration, management compares the actual amount spent for labor to the targeted amount to be spent. The targeted amount to be spent, if determined correctly, takes into account the level of service at which management expects its operations to perform. Sufficient hours scheduled in the kitchen will result in an excellent product being sent out in a prompt manner. Likewise, the correct number of servers to take orders and serve efficiently will ensure good food and service.

It is important to recognize that management determines a standard based on many factors, not the least of which is profit. When considering a labor standard, management takes into account producing a quality product and providing quality service. To go below the standard could sacrifice product or service quality and, as a result, long-term profitability. For that reason, it is important that an operation *spends* what is needed to achieve the standard as well as *reduces costs* to achieve the standard.

In addition to comparing actual costs to standard costs, management also compares actual costs to historical costs. **Historical costs** are those costs that have been incurred in the past. By comparing these two figures, management can determine if the operation is improving.

When comparing actual costs to historical costs, it is important to remember that similar periods must be compared. Thus, January's labor cost is compared to January's labor cost of the previous year, or Monday's sales this week are compared to Monday's sales of last week. Special events or unusual circumstances should also be taken into account when comparing historical costs. For example, comparing this Sunday's sales to last Sunday's sales, which happened to be Mother's Day and the busiest day of the year for many operations, would not be a good comparison.

3. Take Corrective Action as Appropriate

Over time, even small changes in costs can add up to significant losses. When costs are determined to be out of line, the cause should be investigated. If the budget and actual expenses incurred do not match, the costs must be analyzed

THINK ABOUT IT . . .

When would using a lower-quality ingredient in a menu item not be a good idea, even if it does result in lower food cost?

to see what could have caused the problem. If there is a variance, management should take action to correct the variance. For example, if food cost is too high, purchasing, receiving, and preparation procedures should be investigated. If labor cost shows a variance, scheduling and work production standards should be analyzed.

As soon as the cause for a variance is identified, the manager should take steps to correct the problem. These steps are called **corrective actions**. As explained in chapter 3, restaurant and foodservice managers have more control over some costs than they do over others. Corrective actions, by nature, can be used only to affect controllable costs.

Exhibit 7.3 lists some examples of corrective actions that can be taken to control various costs. For example, if sales are lower than expected, the hours included on the employee work schedule (*Exhibit 7.4*) might need to be reduced to lower labor costs.

In addition to taking corrective actions, it may also be necessary to reforecast revenue or make other changes to the operation's budget. As circumstances change, some forecasts used to prepare the original budget may no longer be accurate. Reviewing forecasts, at least on a monthly basis, will help managers make realistic adjustments to the budget for upcoming periods.

Managers who seek to effectively control all of their operating costs can do so by developing specialized procedures in the three key areas of foodservice cost:

- Food cost
- Labor cost
- Other expenses

Exhibit 7.3

SAMPLE CORRECTIVE ACTIONS FOR COST CONTROL

To Reduce	Implement These Corrective Actions
Food cost	Reduce portion size. Replace current ingredients with more cost-effective ingredients. Feature menu items with higher profit margins. Raise menu prices if appropriate.
Food waste	Monitor portion control. Monitor food storage and rotation. Monitor food ordering. Improve order communication to reduce production errors.
Inventory cost	Order appropriate quantities—avoid having too much or too little in storage.
Labor cost	Reduce number of employees on schedule. Ask employees to end their shifts early. Schedule cross-trained staff (for example, server/cashier/host).

Exhibit 7.4

FOOD COST CONTROL

Food cost information is usually determined by reviewing inventory and purchasing records for a period. Most restaurant and foodservice operations calculate their food cost on a monthly basis. Some quick-service restaurants will do so as often as weekly or even daily.

Many people, including some restaurant and foodservice managers, have the misconception that when food is purchased it becomes food cost. This is not true. Purchases certainly are an integral part of food cost. However, food cost is, in reality, the dollar value of the food that was actually used during a certain period. In the restaurant and foodservice industry, the terms *food cost* and *cost of food sold* are used interchangeably.

Fortunately, there is a formula for calculating food cost that takes into account the multiple purchases of the many items used in a typical establishment. To determine the value of the food that has been used, managers must first calculate their operation's beginning, or opening, inventory values. Then they must calculate their ending, or closing, inventory values.

Beginning inventory is the total value of products on hand at the beginning of the accounting period for which food cost is being calculated. **Ending inventory** is the total value of products on hand at the end of that same accounting period. When those two values are known, food cost is calculated as follows:

(Beginning inventory + Purchases) − Ending inventory = Food cost

Exhibit 7.5	
CALCULATION OF FOOD COST FOR ONE WEEK	
$1,000	Value of beginning inventory at beginning of week
+ $5,000	Purchases of food during week
= $6,000	Total value of available food
− $2,000	Value of ending inventory at end of week*
= $4,000	Food cost

*Note that the value of ending inventory for this week is the beginning inventory for the next week.

Exhibit 7.5 shows how food cost is calculated. In one week, an opening food inventory was valued at $1,000, food purchases were $5,000, and the operation's closing food inventory was valued at $2,000.

It is important to recognize that when one accounting period ends, a new accounting period begins. In other words, the ending inventory for one period becomes the beginning inventory for the next accounting period.

Some managers also refer to their food cost, or their beverage cost, as cost of goods sold or cost of sales. See chapter 3. Regardless of the many terms used, however, the total food cost must be determined to properly calculate an operation's food cost percentage.

Food Cost Percentage

Now that the actual cost of food has been determined, the next management task is to calculate the actual food cost percentage. As explained in chapter 3, food cost percentage is a measurement of the relationship between sales and the amount spent on food in order to generate those sales. Once managers have determined their actual food cost information, food cost percentage is calculated using the following formula:

Food cost ÷ Food sales = Food cost percentage

For example, if an establishment's food sales are $24,000 for a given week, and the food cost is $7,000 for the same week, then the food cost percentage for that week is 29.2 percent:

$$\underset{\textbf{Food costs}}{\$7,000} \quad \div \quad \underset{\textbf{Food sales}}{\$24,000} \quad = \quad \underset{\textbf{Food cost percentage}}{\textbf{0.292 or 29.2\%}}$$

Another way to state this is to say that out of every dollar of sales, food cost accounted for approximately $0.29.

Many managers calculate their food cost percentage for a given accounting period, such as a week or a month. This calculation can be broken down into further levels of detail, such as by menu item, menu category, or even meal period. For instance, the average breakfast food cost percentage might be lower than the average dinner food cost percentage. Food cost percentage is most often compared to the operation's preestablished standard, a company standard, historical costs, or even industry standards. To control food costs, managers develop and maintain control systems in several key areas:

- Purchasing controls
- Inventory controls
- Product theft controls
- Production controls

PURCHASING CONTROLS

The control of purchasing in a restaurant or foodservice operation is essential. Managers want to buy no more and no less than their required amount of food and beverage products. Also, they want to purchase these items at prices that are known in advance. Excessive purchasing can lead to higher food costs due to increased product spoilage or deterioration. To maintain an effective purchasing program, managers ensure that several requirements are in place and consistently followed:

- Only employees expressly authorized to purchase items may do so.
- Purchases are made only from predesignated and preapproved vendors.
- A purchase order (PO) is initiated for all major purchases.

OPEN FOR BUSINESS

MANAGER'S MATH

Read the following examples and answer the questions related to food cost and food cost percentage.

1. Breakfast sales for last week equaled $17,000. To prepare the breakfast items for the week, the food cost was $2,900. What is the food cost percentage for breakfast last week?

2. Shrimp cocktail has a food cost of $3.65 per order and is listed on the menu at a sales price of $9.50. What is the food cost percentage for shrimp cocktail?

3. A sandwich shop menu lists 17 sandwiches with an average sales price of $5.00 per sandwich. If total sales for a given period are $8,500, about how many sandwiches sold during this period?

4. Using the same information as in question 3, assume that the average food cost per sandwich is $1.19. What is the average food cost percentage per sandwich?

(Answers: 1. 17.06%; 2. 38.42%; 3. 1,700; 4. 23.8%)

Manager's Memo

Two things must be in place to calculate food cost. First, standardized recipes must be used. A standardized recipe includes the instructions needed to produce a menu item that will meet an operation's quality and quantity standards. When standardized recipes are used, managers will know what ingredients, and the amount of each, that were used. Second, the current cost of all ingredients must be known. Then the amount of each ingredient used must be calculated to determine the food cost of the ingredients used.

Most establishments sell an entrée with other items for a specified price. For example, a chicken dinner may include the chicken entrée, salad with dressing, potato, vegetable, and a bread roll and butter. The food cost for each of the meal components must be added together to calculate the total food cost for menu item pricing purposes.

- PO information is matched to delivery invoices when products are received.
- Discrepancies between POs and delivery invoice amounts are noted on credit memos.
- Systems are in place to ensure that invoices are paid only once and for the proper amount.
- Invoices are authorized by managers prior to payment.

Security concerns can also relate to issues that arise during the product receiving process.

- **Short weights:** A carton containing, for example, 45 pounds of fresh steaks should be weighed. Ideally, steaks will be removed from the cardboard carton to determine their exact weight. When fresh seafood or fresh poultry is packed in heavy, waxed cardboard containers containing ice, these products should be removed from the ice prior to weighing.

- **Assorted contents:** A carton containing 40 pounds of ground beef and 40 pounds of pre-portioned steaks weighs the same as a carton containing 60 pounds of ground beef and 20 pounds of fresh-cut steaks. The latter costs much more. Different items must be weighed separately when their costs are different.

- **Missing items:** In instances of missing items, credit memos indicating the shorted item and their cost are prepared and attached to the delivery invoice. This helps ensure that the vendor will be paid only for delivered items.

Another potential security-related problem at the time of product delivery occurs when delivery personnel gain access to the operation's storage areas. Consider, for example, the possibility of theft when delivery personnel are allowed access to storage areas containing liquor or expensive meats. To prevent this occurrence, no unauthorized person should be allowed into an operation's product storage areas.

INVENTORY CONTROLS

An operation's cost of food is based, in part, on the amount of product remaining in inventory at the end of an accounting period. It is easy to see that theft or other loss of items stored in inventory will cause food costs to increase. For that reason, managers must carefully monitor the amounts they have in inventory. This includes the length of time that the items have been held in storage and the amount of any inventory write-offs. Write-offs are recorded reductions in the stated value of inventories. Write-offs are taken as a result of shrinkage, which is product spoilage, product waste, or theft of inventory.

The first step in protecting products in inventory is proper storage. There are three basic types of food storage with which kitchen managers must be familiar:

Exhibit 7.6

- **Dry storage (50°F–70°F [10°C–21°C]):** This is for grocery items such as canned goods, condiments, bakery products such as flour and sugar, herbs and spices, and some beverages (*Exhibit 7.6*).

- **Refrigerated storage (below 41°F [5°C]):** This is for items such as fresh meat, produce, seafood, dairy products, and some beverages.

- **Frozen storage:** The proper frozen-storage temperature varies from product to product. A temperature that is good for one product may affect the quality of another product. Frozen storage is for items such as frozen meat, seafood, French fries, and vegetables purchased in this market form.

Food and beverage products available in inventory have been purchased with the intent that they will be used to generate revenues. If, instead, they are stolen or wasted, money will have been spent with no resulting revenue. Therefore, costs will be greater than necessary. As a result, profitability will be lower than expected.

Managers count and assign a value to their product inventories at the beginning and end of each accounting period for which they wish to calculate food costs. They then multiply the numbers of items in inventory by the value of each item to arrive at the inventory's total value.

Ingredients may be purchased in cases, cans, boxes, bags, cartons, gallons, pounds, and other measurements. Regardless of how it is received, the purchase unit (PU) represents the measurement in which the item is purchased and stored.

When taking inventory, it is a good idea to have one person count the items in storage. Then a second person who is helping take inventory verifies the count. Having two people count and value inventory speeds up the process, and helps ensure the items in storage are counted accurately and honestly.

To make the inventory valuation process easier, some products can be priced early in the storage process. This involves printing information such as the date delivered and invoice cost on product containers

MANAGER'S MATH

OPEN FOR BUSINESS

Calculate the inventory value of each of the examples listed.

Inventory Item	Purchase Unit (PU)	Units in Inventory	Cost per PU	Value of Inventory
1. Salmon steak	Pound	15	$ 9.50	—
2. Tomato paste	Case	2.5	38.50	—
3. Parsley	Bunch	4	2.90	—
4. Milk	Gallon	4	2.60	—
5. Eggs	Carton	1.25	68.50	—
			TOTAL	—

What is the total value of inventory for the items listed?

(Answer: $346.38)

entering storage. When this is done, managers and others can easily check **stock rotation**. This is the practice of ensuring products in storage the longest are used first. Some operations require managers to take inventory very frequently. Including product cost information on cases and other containers makes this task easy to do.

Inventory values that vary greatly from one accounting period to another can be cause for concern. Most operations seek to maintain fairly consistent amounts of product in inventory from one accounting period to the next. Therefore managers should carefully investigate wide inventory value fluctuations. These can indicate product theft, spoilage, or waste.

PRODUCT THEFT CONTROLS

Products kept in storage can be considered money in a bank. Storage areas then could be considered bank vaults, and procedures used for storage should address the question: How should money be managed in a bank vault?

Some basic approaches to safeguard and prevent shrinkage of an operation's products by employees and others include keeping them in locked areas with walls extending to the ceiling, and limiting access to storage areas to authorized persons. Some properties use employee package inspection programs to reduce the possibility of employees hiding items to be stolen in lockers or in bags, and then removing the items when the employee leaves work. If managers suspect an employee, vendor, or even a guest of stealing from inventory, they can take steps to minimize the opportunity for theft:

- Store inventory items in a safe and lockable room or cabinet.
- Restrict access to high-cost inventory items, such as fine wines or premium meat cuts, to only managers or supervisors.
- Increase the frequency of taking inventory for some or all stored items.
- Restrict employee meals to designated areas and to allowed menu items.
- Ensure no products can be removed by vendor representatives or guests.
- Consider implementing legal search procedures to ensure employees do not leave the premises with any products they have not purchased. Advice of legal counsel should be followed when considering this action.
- Install security cameras, and ensure that they are in good operating condition and are inspected regularly.
- Periodically review inventory control procedures with all managers, supervisors, and staff.

PRODUCTION CONTROLS

Chapter 8 of this book examines the methods managers use to establish the selling prices of their products. Every objective method of establishing menu selling prices is based, at least in part, on the cost of the food item being sold. That cost is determined, in large part, by the way kitchen production staff prepares menu items. When the production staff is well trained and its members work carefully, food costs most often remain in line. If the staff is not well trained or works in a haphazard manner, food costs can easily rise above acceptable levels. As a result, how production staff members measure, count, weigh, combine, and portion menu items will have a direct impact on an operation's food costs.

Managers who operate all-you-can-eat facilities such as college cafeterias and buffets (*Exhibit 7.7*) face special food cost challenges. Some of these can be addressed by implementing special production and service procedures. Is there any way to control food cost when portioning is done by the guests rather than the kitchen manager's staff? The answer is yes, and there are actually several things managers can do.

First, managers must understand that food waste benefits neither guests nor a restaurant or foodservice operation. Food that is produced, taken by guests but not eaten, and then discarded does not benefit anyone.

Managers can observe actual plate waste by walking through the dining room during meal service. They can also examine dish return areas and dish-washing areas to see where food items have been returned by guests. The use of basic portion control techniques in self-service food areas is helpful in reducing costs. There are other actions managers can take:

Exhibit 7.7

- Pre-portion items onto smaller plates or bowls.
- Cut large items such as chicken or ham into smaller pieces.
- Serve half-sized desserts and cookies at dessert bars rather than larger servings.
- Use serving utensils that make it easiest for guests to take management approved portion sizes.
- Use smaller-sized glassware and cups for beverages.
- Use signage to politely remind guests they are allowed to return to the self-service unit for additional servings to encourage them to take smaller servings initially.

THINK ABOUT IT . . .

Managers of operations serving food in all-you-can-eat settings are also concerned about their food costs. What are some customer-friendly ways these managers can work with guests to help reduce food waste?

One of the best ways to help reduce food expense in any operation is directly related to monitoring food product waste. **Food product waste** is a measurement of how much food product is purchased and taken from inventory, but not actually sold. This waste figure includes costs for mistakes made during preparation, food that must be discarded, or food items that have been stolen or misused by staff. Food product waste is also called shrinkage.

Measuring the cost of food product waste is important, as it helps managers identify where steps must be taken to reduce waste. Food product waste can be determined by comparing sales reports to the actual amount of food product inventory used. Items that have been used, but are not included in the sales report, are usually considered waste.

For example, if sales reports indicate that 20 strip steaks were sold, yet the inventory records show 25 steaks were actually taken from inventory, then 5 steaks are missing and considered wasted. If each steak costs the operation $2.07, then the food product waste for strip steaks is $10.35 for the period.

Some waste cannot be avoided. Most operations expect to have some amount of waste over time. The most perishable and expensive food products are at greater risk for higher waste costs. This is because just a few mistakes can be very costly. Whether waste amounts are acceptable can be determined by comparing actual waste amounts to ideal, or standard, waste targets that managers have established for their unique operations.

This comparison between actual costs and ideal costs, or standards, can be performed for both total waste and individual ingredient or menu item product costs.

There are several techniques that can be used to help prevent or reduce food product waste. *Exhibit 7.8* lists a few of these techniques. There are countless other waste-reduction practices in place in the restaurant and foodservice industry.

Exhibit 7.8

TIPS FOR REDUCING FOOD PRODUCT WASTE

- Set ideal values of prep items to avoid overproduction.
- Track ordering and cooking mistakes. This will help pinpoint food waste problems or patterns.
- Reuse product scraps and leftovers where appropriate. For example, turn day-old bread that has not been served into homemade salad croutons.
- Store food items at the correct temperatures to prevent spoilage.
- Provide proper training to new production staff.
- Keep inventory of food items secure—lock storerooms and freezers.

LABOR COST CONTROL

Often, the terms *labor cost* and *payroll cost* are used interchangeably in the restaurant and foodservice industry. They are, in reality, two different things. **Payroll cost** is the amount of money that is spent for employee wages, both fixed and variable. Thus, payroll generally means only the total salaries and wages paid to employees. **Labor costs**, however, consist of more than just payroll and include all other labor-related costs:

- FICA (Social Security taxes)
- Unemployment and Workers' compensation taxes
- Employee health, dental, and vision insurance premiums paid by the employer
- Vacation time, sick leave, and personal days
- Employee meals
- Employee training expenses

Restaurant and foodservice managers should include all related costs when calculating their labor cost.

When labor cost is determined to be out of line, corrective actions are taken. These can include re-forecasting the labor budget and adjusting the work schedules. Managers can use a variety of techniques to analyze labor costs. Suppose sales are fairly consistent from week-to-week or month-to-month. Then the total hours worked by employees in each period could provide accurate labor-related information. If, however, sales fluctuate from day-to-day, week-to-week, or month-to-month, this approach to labor cost control is less valuable.

To illustrate, consider the manager of a hospital foodservice department that has a consistent patient count. This manager can easily compare the total hours worked from one week to the next to see if the labor cost is consistent with a preestablished budget. Conversely, the manager of a restaurant across the street from a convention center cannot use this method. This is because the sales would likely vary greatly each period depending on the number of events booked at the center. In a well-operated establishment, managers do much more than add all employee hours together to assess their labor costs.

Controlling Variable Labor

There are a variety of alternative ways to evaluate labor cost. Performance and productivity ratios provide added detail in order to perform accurate and meaningful analysis. Some of the more common calculations for measuring and analyzing labor costs include those listed in *Exhibit 7.9*. Each of these deserves a closer look.

Exhibit 7.9

PERFORMANCE AND PRODUCTIVITY RATIOS USED TO ANALYZE LABOR COST

- Labor cost percentage
- Sales per labor hour
- Average wage per hour
- Covers per hour
- Sales per cover

LABOR COST PERCENTAGE

When analyzing labor cost, it is important to convert costs into a percentage. To simply look at the dollars spent on labor is to see only part of the picture. By looking at labor cost as a percentage, the relationship between the labor cost and sales is taken into account. Labor cost is converted into a **labor cost percentage** by dividing the actual labor cost by sales as shown in the following formula:

$$\text{Labor cost} \div \text{Sales} = \text{Labor cost percentage}$$

For example, if an operation's sales are $12,000 for a given week and the labor cost is $4,000 for the same week, then the labor cost percentage for that week is about 33.3 percent:

$$\underset{\text{Labor cost}}{\$4,000} \quad \div \quad \underset{\text{Sales}}{\$12,000} \quad = \quad \underset{\text{Labor cost percentage}}{0.333 \text{ or } 33.3\%}$$

While most operations look at labor cost percentage monthly, many will analyze labor cost percentage weekly and some will even do it daily. Analyzing labor cost percentages daily can ultimately produce positive results. If the daily percentage is in line, then the weekly percentage will be in line, as will the monthly percentage. By looking at daily figures, actions can be taken immediately to remedy the cost if it is not meeting the operation's labor cost target.

When analyzing labor cost percentages, results are most often compared to the operation's preestablished standard. They can, however, be compared to historical costs, and they can also be compared to industry standards. Caution should be exercised when comparing to industry standards, however, as operations differ greatly. Urban versus rural, union versus nonunion, self-service versus full-service, complexity of the menu, and employee costs incurred in different sections of the country all have an effect on labor cost and thus labor cost percentage.

SALES PER LABOR HOUR

Sales per labor hour gives an indication of how productive the staff is. Sales per labor hour is normally figured for hourly, or variable-cost, employees only, since salaried employees normally do not work a fixed number of hours. Instead, they work the hours necessary to get the job done. Hourly employees, on the other hand, are paid for the actual number of hours they work.

Sales per labor hour can be figured for any sales period—hour, day part, meal, day, week, month, or year. To calculate sales per labor hour, managers determine revenue achieved for a period and divide by the number of hours worked for that same period:

$$\text{Sales} \div \text{Number of hours worked} = \text{Sales per labor hour}$$

For example, if sales for April are $60,000, and the number of hours worked by hourly employees is 300, then the sales per labor hour is $200:

$$\underset{\text{Sales}}{\$60,000} \div \underset{\substack{\text{Number of}\\\text{hours worked}}}{300} = \underset{\substack{\text{Sales per}\\\text{labor hour}}}{\$200}$$

If sales per labor hour declines or is below standards, managers should ask some important questions: Are the tables being turned over quickly enough? Is the host seating guests in an efficient manner? Are the busers who clear and reset tables performing to standard? Is the waitstaff taking orders quickly? Is the waitstaff selling or merely taking orders? Are the cooks turning the orders out of the kitchen in a timely manner? At the same time, it is entirely possible that a drop in sales per labor hour could simply be due to a drop in sales, and not staff performance.

AVERAGE WAGE PER HOUR

Like sales per labor hour, the average wage per hour is normally figured for variable cost employees only. To calculate the average wage per hour, managers take the total variable labor cost and divide it by the total number of hours worked:

$$\underset{\substack{\text{Total variable}\\\text{labor cost}}}{\text{Total variable}} \div \underset{\substack{\text{Number of hours worked}\\\text{by variable cost employees}}}{\text{Number of hours worked}} = \underset{\substack{\text{Average wage}\\\text{per hour}}}{\text{Average wage}}$$

For example, if the total variable payroll costs for October are $30,000, and the number of hours worked by hourly employees is 4,000 hours, then the average wage per hour is $7.50:

$$\underset{\substack{\text{Total variable}\\\text{labor cost}}}{\$30,000} \div \underset{\substack{\text{Number of hours worked}\\\text{by variable cost employees}}}{4,000} = \underset{\substack{\text{Average wage}\\\text{per hour}}}{\$7.50}$$

Quite often, the average wage per hour is broken down by department, such as front of the house and back of the house. Front of the house can then be separated into waitstaff, hosts, and bartenders, while back of the house could be broken down into cooks and dish washers. Looking carefully at each department and position helps management determine more clearly where scheduling problems are occurring. Also, there may be a rather large wage gap among job classifications. For example, line cooks might average $15 per hour (*Exhibit 7.10*), while the waitstaff might average $6 per hour because they receive tips. Calculating a single figure for all of these wage groups together could give a distorted average.

Exhibit 7.10

Average wage per hour can be used to compare wages in one operation against the community standard. Suppose one establishment pays an average of $10 for line cooks, and the other operations in the area are paying an average of $12.50. This could explain why one particular establishment has a high turnover of line cooks. As noted in chapter 4, average wage per hour is also useful in the budgeting process and for preparing work schedules.

COVERS PER HOUR AND SALES PER COVER

When analyzed together, covers per hour and sales per cover will indicate who the best servers are. This is done in terms of productivity, or table turnover, and sales ability, or average check size. These numbers can be used to develop a standard by which all servers are measured.

Covers per hour is a measure of a server's productivity. In figuring covers per hour, one cover is equal to one customer meal served. Thus, covers per hour could also be expressed as customer meals served per hour.

To calculate covers per hour, managers determine the number of covers served by a server for a shift, day, week, or month, and divide by the number of hours that person worked:

Number of covers ÷ Hours worked = Covers per hour

For example, Sue Ellen worked 30 hours last week and served 575 covers or customer meals:

575	÷	30	=	19.2 (rounded)
Number of covers		**Hours worked**		**Covers per hour**

Contrast this to Carl, who worked 35 hours and served 600 covers:

600	÷	35	=	17.1 (rounded)
Number of covers		**Hours worked**		**Covers per hour**

Based on this information, Sue Ellen was able to serve more customers per hour on average than Carl.

Sales per cover measures the sales ability of a server. The higher the figure, the more that person is selling, on average, to each customer. Sales per cover can be calculated by the hour, shift, day, week, month, or year. To calculate sales per cover, managers determine the total sales achieved by a server and divide by the number of covers served by that worker:

Total sales per server ÷ Number of covers serviced = Sales per cover

To illustrate sales per cover, assume that LaToya had sales of $900 last Saturday evening and served 55 covers:

$$\underset{\substack{\textbf{Total sales} \\ \textbf{per server}}}{\$900} \quad \div \quad \underset{\substack{\textbf{Number of} \\ \textbf{covers serviced}}}{55} \quad = \quad \underset{\textbf{Sales per cover}}{\$16.36}$$

Contrast this to Hunter, who had $1,050 in sales for the same meal period and served 70 covers:

$$\underset{\substack{\textbf{Total sales} \\ \textbf{per server}}}{\$1,050} \quad \div \quad \underset{\substack{\textbf{Number of} \\ \textbf{covers serviced}}}{70} \quad = \quad \underset{\substack{\textbf{Sales per} \\ \textbf{cover}}}{\$15.00}$$

Even though Hunter had a higher sales total and served more customers, his sales per cover was lower than LaToya's. This means LaToya sold more to each of her customers than Hunter did to his.

Conclusions on server productivity and performance should not be drawn from one week's numbers. Analysis should be done over a period of time, as there are too many external factors that could distort figures for only one shift.

For example, a server who normally has a high number of covers per server rate could have a shift where several guests are content to sit and talk. Consequently, this lowers that server's table turnover. Managers should also recognize that the covers per hour and sales per cover performance between workers need to be compared for the same time period. To compare one server's lunch sales with another server's dinner sales would give a distorted figure. Average lunch checks are generally lower than average dinner checks. Another use for analyzing covers per server is to schedule the waitstaff. By anticipating the total number of covers to be sold for a particular meal period, management can determine the number of servers to schedule.

Controlling Fixed Labor

Salaried workers are considered a fixed labor cost. Some managers facing rising labor costs consider if certain employees should be paid a salary rather than a wage. Their reasoning is that salaried employees can then work more than 40 hours weekly without receiving overtime pay. However, there are strictly enforced laws governing precisely who is legally considered a salaried employee. Current regulations regarding salaried workers and their overtime pay can be reviewed at the U.S. Department of Labor's Web site.

Managers should also be aware that pay for salaried employees cannot fluctuate based on their quantity of work. If a salaried employee works only a part of the day, compensation cannot be reduced for missing part of that day.

THINK ABOUT IT …

What is the maximum number of hours you think a salaried worker should be scheduled to work? When would it be advisable to exceed that number of hours?

OPEN FOR BUSINESS

MANAGER'S MATH

A manager's operation had the following labor- and sales-related operating results last week.

Sales: $23,000   Guests served: 2,000

Labor hours used: 460   Labor cost: $5,750

Review the operating information, then answer the questions that follow.

1. What was the operation's labor cost percentage last week?

2. What were the operation's sales per labor hour last week?

3. What was the operation's average wage per hour last week?

4. What was the operation's covers per hour last week?

(Answers: 1. 25%; 2. $50.00; 3. $12.50; 4. 4.35 (rounded))

OPEN FOR BUSINESS

RESTAURANT TECHNOLOGY

A restaurant or food-service operation's POS is not typically programmed to monitor other expenses. Tracking other expense costs is, however, made easier with the use of software designed specifically for that purpose.

Advancements in cost control technology have come primarily through advancements in total accounting packages marketed by a number of firms. To learn more about these, go online and enter *restaurant accounting packages* in your favorite search engine.

However, salaried employees may have compensation reduced for missing an entire day for personal reasons in keeping with appropriate company policies. In addition, if the employee is paid a salary, he or she must meet certain defined requirements:

- At least 60 percent of an employee's primary duties must involve managing the business or a department within it.

- The employee must regularly direct the work of two or more other employees.

- The employee must have the authority to hire, fire, or recommend these courses of action.

Violations of these regulations can subject an operation to significant penalties and fines. Requirements must be carefully followed. Many salaried employees are hired to work 40 or more hours weekly. However, managers should not schedule salaried employees beyond a reasonable number of hours each week. The inevitable result will be increased employee dissatisfaction and lessened productivity.

OTHER EXPENSE CONTROL

While food and labor are typically a restaurant or foodservice manager's largest costs, they are not the only costs that must be controlled. Other expenses, which are also called other operating expenses, are the nonfood and nonlabor costs of operating a business. The number of and types of controllable (chapter 3) cost categories that are used for invoice expense coding (chapter 6) that are related directly to operating a business are many. They are detailed in the Uniform System of Accounts for Restaurants (USAR), including direct operating expenses:

- Auto or Truck Expenses

- Banquet and Catering

- Bar Utensils and Supplies

- Cleaning Supplies

- Contract Cleaning

- Equipment/Other Rentals

- Flowers and Decorations

- Freight and Fuel Surcharges

- Glassware

- Guest Supplies
- Kitchen Utensils and Supplies
- Laundry and Dry Cleaning
- Linen and Linen Rental
- Menus and Drink Lists
- Miscellaneous
- Paper and Packaging
- Parking
- Pest Control
- Tableware and Service Ware
- Uniforms

There are a large number of cost categories that can be used to code controllable music and entertainment-related expenses:

- Audio Broadcast Service
- Bands and Musicians
- Comedians and Entertainers
- Meals Served to Musicians and Entertainers
- Music Licensing Fees
- Television Broadcast Service

There are a large number of cost categories that can be used to code marketing-related expenses:

- Advertising
- Advertising/Marketing Fees
- Agency Commissions and Fees
- Print Media
- Online Advertising
- Outdoor Signs
- Radio and Television
- Theaters
- Direct Response Marketing
- Birthday Club
- Customer Database

In addition to the other expenses already listed, there are several additional areas of expense that fall under this heading. *Exhibit 7.11* lists some additional operating expenses.

Exhibit 7.11

ADDITIONAL OPERATING EXPENSES

Miscellaneous Expenses

- Email Service
- Loyalty Program
- Mailing Lists
- Newsletter
- Postage
- Printing and Mail Services
- Public Relations and Publicity
- Civic and Community Projects
- Donations and Gifts
- PR Agency Fees
- Sports Team Sponsorship
- Research
- Customer Surveys and Focus Groups
- Outside Research Agency
- Product Testing
- Travel in Connection with Research Other
- Complimentary Meals
- Discounts and Coupons
- Gift Cards
- Logoed Products
- Reservation System
- Restaurant Web Site
- Other

Utilities

- Electricity
- Gas
- Heating Oil and Other Fuel
- Recycling Credits
- Trash Removal
- Water and Sewage

Administrative Costs

- Accounting and Payroll
- Bad Debts
- Bank Charges
- Cash Over/Short
- Claims and Damages Paid
- Collection Fees
- Computer and Data Processing Costs
- Consulting and Coaching Services
- Credit Card Fees
- Directors' or Officers' Fees
- Dues and Subscriptions
- Franchise Fees
- Insurance—Liability and General
- Licenses and Permits
- Miscellaneous
- Office Printing and Supplies
- Personnel Expenses
- Postage and Delivery
- Professional Services
- Sales (or Beverage) Taxes
- Security and Deposit Services
- State Business Taxes
- Telephone and Communications
- Training Programs and Materials
- Travel

Repairs and Maintenance

- Building and Structure
- Equipment and Furniture
- Grounds and Parking Lot

As shown, there are a variety of different costs incurred in the operation of a restaurant or foodservice facility. Costs in general, however, can also be classified based on the nature of the cost. Cost classification is used when preparing budgets and forecasts, and calculating important operating ratios. In the restaurant and foodservice industry, the most common classifications are controllable and noncontrollable costs, as well as variable, semivariable, step, and fixed costs.

In general, it can be said that managers are responsible for managing only their controllable costs. To better understand how controllable operating costs are managed, operators must understand well the various types of costs:

- Variable costs
- Semivariable costs
- Step costs
- Fixed costs

Variable Costs

Variable costs are those costs that go up and down as sales go up and down, and do so in direct proportion. An example of a variable cost that is classified as an other expense is tablecloths and napkins (see *Exhibit 7.12*). If each guest in an establishment uses one cloth napkin, as the number of guests served increases, the number of cloth napkins used will increase in direct proportion.

Semivariable Costs

Semivariable costs go up and down as sales go up and down, but not in direct proportion. Semivariable costs are made up of both fixed costs and variable costs. Cleaning supplies are an example of an other expense that is semivariable. For example, the cleaning supplies needed to wash windows will be the same regardless of sales volume. The amount of dish machine chemicals used to clean dishes, however, will increase as more guests are served and more dishes are washed.

Step Costs

A **step cost** is a fixed cost that increases to a new level in step with significant changes in activity or usage. A step cost is relatively fixed over a small volume change but is variable over a large range of volume. For example, assume a manager's operation is charged a per-pickup fee for trash collection twice per week. The manager's operation experiences a 25 percent increase in volume, which means an additional trash pickup day is required. In this case, trash pickup

Exhibit 7.12

Manager's Memo

In most operations, fixed costs must be paid every month. As a result, they are sometimes referred to as sunk costs because, at the present, they are beyond the manager's control. Fixed costs are generally paid out of the money earned from an operation's sales. As a result, if the operation can sell more products, the fixed costs will be a smaller part of income.

Some managers seek to sell more products, and thus reduce fixed costs by adding items to their menus or expanding their operating hours. Those may be good strategies, but each of these strategies may also increase variable costs—for additional food, labor, or other operating expenses such as utilities.

Although it is possible to improve an operation's profitability by expanding its offerings, there is no guarantee this approach will always work. As a result, an emphasis on controlling variable costs and providing excellent service must always be an important part of every manager's expense-control efforts.

cannot be increased by 25 percent. Rather, the additional pickup day added to the operation's scheduled pickup dates would cause a 50 percent step up in trash collection costs because the operation would now pay for three, rather than two, pickups per week.

Managers who schedule labor are also familiar with the concept of step cost. For example, a manager who regularly schedules four service staff members during lunch periods cannot increase servers by 10 percent to accommodate a 10 percent increase in sales. That manager must either maintain a staff of four or add another person, which would result in a 25 percent step cost increase in that area of labor expense. To illustrate, assume each server is paid $20 per meal period. The cost of four servers is $80:

$$4 \times \$20 = \$80$$

Number of servers	Cost per server	Server labor cost

If a fifth server were added to the schedule, the new cost of labor would be $100:

$$5 \times \$20 = \$100$$

Number of servers	Cost per server	Server labor cost

The step increase in labor cost in this example would be 25 percent:

$$(\$100 - \$80) \div \$80 = 0.25, \text{ or } 25\%$$

Increased labor cost	Original labor cost	Original labor cost	Step increase

Fixed Costs

Fixed costs are those costs that remain the same regardless of sales volume. Web site hosting fees are an example of a fixed other expense cost. That is, the charge for hosting an operation's Web site will not vary if sales levels increase, nor will the charges be reduced if sales levels decline.

Many fixed costs relate to those expenses incurred by an operation's occupancy of its physical space. For the restaurant or foodservice manager who is not the operation's owner, these occupancy costs (chapter 4) will most often be noncontrollable. Rent, taxes, and interest on loans are real costs, but they cannot typically be controlled by a manager. For owners, however, occupancy costs can have a large impact on profit and investment returns. If occupancy costs are too high, an operation may have a difficult time generating profits, even if all other costs are well managed.

Regardless of the cost type under assessment, managers can apply the three-step cost control system presented in this chapter as they seek to optimize profitability in their businesses.

SUMMARY

1. **Describe the steps needed to implement a foodservice cost control system.**

   To implement a total cost control system managers take three important steps. In step 1, managers collect accurate sales and cost data. These historical data are obtained from information contained in the operation's income statements (profit and loss reports, or P&Ls). Step 2 of the control process requires managers to carefully monitor current sales and costs. They do so by recording actual costs and conducting line item reviews that compare actual expenses with budgeted or targeted expenses. Finally, in step 3, managers take corrective action, when needed, to implement operational changes that will bring costs back in line with expectations and established goals.

2. **List the four key areas related to controlling food costs.**

   The four key areas managers must address to control food-related costs are purchasing, inventory management, product theft, and food production. The effective control of purchasing requires purchasing authority to rest with only properly designated individuals. Deliveries of products should then be checked against original purchase orders to ensure that all items purchased have been delivered. Also, the vendor invoices to be paid for items purchased must be authorized prior to their payment and must be paid only once. Control of inventory relates to minimizing loss due to improper storage techniques, ensuring proper stock rotation, and the regularly scheduled counting of inventory items. Minimizing theft requires managers to secure storage areas against potential theft by employees, vendors, and even customers. Production control requires that managers train their staff well in the production and portioning techniques that will minimize food loss and waste.

3. **Describe the methods used to assess variable labor costs.**

   Operators seeking to manage and control variable labor costs can choose from a variety of assessment tools. These include the labor cost percentage, which is obtained by dividing the cost of labor by unit revenue achieved. Sales per labor hour is an assessment tool obtained by dividing total revenue achieved in a designated time period by the number of labor hours used in that period.

   Average wage per hour is calculated by dividing the cost of labor for a time period by the number of labor hours used in the period. Covers per hour is an assessment tool calculated by dividing the number of covers (guests) served by the number of labor hours used to serve the guests. Sales per hour is an assessment tool obtained by dividing unit revenue by the number of employee hours used to generate the revenue.

4. **Explain the importance of controlling fixed labor costs.**

   Because fixed labor costs do not vary with volume, excessively high levels of fixed or salaried labor are to be avoided. Legally, the pay for salaried employees cannot fluctuate based on their quantity of work. If a salaried employee works only a part of the day, compensation cannot be reduced for missing part of that day.

   Managers should avoid seeking to reduce fixed labor cost by scheduling salaried workers for excessively large numbers of hours per week. Doing so can lead to increased employee dissatisfaction and reduced productivity.

5. **Describe the different types of costs included in an operation's other operating expenses.**

Restaurant and foodservice managers encounter four basic other expense cost types. These are variable, semivariable, step, and fixed costs. Managers typically can control some, but not all, of these costs. Variable costs vary in direct proportion to sales, increasing as sales increase and decreasing as sales decrease. Fixed costs do not vary with changes in sales levels. Semivariable costs have both fixed and variable components and thus vary with sales, but not in direct proportion. Step costs are those that can only be increased or decreased in predetermined amounts, or steps, which are unique to the specific type of step cost incurred.

APPLICATION EXERCISE

Gary is the cafeteria manager at the Sunshine Community Hospital. He is reviewing the sales and cost records for the months of June and July. His manager has provided him with food and labor cost control standards for the cafeteria so that Gary can accurately analyze this information.

Sunshine Community Hospital Public Cafeteria Cost Control Standards

Food cost percentage should be lower than 32 percent.

Labor cost percentage should be between 24 and 26 percent.

SUNSHINE COMMUNITY HOSPITAL PUBLIC CAFETERIA SALES AND COST RECORDS

	June	July
Sales		
	$19,700	$16,900
Opening inventory	June 1	July 1
	13,000	14,105
Closing inventory	June 30	July 31
	14,105	17,105
Food purchases		
	8,000	6,500
Labor expenses		
	5,000	5,000

Given this information, answer the following questions:

- What is the cafeteria's food cost for June? For July?
- What is the cafeteria's food cost percentage for June? For July?
- What is the cafeteria's labor cost for June? For July?

- What is the cafeteria's labor cost percentage for June? For July?
- Which costs were outside acceptable standards for June? For July?
- What recommendations should Gary propose to control costs in the upcoming months?

REVIEW YOUR LEARNING

Select the best answer for each question.

1. What is the first step to be taken in the development of a cost control system?
   A. Taking corrective action
   B. Monitoring current expenses
   C. Analyzing current sales data
   D. Collecting accurate sales and cost data

2. What is the purpose of a line item review?
   A. To establish initial cost targets
   B. To compare actual costs to budgeted costs
   C. To monitor revenue levels by accounting period
   D. To provide information needed to reduce fixed costs

3. A manager had sales of $100,000 and purchases of $15,000 in a month. That month's beginning inventory was $15,000 and ending inventory was $5,000. What was the operation's food cost percentage for that month?
   A. 10%
   B. 25%
   C. 50%
   D. 75%

4. What is the result of proper product stock rotation?
   A. Credit memos for missing items are simplified.
   B. Purchase order preparation for needed items is simplified.
   C. Those inventory items held longest in storage are used last.
   D. Those inventory items held longest in storage are used first.

5. Lamb shanks have an inventory value of $4 per pound. The ending inventory counted 2.5 cases of lamb shanks weighing 10 pounds per case. What is the ending inventory value of lamb shanks?
   A. $10
   B. $40
   C. $100
   D. $400

6. An operation had total sales of $40,000 in a week. It employed 15 workers and the total cost of labor for the week was $10,000. What was the operation's labor cost percentage for that week?
   A. 10%
   B. 15%
   C. 25%
   D. 40%

7. An operation used five servers and 35 labor hours to serve 560 covers on a day last week. What was this operation's covers per hour on that day?
   A. 7
   B. 16
   C. 62.5
   D. 112

8. An operation used six servers and 40 labor hours to serve 180 covers on a day last week. What was this operation's covers per server on that day?
   A. 4.5
   B. 22.2
   C. 30
   D. 40

9. In which cost classification would managers consider the monthly charges for outdoor billboard signs advertising their restaurant?
   A. Step
   B. Fixed
   C. Variable
   D. Semivariable

10. What labor expense is an example of a fixed labor cost?
    A. Bartenders' wages
    B. Managers' salaries
    C. Cooks' hourly pay rates
    D. Service charges shared with waitstaff

8 Profitable Pricing

INSIDE THIS CHAPTER

- Price and Value
- Price and Profits
- Establishing Food and Beverage Prices
- Wine Pricing
- Analyzing the Menu Sales Mix
- Menu Modification and Price Adjustment

CHAPTER LEARNING OBJECTIVES

After completing this chapter, you should be able to:

- Describe the relationship between price and value.

- Explain the relationship between price, revenue, and profits.

- Explain the methods managers use to establish food and beverage prices.

- Describe the procedure used to analyze a menu sales mix.

- State the process used to make needed modifications to menu items and prices.

KEY TERMS

CASE STUDY

"This isn't good," said Loretta, the assistant manager at the Old Bronze Bell steakhouse. She had just called Josh, the manager of the restaurant, at home and was speaking to him on his day off.

"What's the problem?" asked Josh.

"Sea bass is the problem," replied Loretta. "I just got off the phone with our vendor and he said the price per pound had gone up over $5 in the last week, and he didn't see it going down anytime soon."

"That's one of our most popular items," said Josh. "If we don't raise the price of it a lot, that's really going to hurt our profits."

"Tell me about it," agreed Loretta. "Our customers won't like a big price increase, but I actually think we will lose money on every order we sell if we don't do something!"

1. What do you think Loretta and Josh should do about this price increase on sea bass?

2. Why do you think it is important for managers to know how much money they make on each menu item they sell and on each guest they serve?

THINK ABOUT IT . . .

Have you ever decided not to return to a business because the value you received on your first visit was not good enough to return? What specifically caused you to make that decision?

THINK ABOUT IT . . .

Quick-service restaurants may sell combination or value meals that include a sandwich, order of French fries, and a drink. What challenges do you think managers face when they are responsible for pricing such multi-item meals?

OPEN FOR BUSINESS

BY THE CUSTOMER/FOR THE CUSTOMER

Reviews posted on social networking sites often refer to establishments' prices. Some of these comments are very direct, such as:

This restaurant was outrageously expensive!

Or,

The prices charged at this restaurant are really very reasonable!

Other comments are less direct, but still relate to pricing. These include comments like:

I felt like we really got a lot for our money at this restaurant!

Or,

My mother felt they charged too much for what she ordered.

Pricing is always important. Managers monitoring social media sites for reviews should carefully watch for any comments related to pricing so they can better understand their customers' perceptions of the operation's price structure, and make price adjustments if appropriate.

PRICE AND VALUE

Menu prices are an important part of a restaurant or foodservice operation's ability to meet its profit goals. Managers and accounting professionals with a strong understanding of menu pricing can establish prices that help ensure profitability and build customer loyalty. In fact, acquiring a full understanding of pricing is one of a manager's most critical responsibilities.

Nearly all owners and managers establish prices. In many cases, they do so with two primary goals: attracting as many customers as possible, and ensuring that profit goals are met.

From an accounting perspective, prices must be low enough to attract guests, but high enough to make profitable sales. In some cases, managers price items they sell on **à la carte menus**, where each item is priced separately. In other operations, managers offer a **prix fixe menu** (pronounced *prefix*), which consists of predetermined items presented as a multicourse meal and at a set price. On a prix fixe menu, for example, a meal including an appetizer, entrée, and dessert would all be sold for one set price.

Pricing is important because, to stay in business, every operation must charge prices high enough to cover all of its costs. The best managers, however, know they must consider the reaction of customers *and* their costs when they establish menu prices. This is because prices charged and customer perceptions of value received are closely related.

While managers must consider their operating costs when establishing selling prices (see chapter 7), it is important to note that customers are typically indifferent to an operation's costs. For customers, only one factor is important: perceived value.

If the products and services purchased convince customers that they have received good value for their money, they will likely become repeat customers. If customers do not feel they received good value, they are unlikely to buy from that establishment again.

It is critical to remember that the relationship between price and value must be a good one for guests. Menu items that are priced too high will not sell well. But, if they are priced too low, a business may not be able to operate profitably. Proper menu item pricing requires a delicate balance to ensure that customers are willing and able to buy. This must occur without managers sacrificing the overall financial health of their operations.

PRICE AND PROFITS

The process of setting prices to ensure profitability in the restaurant and foodservice industry is both important and complex. To better understand why, consider that the three major areas of business are manufacturing, retailing, and service. Manufacturers convert raw materials into products. Prices for manufactured products must cover the expense of the raw materials used, as well as any costs incurred in the production of the item.

Retailers purchase pre-made products from manufacturing suppliers and sell those products at a markup to the consumer. A retailer's prices must cover the cost of the products and the operating expenses incurred. They must also provide for a profit.

Restaurant and foodservice pricing is more complicated than either manufacturing or retail pricing. Often, establishments both produce and resell items. Managers must know how to price the products they manufacture, such as pies and steaks, as well as pre-made items they offer for retail sale, such as pre-made desserts, beers, and wines. In addition, restaurant and foodservice businesses also sell service levels of various types. These include the convenience of a quick-service restaurant (QSR) drive-through, or the elegance of a meal served in a fine-dining operation.

In the restaurant and foodservice industry, proper pricing is both a science and an art. The science of pricing requires managers to use math skills to calculate costs and arrive at suggested menu prices. The art of pricing means managers continually recognize the very subjective customer perception-related aspects of pricing. They must take them into account when arriving at final selling price decisions.

Exhibit 8.1

Managers responsible for pricing must understand that there are laws enacted at the state and federal levels to ensure customers are informed, in advance, about their prices such as on a menu or on signs (*Exhibit 8.1*). As a result, all prices must be presented fairly. The question of how to ensure that prices are presented fairly can be a complex one.

Certainly, it is fair for managers to use their knowledge of customer buying habits to predict how their customers will react to different pricing strategies. For example, managers that end menu prices in $0.95 or $0.99 can do so fairly. These managers know, for example, that customers do not perceive much difference between a price of $7.50 and $7.99 for an item. However, because an $8.00 price so clearly seems higher than a 7.00 price, psychologically customers would perceive the difference between $7.95 and $8.44 as quite large. In both cases, however, one price is $0.49 higher than the other. Intentionally deceptive pricing, however, such as advertising one price for a menu item but charging a higher price would be unethical and illegal.

Impact of Price on Total Revenue

Chapter 1 introduced the profit formula:

$$\textbf{Revenue} - \textbf{Expense} = \textbf{Profit}$$

The formula is a simple one, but to truly comprehend it managers must understand each of its components. Revenue is the total amount of sales achieved by an operation. The revenue formula is shown below:

$$\textbf{Selling price} \times \textbf{Units sold} = \textbf{Revenue}$$

It is easy to see, from this formula, the importance of proper pricing. Managers who do not truly understand pricing might assume that increasing selling prices would always yield an increase in revenue. That is not always the case. In fact, if prices are raised too high, customers may respond by taking their business elsewhere. Then the number of units sold would decline and revenue levels would decrease, not increase.

The alternative strategy of lowering prices to increase the number of units sold can sometimes be a good one. However, as presented in chapter 7, there are fixed and variable costs associated with each sale in a restaurant or foodservice operation. These must be recovered before profits can be generated. The relationship between revenue, expense, and profit is a complex one, and managers must understand it well. One way to better understand it is to perform a break-even analysis.

Break-Even Analysis

Experienced managers know that some times of the year and some accounting periods are more profitable than others. This is often the case when revenue levels in an operation vary greatly based on the time of year.

This would likely be the situation, for example, in an operation that features ice cream and is located in a busy summer resort area. This ice cream shop would likely experience good business, high revenue levels, and strong profitability during the tourist season. But the same operation would likely experience greatly reduced revenue levels and profitability, or could even be closed, at the time of year when very few tourists are visiting the resort area.

It is also important to recognize that many operating cost percentages change with changes in sales volume. For example, if an operation's fixed cost for rent is $1,000 and revenue is $20,000, the fixed rent cost percentage is 5 percent.

$$\underset{\textbf{Rent}}{\$1,000} \div \underset{\textbf{Revenue}}{\$20,000} = \underset{\substack{\textbf{Fixed cost} \\ \textbf{percentage}}}{0.05, \text{ or } 5\%}$$

THINK ABOUT IT . . .

Restaurant and foodservice operations near ocean beach areas and in ski resorts are examples of locations that can experience wide seasonal fluctuations in sales volume. What are some other examples?

If, however, the operation's sales volume dropped to $10,000, the fixed rent cost percentage increases to 10 percent.

$$\$1,000 \div \$10,000 = 0.10, \text{ or } 10\%$$

Rent   Revenue   Fixed cost percentage

In this example the operation's rent, as a percentage of sales volume, would double. This leaves fewer dollars available to pay for the operation's food, labor, and other expenses. Because fixed expense percentages vary with sales volume, more dollars are available to pay expenses and generate profits when an operation's sales volume is high. Similarly, fewer dollars are available to pay expenses and generate profits when sales volume is low.

Because selling prices affect revenue levels, and revenue levels affect profitability, managers want to know key information:

- At what sales level will my operation begin to make a profit?
- At what sales level will my operation fail to make a profit?

Managers can calculate the sales required to reach their break-even point by performing a cost/volume/profit analysis. A **break-even point** is the level at which the revenue achieved in an operation equals its expenses. Further, managers can calculate the number of guests that must be served to reach their break-even point.

The relationship between an operation's costs, sales volume, and profits is graphically represented in *Exhibit 8.2*.

Exhibit 8.2

BREAK-EVEN CHART

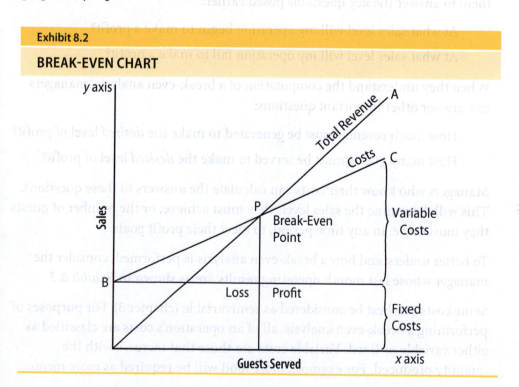

When examining *Exhibit 8.2*, it is important to understand several things:

- The horizontal axis represents the number of guests served in an operation. The number increases from left to right.
- The vertical axis represents the sales volume in an operation. It is increasing from bottom to top.
- Line *A* represents the total revenue achieved in the operation.
- Point *B* represents the operation's fixed costs, costs that must be paid even if no guests are served.
- Line *C* represents the sum of the operation's fixed and variable costs at differing total revenue levels.
- Point *P* represents the break-even point. This is where the revenue and cost lines intersect. At this point the total revenue achieved is equal to the amount needed to pay the operation's fixed and variable costs.

A thoughtful examination of *Exhibit 8.2* reveals critical information to managers:

- Below the break-even point costs are higher than revenues, so losses occur.
- Above the break-even point revenues exceed costs and fixed costs have been paid, so significant profits are generated on sales dollars achieved.

When operating costs are known, managers can calculate their break-even points on an annual, monthly, weekly, or even daily basis. Doing so allows them to answer the key questions posed earlier:

- At what sales level will my operation begin to make a profit?
- At what sales level will my operation fail to make a profit?

When they understand the computation of a break-even analysis, managers can answer other important questions:

- How much revenue must be generated to make the *desired* level of profit?
- How many guests must be served to make the *desired* level of profit?

Managers who know their costs can calculate the answers to these questions. This will determine the sales levels they must achieve, or the number of guests they must serve, in any time period, to meet their profit goals.

To better understand how a break-even analysis is performed, consider the manager whose last month operating results are as shown in *Exhibit 8.3*.

Some costs can best be considered as semivariable (chapter 3). For purposes of performing a break-even analysis, all of an operation's costs are classified as either variable or fixed. Variable costs are those that increase with the quantity produced. For example, more food will be required as more menu

Exhibit 8.3

SAMPLE OPERATING RESULTS

Guests served:	20,000
Sales:	$250,000
Variable costs:	$100,000
Fixed costs:	$120,000
Total costs:	$220,000
Profit:	$ 30,000

items are sold (*Exhibit 8.4*). Fixed costs, however, are those that will be incurred by the company even if no sales are made. Examples include rent, the cost of insurance, and any fees paid for licenses that are required for the operation of a business.

When total sales and variable costs are known, managers can calculate a **contribution margin (CM)**. This is the amount of sales remaining after variable costs have been subtracted. In a break-even analysis, this is the formula for calculating CM:

Sales − Variable costs = Contribution margin (CM)

For purposes of an operational break-even analysis, CM is calculated using total sales and total variable costs. In this example from *Exhibit 8.3*, CM would be calculated as:

$$\underset{\text{Sales}}{\$250,000} - \underset{\substack{\text{Variable} \\ \text{costs}}}{\$100,000} = \underset{\substack{\text{Contribution} \\ \text{margin (CM)}}}{\$150,000}$$

Exhibit 8.4

A manager may view contribution margin as the amount of money left over to pay for fixed costs, and to create profits after all variable costs have been subtracted from sales.

Managers can calculate their **average sale per guest** from the data in *Exhibit 8.3* by applying the average sale per guest formula:

Sales ÷ Guests served = Average sale per guest

In this example, the average sale per guest is:

$$\underset{\text{Sales}}{\$250,000} \div \underset{\substack{\text{Guests} \\ \text{served}}}{20,000} = \underset{\substack{\text{Average sale} \\ \text{per guest}}}{\$12.50}$$

Exhibit 8.5 shows the average sale per guest, variable costs, and contribution margin in this example. These are expressed in total dollars, in dollar amount per average guest sale, and by percentage.

Exhibit 8.5

DATA FOR BREAK-EVEN CALCULATIONS: 20,000 GUESTS SERVED

With 20,000 Guests Served	Total: All Guests	Percentage	Per Guest	Percentage
Sales	$250,000	100%	$12.50	100%
Variable cost	100,000	40	5.00	40
CM	150,000	60	7.50	60

The variable cost percentage for all guests shown in *Exhibit 8.5* is calculated as

$$\text{Variable costs} \div \text{Sales} = \text{Variable cost percentage}$$

In this example:

$$\underset{\substack{\text{Variable}\\\text{costs}}}{\$100{,}000} \div \underset{\text{Sales}}{\$250{,}000} = \underset{\substack{\text{Variable cost}\\\text{percentage}}}{0.40, \text{ or } 40\%}$$

The CM percentage for all guests shown in *Exhibit 8.5* is calculated as

$$\text{CM} \div \text{Sales} = \text{CM percentage}$$

In this example:

$$\underset{\text{CM}}{\$150{,}000} \div \underset{\text{Sales}}{\$250{,}000} = \underset{\text{CM percentage}}{0.60, \text{ or } 60\%}$$

The per guest variable cost shown in *Exhibit 8.5* is calculated as

$$\text{Variable costs} \div \text{Guests served} = \text{Per guest variable costs}$$

In this example:

$$\underset{\text{Variable costs}}{\$100{,}000} \div \underset{\text{Guests served}}{20{,}000} = \underset{\substack{\text{Per guest}\\\text{variable costs}}}{\$5.00}$$

The per guest CM shown in *Exhibit 8.5* is calculated as

$$\text{CM} \div \text{Guests served} = \text{Per guest CM}$$

In this example:

$$\underset{\text{CM}}{\$150{,}000} \div \underset{\text{Guests served}}{20{,}000} = \underset{\text{Per guest CM}}{\$7.50}$$

The relative percentages for variable costs and CM are of course the same, at 40 percent for variable cost and 60 percent for CM, for both total sales and per guest sales.

Note that the information in *Exhibit 8.5* includes per guest information and percentage calculations for sales, variable costs, and CM. However, fixed costs are not calculated on a per guest or percentage of sales basis, because fixed costs do not increase as sales volume increases.

OPEN FOR BUSINESS

MANAGER'S MATH

A manager is preparing a break-even analysis and has taken the following data from his operation's income statement. Help the manager complete his break-even analysis by answering the questions that follow:

	Amount	Percentage
Sales	$750,000	_____
Variable costs	400,000	_____
Fixed costs	200,000	_____
Contribution margin (CM)	_____	_____

1. What is the variable cost percentage in this operation?

2. What is the fixed cost percentage in this operation?

3. What is the contribution margin (CM) amount in this operation?

4. What is the contribution margin (CM) percentage in this operation?

5. What sales level must this operation achieve to break even?

(Answers: 1. 53.3%; 2. 26.7%; 3. $350,000; 4. 46.7%; 5. $428,265.52)

After managers have made the calculations for the information shown in *Exhibit 8.5*, they can calculate the sales required to break even by using the break-even point sales formula:

$$\frac{\text{Fixed}}{\text{costs}} \div \frac{\text{CM}}{\text{percentage}} = \frac{\text{Break-even}}{\text{point for sales}}$$

Using the information in *Exhibit 8.3* and *8.5* in this example, the calculation would be:

$$\underset{\text{Fixed costs}}{\$120,000} \div \underset{\text{CM percentage}}{0.60, \text{ or } 60\%} = \underset{\substack{\text{Break-even} \\ \text{point for sales}}}{\$200,000}$$

In this operation, $200,000 in sales must be achieved before the operation can begin to make a profit. If achieved sales are below $200,000 an operating loss will occur.

Managers can calculate the number of guests that must be served to break even using the formula:

$$\frac{\text{Fixed}}{\text{costs}} \div \frac{\text{CM per}}{\text{guest}} = \frac{\text{Break-even point}}{\text{for guests served}}$$

Using the information in *Exhibit 8.3* and *8.5* in this example, the calculation would be:

$$\underset{\text{Fixed costs}}{\$120,000} \div \underset{\text{CM per guest}}{\$7.50} = \underset{\substack{\text{Break-even point} \\ \text{for guests served}}}{16,000}$$

In this example, 16,000 guests must be served per month before the operation can begin to make a profit. If the number of guests served is below 16,000 an operating loss will occur.

When calculating sales and guests needed to break even, managers must follow two break-even formula rules that are easy to remember:

1. CM percentage is used to calculate sales dollars needed to break even.

2. CM per guest is used to calculate the number of guests needed to break even.

Managers who can calculate their break-even points can make changes in costs and in selling prices that can help them achieve their profit goals.

MANAGER'S MATH

A manager is preparing a break-even analysis and has taken the following data from her operation's income statement and sales histories. Help the manager complete the break-even analysis by answering the questions that follow:

	Amount	Percentage
Sales	$1,800,000	
Guests served	150,000	
Sale per guest		
Variable cost per guest	6.00	
Fixed cost per guest	4.00	
Contribution margin (CM) per guest		
Total fixed cost		
Total contribution margin (CM)		

1. What is the average sale per guest in this operation?

2. What is the variable cost per guest percentage in this operation?

3. What is the fixed cost per guest percentage in this operation?

4. What is the total fixed cost in this operation?

5. What is the contribution margin (CM) amount per guest in this operation?

6. What is the total contribution margin (CM) percentage in this operation?

7. How many guests must this operation serve to achieve its break-even point?

(Answers: 1. $12.00; 2. 50%; 3. 33.3%; 4. $600,000; 5. $6.00; 6. 50%; 7. 100,000)

ESTABLISHING FOOD AND BEVERAGE PRICES

Proper pricing helps the operation meet its financial goals while providing the exceptional value to customers that will keep them coming back (*Exhibit 8.6*).

Exhibit 8.6

Because of this, pricing is too important to be left to guesswork. The best managers use objective methods when calculating their menu prices. While there are several approaches that can be used to properly establish menu prices, four are used most frequently. Many managers use these approaches for both food and beverage pricing, with the exception of wine pricing, which is further explained later in the chapter.

• Food cost percentage pricing method

• Contribution margin pricing method

• Prime cost pricing method

• Ratio pricing method

Note that to use objective pricing methods, managers must have standardized recipes to accurately calculate portion costs. Calculating portions properly involves determining the cost to produce one serving of a recipe. It considers the required ingredients, current costs for the ingredients, and the number of servings a recipe will produce. Often, the most challenging calculations involve determining the food cost for each recipe ingredient.

Today, computerized recipe management programs are readily available. These help managers make the calculations they need to accurately find the portion costs of their recipes, and arrive at proper menu prices.

Food Cost Percentage Pricing Method

The **food cost percentage pricing method** is the simplest of all menu pricing methods because it is based only on the cost of food required to make a menu item. As a result, the approach is very popular in the restaurant and foodservice industry. The method actually goes by several names including the **simple markup pricing method** and the **factor pricing method**. The terms *food cost percentage*, *markup*, and *factor* come from the fact that each of these concepts is used in some way when applying this method of menu pricing.

The formula used to calculate a menu price using the food cost percentage pricing method is:

Food cost ÷ Target food cost percentage = Selling price

Thus, if an item cost $4.00 to make, and the manager wished to achieve a desired target of a 25 percent food cost percentage, the pricing formula would be calculated as follows:

$$\underset{\text{Food cost}}{\$4.00} \div \underset{\substack{\text{Target food} \\ \text{cost percentage}}}{0.25, \text{ or } 25\%} = \underset{\substack{\text{Selling} \\ \text{price}}}{\$16.00}$$

This formula can be rearranged:

Food cost ÷ Selling price = Target food cost percentage

In this example, applying that formula would yield:

$$\underset{\text{Food cost}}{\$4.00} \div \underset{\substack{\text{Selling} \\ \text{price}}}{\$16.00} = \underset{\substack{\text{Target food} \\ \text{cost percentage}}}{0.25, \text{ or } 25\%}$$

Recall that in chapter 3 the formula for a food cost percentage was presented as:

Cost of sales (food) ÷ Food sales = Food cost percentage

When using the food cost percentage pricing method the "cost of sales (food)" is the amount of money it costs an operation to purchase the food used to make the menu item. Cost of sales (food), food cost, and **portion cost**—the cost of creating one serving of a menu item—are all industry terms used to describe this same expense. For example, if it costs an operation $3.00 to make an apple pie, and the pie will be cut into six pieces, then the cost of sales (food), food cost, and portion cost for one slice of pie would all be $0.50:

$$\underset{\text{Pie cost}}{\$3.00} \div \underset{\text{Slices}}{6} = \underset{\substack{\text{Portion cost} \\ \text{per slice}}}{\$0.50}$$

If any two of the numbers in the food cost percentage formula are known, the third number can easily be calculated. Thus, if food cost and selling price are known, the formula to compute food cost percentage is:

Food cost ÷ Selling price = Food cost percentage

If food cost and targeted food cost percentage are known, the formula to compute selling price is:

Food cost ÷ Target food cost percentage = Selling price

If targeted food cost percentage and desired selling price are known, then the formula to compute the amount the managers may spend for food is:

Selling price × Target food cost percentage = Food cost

Manager's Memo

The food cost percentage method is often referred to as the markup or factor method because managers can use a factor as a shortcut to calculate selling prices.

Dividing 1.00 by any targeted food cost percentage yields a factor that can then be multiplied by the item's food cost to yield its selling price. For example, 1.00 divided by 25 percent yields a factor of 4:

$$1.00 \div 0.25 = 4$$

The factor table shows the factors that result when seeking to achieve some popular food cost percentage targets.

Target Food Cost Percentage	Factor
20%	5.00
25	4.00
28	3.57
30	3.33
32	3.13
34	2.94
36	2.78
40	2.50
42	2.38

For example, if the food cost of an item is $6.00 and the targeted food cost is 25 percent, a manager using the proper factor from the table would calculate the item's selling price as:

$$\underset{\substack{\text{Cost of} \\ \text{food}}}{} \times \text{Factor} = \underset{\substack{\text{Selling} \\ \text{price}}}{}$$

or

$$\underset{\substack{\$6.00 \\ \text{Cost of} \\ \text{food}}}{} \times \underset{\substack{4 \\ \text{Factor}}}{} = \underset{\substack{\$24.00 \\ \text{Selling} \\ \text{price}}}{}$$

MANAGER'S MATH

A manager is calculating proposed menu prices for three new menu items. Using the following information, calculate the selling price the manager should charge for each new menu item. Then use the information to answer the questions.

Item	Food Cost	Target Food Cost Percentage	Selling Price
Rib-Eye Steak	$7.50	40%	
Italian Roast Chicken	4.51	22	
Great Lakes Perch	5.50	25	

1. What is the selling price for rib-eye steak?
2. What is the selling price for Italian roast chicken?
3. What is the selling price for Great Lakes perch?
4. If you were the manager, would you adjust any of these prices up or down prior to printing them on the menu? Which ones? What would be the adjusted prices? Why would you adjust the prices?

(Answers: 1. $18.75; 2. $20.50; 3. $22.00; 4. Answers will vary.)

In the previous example, if the manager wants to sell an item for $16.00, and the targeted food cost is 25 percent, then the allowable food cost would be calculated as:

$$\underset{\text{Selling price}}{\$16.00} \times \underset{\substack{\text{Target food cost} \\ \text{percentage}}}{0.25, \text{ or } 25\%} = \underset{\text{Food cost}}{\$4.00}$$

The food cost percentage pricing method is simple to use after managers master the basic formula. However, the selling price that results from using the food cost percentage formula is often merely a starting point.

To illustrate, assume an item cost $4.11 to make. The manager has a 35 percent target food cost. Using the food cost percentage formula yields a selling price of:

$$\underset{\text{Food cost}}{\$4.11} \div \underset{\substack{\text{Target food} \\ \text{cost percentage}}}{0.35, \text{ or } 35\%} = \underset{\substack{\text{Selling} \\ \text{price}}}{\$11.74}$$

In this case, the manager would likely round the selling price to $11.75, $11.95, or even to $11.99, rather than keep the price at $11.74. Doing so would allow managers to use the same pricing format (*i.e.*, make all prices end in the same digits) for all menu items.

It is important to know that applying the same division or multiplication factors to all menu items may not be in the operation's best interest. Some managers feel the food cost percentage pricing method tends to overprice high food cost items. They also feel it underprices low food cost items, such as soups, pasta, chicken, beverages, and desserts.

Market factors, what potential customers are willing to pay for specific menu items, and what the competition is charging should all influence pricing decisions. Prices should be adjusted up or down based on psychological pricing considerations and other subjective factors.

This may result in the selling prices for many menu items being set at a cost percentage higher than management might desire. However, there will be other items with a lower than average food cost. The goal is for the total menu to average out to a targeted food cost percentage.

Contribution Margin Pricing Method

Contribution margin (CM) is defined as what is left over after the variable food cost of a menu item is subtracted from the menu selling price. That is the amount that each item contributes to paying for labor and other operating expenses, and to provide a profit. The CM pricing method is also easy to use if managers know or can estimate key information:

- The number of customers they will serve in a budget or time period
- Their nonfood operating costs
- Their desired profit

To illustrate, assume that a manager has created a budget that indicates 50,000 customers will be served in the coming year. Also, all nonfood costs, such as labor and all other operating expenses, will be $312,000. The operation's target profit goal is $36,000. To use CM pricing, managers would follow these two steps:

1. Calculate the average CM per customer:

$$\textbf{(Nonfood costs} + \textbf{Profit)} \div \frac{\textbf{Number of}}{\textbf{customers}} = \frac{\textbf{Average CM}}{\textbf{per customer}}$$

In this example:

$$\underset{\textbf{Nonfood costs}}{(\$312,\!000} + \underset{\textbf{Profit}}{\$36,\!000)} \div \underset{\substack{\textbf{Number of} \\ \textbf{customers}}}{50,\!000} = \underset{\substack{\textbf{Average CM} \\ \textbf{per customer}}}{\$6.96}$$

2. Determine the selling price for the menu item.

For example, the base selling price for a menu item with a $4.15 food cost would be:

$$\underset{\textbf{Food cost}}{\$4.15} + \underset{\substack{\textbf{Contribution} \\ \textbf{margin}}}{\$6.96} = \underset{\substack{\textbf{Selling} \\ \textbf{price}}}{\$11.11}$$

Again, the manager would likely adjust the calculated price to a number that could easily be used on the menu. In this case, that might be $10.95, $10.99, or $11.25.

CM menu pricing is easy to use because the necessary information is in the establishment's operating budget or forecast. CM is practical when the nonfood costs, such as labor and other expenses, that are incurred when serving each customers are basically the same. When they are, only the food cost for the individual menu items prepared and served to each guest will vary.

Managers who use the CM pricing method consider the contribution margin per menu item as being as important, or more important, than the food cost percentage. This pricing method reduces the range of selling prices because the only difference in selling price is the cost of food purchased by the customer.

Manager's Memo

The food cost percentage and all other objective menu pricing methods require information about the food cost of the item being priced.

Two things must be in place to calculate the food cost. First, standardized recipes must be used. Then the manager will know what ingredients and the amount of each to use. Second, the current cost of all ingredients must be known. Then the amount of each ingredient used must be calculated to determine the food cost of each ingredient.

Most establishments sell an entrée with other items for a specified price. For example, a chicken dinner may include the chicken entrée, salad with dressing, potato, vegetable, and bread roll and butter. The food cost for each of the meal components must be added together to calculate the total food cost for menu item pricing purposes.

Prime Cost Pricing Method

The prime cost method requires managers to consider the labor cost required to make a menu item as well as the item's food cost. The method gets its name from the fact that in the restaurant and foodservice industry the two highest costs in an operation, food cost and labor cost, are known as the **prime cost**.

The formula used in prime cost pricing is:

$$\left(\begin{array}{c}\text{Labor}\\\text{cost}\end{array} + \begin{array}{c}\text{Food}\\\text{cost}\end{array}\right) \div \left(\begin{array}{c}\text{Target labor}\\\text{cost percentage}\end{array} + \begin{array}{c}\text{Target food cost}\\\text{percentage}\end{array}\right) = \begin{array}{c}\text{Selling}\\\text{price}\end{array}$$

Exhibit 8.7

Use of the prime cost method requires management to determine the amount of direct labor spent in preparing an item (*Exhibit 8.7*). This amount is added to food cost and then divided by the targeted labor cost percentage plus the targeted food cost percentage.

For example, assume food cost for an item is $3.00 and the labor cost required to make it is $2.00. In this case, the prime cost is $5.00.

A selling price based on prime cost is derived by establishing a targeted and combined labor cost percentage and food cost percentage. If the operation desires a 15 percent labor cost and 30 percent food cost, the prime cost percentage would be 45 percent:

15%	+	30%	=	45%
Target labor cost percentage		Target food cost percentage		Prime cost percentage

In this example the selling price formula would be:

$$(\$2.00 + \$5.00) \div (15\% + 30\%) = \begin{array}{c}\text{Selling}\\\text{price}\end{array}$$

$$\left(\begin{array}{c}\text{Labor}\\\text{cost}\end{array} \quad \begin{array}{c}\text{Food}\\\text{cost}\end{array}\right) \left(\begin{array}{c}\text{Target labor}\\\text{cost percentage}\end{array} \quad \begin{array}{c}\text{Target food}\\\text{cost percentage}\end{array}\right)$$

or

$$\$7.00 \div 45\% = \$15.56$$

So, the item with a $7.00 prime cost would be divided by 45 percent to arrive at a $15.56 selling price. Managers could then adjust as needed to match the form of other menu item selling prices.

Ratio Pricing Method

The ratio pricing method considers the relationship or ratio between food costs and CM (nonfood costs and profit) and then uses the ratio to develop base selling prices.

To illustrate, assume that the operating budget for an establishment indicates food costs of $310,000, nonfood costs of $620,000, and a profit goal of $61,000.

1. Calculate the ratio of nonfood costs plus profit to food costs:

$$\textbf{(Nonfood cost + Profit)} \div \textbf{Food cost = Ratio}$$

In this example,

$$\underset{\textbf{Nonfood costs}}{(\$620,000} + \underset{\textbf{Profit}}{\$61,000)} \div \underset{\textbf{Food cost}}{\$310,000} = \underset{\textbf{Ratio}}{2.20}$$

Now the manager knows that, for each $1.00 of revenue to pay for food costs, he or she must generate an extra $2.20 in revenue for nonfood and profit requirements.

2. Calculate the nonfood and profit requirement ratio amount for the menu item. The manager can do this by multiplying the menu item's food cost by the ratio.

For example, in this operation, if a menu item had a food cost of $3.20, the selling price required for the item's contribution margin (CM) would be:

$$\underset{\textbf{Food cost}}{\$3.20} \times \underset{\textbf{Ratio}}{2.20} = \underset{\textbf{CM}}{\$7.04}$$

3. Determine the menu item's selling price by adding the ratio result to the menu item's food cost:

In this example:

$$\underset{\textbf{Food cost}}{\$3.20} + \underset{\textbf{CM}}{\$7.04} = \underset{\textbf{Menu selling price}}{\$10.24}$$

The base selling price for the item with a $3.20 food cost is $10.24.

The ratio pricing method can be very accurate when it is based on accurate budget information.

WINE PRICING

The pricing of wine in restaurants is a special topic. It has been debated for years by those inside and outside the restaurant and foodservice industry, and the debate continues. Some operation managers, wine producers, and wine distributors argue that managers hurt wine sales and overall profitability by marking up the selling prices of wines excessively.

These professionals point out that a guest who can buy a bottle of popular wine in a grocery store for $12 may hesitate at paying $40 or more for that same bottle of wine in a restaurant even though at that price the establishment is achieving a profit percentage similar to that of the menu items it sells. To sell more wines, these observers contend, managers should reduce the markups on their wines to no more than two times the manager's cost of the wine. Also, they should mark them up even less if the wines are very expensive.

On the other side of the argument are the establishment managers who have traditionally marked up the price of the raw food and beverage ingredients they purchase by a factor of three, four, or even five times their cost. For

Exhibit 8.8

example, if a manager purchased a wine for $10 per bottle and used a factor of 3 for pricing the wines, the wine would sell for $30. Some managers point out that alternative alcoholic beverages such as cocktails or beer often generate similar markups of three, four, or even five times their cost. Markups of only two times product cost, they maintain, would mean a selling price of $20 for this wine and that would result in reduced profits.

Managers on each side of this issue make valid points that thoughtful professionals responsible for pricing wines should consider. In most cases, excessive markups on wine will result in decreased sales. Wine, however, must be a profitable item or establishments should not sell it. Lost in the argument, perhaps, is the fact that in the minds of many guests meals are more elegant, more memorable, and more festive when wine is included (*Exhibit 8.8*).

An operation's total revenue comes from its guests' total purchases. When wines complement meals and are sold at a fair price, repeat business results and total revenue will increase. Then an establishment's profits will increase as well.

It is impossible to state definitively what managers should charge for a steak listed on the menu. Similarly, it is impossible to declare how much should be charged for a specific wine, or even how its selling price should be determined. But a rational approach to wine pricing should always be used. Such an approach will result in the manager following some reasonable guidelines regarding by-the-bottle markups and prices for wine:

- **Price wines in keeping with the overall price structure of the menu.** Guests who visit moderately priced establishments will expect moderately priced wines. If an establishment is very elegant and higher priced, it makes sense for the wines offered to reflect that. Just as most food menus offer a range of entrée prices, the same should be true of a wine list, the operation's menu of wine offerings. Managers should seek to keep the prices of wine and of food in harmony.

- **Some inexpensive wines should be offered.** The additional cost incurred to serve wine to guests already dining in an operation is minimal. If the operation wants to achieve a reputation as one where wine is a natural part of the dining experience, some inexpensive wines should be offered to encourage even the most cost-conscious diners to try them.

- **Offer something for those who want very high quality.** All of the wines selected for the wine list should be good. However, many operations offer premium wine products for those who desire them. Wine drinkers who want the best of the house should be able to purchase it. This should be reflected in the wine's price.

- **Consider the guest's alternatives when pricing.** Wine is one of several choices guests have when electing to purchase alcoholic beverages as part of their meal. Consider the couple that desires a very nice dining experience. Assume this couple will consume two drinks each during their visit. Their alternatives are many. They could, for example, order before-dinner cocktails and after-dinner drinks. The total cost to this couple of their alcoholic beverage choices will be the price of the four drinks. Alternatively, assume they elect to buy a 750-milliliter bottle of wine that will yield four good-sized glasses. It makes sense that the price of the wine must have some relationship to the costs of these guests' other beverage alternatives.

  If the wine is the same or lower in cost than the four-drink alternative, it will likely sell better than if it is perceived as much more expensive than the four-drink alternative. Managers must evaluate the prices charged for all alcoholic beverages and then price their wines accordingly.

- **Evaluate contribution margin as well as cost percentage.** At the heart of the wine list pricing debate is the issue of the importance of contribution margin (CM) relative to the importance of low product cost percentages. In the case of wine pricing, the issue is less confusing than in other areas of operation pricing. Contribution margin, which is the wine's selling price minus its product cost, must dictate the wine-pricing decision. It should not be dictated by its cost percentage, or the product cost divided by selling price. It is the profit per bottle that is important rather than the wine's cost to selling price ratio.

If the manager elects to use markup factors to price wines, *Exhibit 8.9* suggests commonly used markup factors for various types of wine.

Exhibit 8.9	
SUGGESTIONS FOR MARKUP FACTORS BY WINE TYPE	
Wine Type	**Markup Factor**
Inexpensive bulk wines, such as box, carafe, and lower-cost house wines	4–5 times cost
Inexpensive bottled wines	3 times cost
Moderately expensive bottled wines	2 times cost
Highest-priced bottled wines	Less than 2 times cost

ANALYZING THE MENU SALES MIX

An operation's profitability is directly tied to its **menu mix**. This is the frequency with which a menu item is ordered compared to other menu items. Managers should conduct a periodic menu sales mix analysis. A sales mix analysis, also called menu engineering, is a study designed to determine the popularity and profitability of competing items on a menu.

Exhibit 8.10

A major purpose of the analysis is to monitor the effectiveness of menu items to best meet the needs of customers and maximize the profits for the operation. The results of the analysis determine whether changes in menu pricing and menu design are needed (*Exhibit 8.10*).

There are several steps involved in performing a sales mix analysis:

1. Select items to compare.
2. Determine menu mix percentage, or popularity rate.
3. Compare menu items and menu mix popularity percentage.
4. Determine menu item contribution margins.
5. Determine average contribution margin, or profitability.
6. Compare menu item and average contribution margins.
7. Classify menu items.

The menu sales mix analysis is done using a format similar to *Exhibit 8.11*. While it suggests a manual tally of the information, software is also available.

Exhibit 8.11

SAMPLE MENU SALES MIX ANALYSIS

A Menu Item	B Number Sold	C Menu Mix (MM)% (B ÷ Sum of B)	D Selling Price	E Item Food Cost	F Item Contribution Margin (D − E)	G Total Item CM (B × F)	H MM% Category	I CM Category	J Menu Item Classification
Sea Bass	74	20.0%	$13.95	$4.81	$ 9.14	$ 676.36	High	Low	Plow horse
Loin of Pork	49	13.2	16.50	6.02	10.48	513.52	High	High	Star
Strip Steak	81	21.9	15.95	5.68	10.27	831.87	High	High	Star
Rosemary Chicken	57	15.4	13.95	3.67	10.28	585.96	High	High	Star
Grilled Salmon	27	7.3	16.95	6.20	10.75	290.25	Low	High	Puzzle
Beef Stroganoff	43	11.6	12.50	4.48	8.02	344.86	High	Low	Plow horse
Veal Shank	20	5.4	14.50	7.45	7.05	141.00	Low	Low	Dog
Filet Oscar	19	5.1	16.95	8.18	8.77	166.63	Low	Low	Dog
Total	**370**					**$3,550.45**			

1. **Select items to compare:** A menu sales mix analysis is done on competing items in a single menu classification, such as appetizers or entrées.

   The first step in a menu sales analysis is to list the menu items to be analyzed in column A of the analysis worksheet. *Exhibit 8.11* lists the entrées offered in this operation, taken directly from its menu.

2. **Determine menu mix percentage, or popularity rate:** In column B, list the number of each entrée sold during the time period covered by the analysis. Then calculate the total by adding the individual sales. Note that a total of 370 entrées were sold, as shown at the bottom of column B.

   The menu mix percentage for each entrée can be calculated by dividing the number of each specific item sold by the total number of items sold. For example, sea bass sold 74 entrées and represents 20.0 percent of all entrées sold:

$$74 \quad \div \quad 370 \quad = \quad 20.0\%$$

Number of sea bass entrées sold	Total entrées sold	Menu mix Percentage

Menu mix percentages, abbreviated MM%, for each item are recorded in column C.

The sales mix analysis model assumes that a menu item is popular if it sells at least 70 percent of the expected sales for a menu item. This is calculated by dividing 100 percent by the number of menu items being analyzed and then multiplying that number by 70 percent. The result is the **menu mix popularity percentage**. This is the percentage of total menu items that must be sold for a menu item to be considered popular. The menu mix popularity percentage is a baseline against which all menu items are compared during sales mix analysis to determine item popularity.

In this example, the operation features eight entrées (column A). Therefore, 70 percent of the expected sales mix percentage is 8.75 percent:

$$100\% \quad \div \quad 8 \quad = \quad 12.5\%$$

Total sales	Number of different entrées	Expected sales mix percentage

$$12.5\% \quad \times \quad 70\% \quad = \quad 8.75\%$$

Expected sales mix percentage	Allowable sales percentage	Menu mix popularity percentage

The analysis shows that those menu items selling to at least 8.75 percent of guests would be considered popular. So 8.75 percent is the baseline against which all entree items in this sales mix analysis are compared to determine item popularity.

3. **Compare menu items and menu mix popularity percentage:** After the menu mix popularity percentage is calculated, the MM% of each menu item is compared to this benchmark to determine whether the item is popular and sells well or is less popular.

- Items with an MM% at or above the menu mix item popularity percentage are considered popular sellers. In this example, any item that has an MM% above 8.75 percent would be considered popular.

- Items with an MM% below the menu mix popularity percentage are considered unpopular. In this example, any item that has an MM% below 8.75 percent would be considered unpopular.

If an item is considered popular, *high* is recorded in the MM% Category (column H). If an item is considered unpopular, *low* is recorded.

In this example, the MM percentage of sea bass is 20.0 percent (column C). This is significantly higher than the MM popularity percentage of 8.75 percent, so the popularity of sea bass is high.

Exhibit 8.11 shows the menu mix percentage category (abbreviated MM% category) of each item. The comparison process used to reach these results is shown in *Exhibit 8.12*.

MANAGER'S MATH

The menu mix popularity percentage is a baseline against which all menu items are compared during sales mix analysis to determine item popularity.

What is the expected sales mix (popularity) percentage in the following cases?

1. The menu has 30 competing items.
2. The menu has 18 competing items.
3. The menu has 10 competing items.

(Answers: 1. 3.33%; 2. 5.56%; 3. 10.0%)

Exhibit 8.12

SAMPLE MENU MIX PERCENTAGE CATEGORY RESULTS

A Menu Item	B Number Sold	Menu Mix Popularity %	C Menu Mix (MM) %	H MM% Category
Sea Bass	74	8.75%	20.0%	High
Loin of Pork	49	8.75	13.2	High
Strip Steak	81	8.75	21.9	High
Rosemary Chicken	57	8.75	15.4	High
Grilled Salmon	27	8.75	7.3	Low
Beef Stroganoff	43	8.75	11.6	High
Veal Shank	20	8.75	5.4	Low
Filet Oscar	19	8.75	5.1	Low
Total	**370**			

4. **Determine menu item contribution margins:** The fourth step in sales mix analysis is to determine each menu item's contribution margin (CM). Start by listing the selling price of each entrée in column D. See *Exhibit 8.11*. For example, the menu price for sea bass is $13.95.

Next, list the food cost of each item in column E. Note that the food cost for sea bass is $4.81.

Recall that a menu item's CM is the difference between the item's revenue or selling price and its food cost.

The CM for each entrée in the sample menu is shown in *Exhibit 8.11*.

Note that the CM from the sale of one serving of sea bass is $9.14. It is calculated as follows:

$$\underset{\substack{\text{Item selling price} \\ \text{(column D)}}}{\$13.95} \quad - \quad \underset{\substack{\text{Item food cost} \\ \text{(column E)}}}{\$4.81} \quad = \quad \underset{\substack{\text{Item contribution} \\ \text{margin (column F)}}}{\$9.14}$$

The CM from total sales of each menu item is determined by multiplying the number of items sold (column B) by the item's CM (column F). The total CM from the sale of all 74 servings of sea bass is shown in column G:

$$\underset{\substack{\text{Item contribution} \\ \text{margin (column F)}}}{\$9.14} \quad \times \quad \underset{\substack{\text{Number of items} \\ \text{sold (column B)}}}{74} \quad = \quad \underset{\substack{\text{Total item} \\ \text{contribution} \\ \text{margin (column G)}}}{\$676.36}$$

The total CM for all entrées sold in this example was $3,550.45, shown at the bottom of column G.

5. **Determine average contribution margin, or profitability:** The average CM for all entrées is determined by dividing the total CM (bottom of column G) by the total number of entrées sold (bottom of column B):

$$\underset{\substack{\text{Total contribution} \\ \text{margin (column G)}}}{\$3,550.45} \quad \div \quad \underset{\substack{\text{Total number of} \\ \text{items sold (column B)}}}{370} \quad = \quad \underset{\substack{\text{Average contribution} \\ \text{margin}}}{\$9.60}$$

6. **Compare menu item and average contribution margins:** The CM of each menu item should be compared to the average CM to determine the item's profitability. If the item's CM is higher than the average, then *high* is recorded in column I. If the item's CM is lower than the average, *low* is recorded.

In *Exhibit 8.11*, note that the CM of $9.14 for sea bass (column F) is lower than the average CM of $9.60. Therefore, it has a low CM (column I).

The contribution margin for each item in the example is shown in column F of *Exhibit 8.11*. The comparison process is shown in *Exhibit 8.13*.

Exhibit 8.13

CONTRIBUTION MARGIN CATEGORY RESULTS

A Menu Item	B Number Sold	F Item CM	Average CM	I CM Category
Sea Bass	74	$ 9.14	$9.60	Low
Loin of Pork	49	10.48	9.60	High
Strip Steak	81	10.27	9.60	High
Rosemary Chicken	57	10.28	9.60	High
Grilled Salmon	27	10.75	9.60	High
Beef Stroganoff	43	8.02	9.60	Low
Veal Shank	20	7.05	9.60	Low
Filet Oscar	19	8.77	9.60	Low
Total	**370**			

7. **Classify menu items:** The last step in menu sales mix analysis is to classify the menu items based on a combination of their MM percentage category (column H of *Exhibit 8.11*) and their CM category (column I). The following names are used in the classification system:

- **Star:** An item with a high MM percentage and a high CM
- **Plow horse:** An item with a high MM percentage and a low CM
- **Puzzle:** An item with a low MM percentage and a high CM
- **Dog:** An item with a low MM percentage and a low CM

Menu improvements are based on these classifications. The results of assigning menu item classifications to the entrées in this sample menu are shown in column J of *Exhibit 8.11*. A summary of the process used to classify the individual menu items is shown in *Exhibit 8.14*.

Exhibit 8.14

MENU ITEM CLASSIFICATION RESULTS

A Menu Item	H MM% Category	I CM Category	J Menu Item Classification
Sea Bass	High	Low	Plow horse
Loin of Pork	High	High	Star
Strip Steak	High	High	Star
Rosemary Chicken	High	High	Star
Grilled Salmon	Low	High	Puzzle
Beef Stroganoff	High	Low	Plow horse
Veal Shank	Low	Low	Dog
Filet Oscar	Low	Low	Dog

MENU MODIFICATION AND PRICE ADJUSTMENT

After managers have completed their sales analysis, they consider how they can modify their menus. If needed, they can make adjustments to menu prices. The purpose of learning each menu item's popularity and profitability is to determine how to merchandise the items on the menu.

The specific actions to be taken to modify menu items will vary for each operation. However, the menu sales mix analysis does give managers some guidance on how evaluated menu items should be treated. Managers can use many strategies to improve menu items. It is important to make changes in line with the brand image, company profitability, competitors, production and service considerations, and customer expectations.

Stars

Stars are menu items that are profitable and popular. In *Exhibit 8.11*, Loin of Pork is a star menu item and the following strategies can be used to manage stars (see *Exhibit 8.15*):

Exhibit 8.15

- Do not change the item. These menu items already sell well and make money for the operation.
- Maintain quality standards.
- Ensure that these items are in highly visible menu locations.
- Promote these items aggressively with table tents and suggestive selling. This is to ensure that customers know about the products and services offered by the establishment. **Suggestive selling** means recommending additional or different items to a customer. For example, a server could ask a customer, "Would you like a pastry with your coffee?"

Suggestive selling can actually be a way of providing high-quality customer service. It should be approached as enhancing the guest experience. If done correctly, suggesting a side dish that will enhance an entrée, a wine that complements the main course, or a dessert to complete the meal will influence the guest's perception of value and improve the dining experience.

Plow Horses

Plow horses are menu items that are popular but not profitable. They may bring in customers, but selling a lot of them will not improve profitability. Use these management suggestions:

- Consider a selling price increase. One reason for high sales may be the value these items provide. A small price increase may not affect popularity but will increase profitability.
- If portions are large, reduce them slightly to decrease food cost and increase the CM.

- The menu design may indicate that they are present in a very high-profile position on the menu. If so, a less visible spot will likely lead to reduced sales.

- Combine the item with another menu item that has a much lower food cost to increase profitability. For example, a high-cost twice-baked potato that comes with a menu item might be offered as an à la carte item. Replace the included item with a lower-cost potato or starch.

- If the item requires many labor hours to produce, it could be removed from the menu. Or consider ways to reduce labor costs.

Puzzles

Puzzles are menu items that are profitable, but not many are sold. Use these management strategies to increase popularity:

- Reduce the price to provide greater customer value.

- Promote the items by moving them to a more visible menu position, using table tents, and using suggestive selling.

- Rename the item to increase recognition and sales.

- Remove the item if it creates production or service problems.

Dogs

Dogs are menu items that are unprofitable and unpopular. Use these management strategies:

- Remove the item from the menu.

- Raise the selling price or reduce the cost of ingredients to increase profitability.

- Replace with an alternative menu item that supports the brand image. Properly test the item before it is added to the menu.

When considering major alterations to their menus, managers can follow this list to ensure they have considered all of the important issues related to menu modification:

1. Review and verify previously established optimal menu sales mix and product costs.

2. Verify previously established profitability goals, or recalculate as needed.

3. Change menu mix, cost margins, and profitability goals as needed.

4. Recalculate the price of each suggested food and beverage item on the menu.

5. Compare revised prices to competitor pricing.

REAL MANAGER

OPTIMIZING THE MENU

I was reviewing the menu of one of our restaurant brands. It seemed to be way too big with many items that did not have any real ties to the brand's overall DNA. I started speaking with some of our operators and franchisees about eliminating some of these items and was met with overwhelming resistance. Every time I would bring up an item that should be removed, I received a similar answer: "It will kill my sales!" When I heard this, I would ask what percentage of sales was made up of the item. Nobody could say. When pushed, it basically came down to one or two frequent guests that came in and ordered these items. That was it.

So, we took several restaurants and did a complete menu mix analysis. We found that 9 items were doing less than 2 percent of sales on the menu. Three items were less than 1 percent. We then did a P&L analysis on the current menu and found that those same items were losing money at the current volumes. So, we changed the menu board in half of the restaurants analyzed, removing all of the items below a 2 percent menu mix to give us much more visual space to market the more profitable items. We left the other half as is. The restaurants with no menu change had flat sales for the 90-day test period. The ones where we made the menu change saw an increase in overall restaurant sales of 8 percent for the same period. From this experience, you can see the power of menu mix analysis. In the restaurant and foodservice industry, sometimes less is really more.

6. Adjust the sales forecast to reflect the impact of potential menu changes.

7. Assess the estimated impact of menu changes on operational profitability.

8. Accept the suggested new menu items and modifications or adjust the operation's profitability targets.

9. Update the menu.

10. Reprogram the operation's POS with new menu information and pricing.

In most operations, the manager will not have complete control over the pricing process. The operation's owners will likely make some pricing decisions. Managers can, however, provide valuable insight and information. This can assist owners and others in determining how menu items are best prepared, and at what prices they should be sold.

For all managers, the key to proper pricing is a thorough understanding of what customers value most, and an awareness of operating costs. These two considerations should be foremost in managers' minds. They will then consistently make pricing decisions that are good for their customers and for their operations.

SUMMARY

1. **Describe the relationship between price and value.**

   Pricing is important because every business must charge prices high enough to cover its costs. Experienced managers, however, know that costs as well as the reactions of customers must be considered when establishing menu prices. That is so because prices charged and customer perceptions of value received for money spent are closely related. For customers, only one pricing-related factor is important—perceived value. If the items' prices reflect a high value for money spent, repeat customers are likely. If, however, customers do not feel they received good value for the prices they have paid, they are unlikely to return.

2. **Explain the relationship between price, revenue, and profits.**

   The basic accounting formula is Revenue − Expense = Profits. If revenue is not sufficiently large, expenses can easily result in reduced profits or even the elimination of profits. Revenue, or sales, is defined as the price of an item multiplied by the number of units sold. Therefore the price charged has a direct impact on revenue. If prices are too high, too few units may be sold and revenue may be too low to achieve desired profits. If prices are too low, the number of units sold may be high, but the revenue may again be insufficient to allow an operation to achieve its desired profit level. Proper pricing optimizes sales to guests, ensuring their desire to return and ensuring an operation's ability to achieve its profit goals.

3. **Explain the methods managers use to establish food and beverage prices.**

Managers can choose from a variety of menu pricing methods. Four of the most popular ones are the food cost percentage, contribution margin, prime cost, and ratio pricing methods. When using the food cost percentage pricing method, managers seek to price their items in a way that yields a predetermined food cost percentage. Managers want to ensure that each menu item selling price is equal to an amount needed to cover the average nonfood cost and targeted profit per guest served.

The prime cost pricing method includes detailed labor and food costs in the calculation of a menu item's price. Finally, the ratio pricing method requires managers to consider all operating expenses and desired profit when pricing menu items.

4. **Describe the procedure used to analyze a menu sales mix.**

A sales mix analysis involves determining the popularity and profitability of each menu item, and then comparing these items against the *average* popularity and profitability for all menu items on the menu. Menu items can be classified according to popularity and profitability and, when this information is known, menu improvements can be made.

5. **State the process used to make needed modifications to menu items and prices.**

When considering major alterations to their menus, managers conduct a menu sales mix analysis. This is to identify strong selling and profitable menu items, and to modify or eliminate weaker ones. When menu changes are under consideration, managers implement a specific process that includes a review of the current menu's targets and goals. These are reassessed and changed as needed. Current recipe costs are assessed and prices are evaluated against those of competitors. Profit forecasts are then made based on the new prices. If the forecasted profit results are acceptable, the menu is modified. Programming changes are also made to the operation's POS to reflect the changes.

APPLICATION EXERCISE

Claudia wants to perform a break-even analysis on her very busy casual-dining operation. She has obtained the following operating results from last month's income statement and POS system sales records:

Guests served:	25,000
Sales:	$210,000
Variable costs:	$75,000
Fixed costs:	$110,000
Total costs:	$185,000
Profit:	$25,000

1. What is her average sale per guest?
2. What is her variable cost percentage?
3. What is her fixed cost percentage?
4. What is her contribution margin (CM) percentage?
5. What is her break-even point in sales?
6. What is her break-even point in customers?

REVIEW YOUR LEARNING

Select the best answer for each question.

1. What most affects a customer's opinion of a price?

   A. Perceptions of value delivered

   B. The profit needs of an operation

   C. The restaurant or foodservice operation's costs

   D. Taxes paid on the menu items purchased

2. What is the name for menus that have separate prices for each menu item?

   A. Du jour

   B. Cyclical

   C. À la carte

   D. Table d'hôte

3. What is the formula for an operation's revenue?

   A. Profit − Expense = Revenue

   B. Units sold × Expense = Revenue

   C. Selling price × Expense = Revenue

   D. Selling price × Units sold = Revenue

4. What is the menu pricing markup if the operating budget specifies a 40% food cost?

   A. 0.25

   B. 0.4

   C. 2.5

   D. 4.0

5. What is the formula used to calculate contribution margin (CM) when determining how much to charge for a menu item?

   A. Food cost − Revenue = CM

   B. Food cost + Labor cost = CM

   C. Selling price − Food cost = CM

   D. Selling price − Labor cost = CM

6. What is the CM percentage if sales are $500,000, there are 20,000 customers, and variable costs are $125,000?

   A. 2.5%

   B. 7.5%

   C. 25%

   D. 75%

7. What is the per guest CM if sales are $500,000, there are 20,000 customers, and variable costs are $125,000?

   A. $16.75

   B. $17.75

   C. $18.75

   D. $19.75

8. A menu item sells for $10. It has a 40% food cost. What is the menu item's contribution margin (CM)?

   A. $0.40

   B. $0.60

   C. $4.00

   D. $6.00

9. A plow horse is a menu item that is

   A. popular and profitable.

   B. unpopular but profitable.

   C. popular but unprofitable.

   D. unpopular and unprofitable.

10. Which is a good strategy for modifying a menu item that has been designated as a puzzle by a menu sales mix analysis?

    A. Replace the item with a new item.

    B. Improve the item's placement on the menu.

    C. Move the item to a less prominent part of the menu.

    D. Maintain the same selling price but reduce the item's portion size.

FIELD PROJECT

Visit a commercial or noncommercial restaurant or foodservice operation. Ask the manager some questions about the way menu modification decisions are made in his or her operation. Ask the manager:

1. Are standardized recipes used?

2. How often are the (portion) costs of preparing the standardized recipes updated?

3. Is a formal menu sales mix analysis performed in the operation? If so, how often is it performed?

4. What criteria are used to determine if an item should be dropped from the menu?

5. What criteria are used to determine if an item should be added to the menu?

6. What criteria are used to determine if an item's price should be changed?

7. Who is responsible for suggesting potential changes in menu items to be served, and the prices at which the items will be sold?

8. Who has the final authority for determining which suggested changes are implemented?

9 Assessing Actual Performance

INSIDE THIS CHAPTER

- Comparing Budgeted to Actual Performance
- Revising the Budget

CHAPTER LEARNING OBJECTIVES

After completing this chapter, you should be able to:

- Explain the purposes for comparing budgeted results to actual operating results.

- Describe the way managers calculate budget variances and budget variance percentages.

- Identify reasons for variation in revenue, expense, and profit line items.

- State factors that could result in revenue or expense-related budget revisions.

- State factors that could result in profit-related budget revisions.

KEY TERMS

CASE STUDY

"We budgeted only $5,000 for labor last week," said Cindy, the manager of Villa Park Country Club. "But our payroll report from accounting said we spent over $6,000 last week. We've got to cut back!"

"But that doesn't make any sense," said Sandy, the club's grill manager. "We had a great week last week. It was sunny every day and the golfers were out in droves. I think we had the best sales week we have had all year. Our revenue was way higher than expected, too!"

"Is that why you had so much overtime?" asked Cindy. "Accounting said we used a ton of overtime."

"We did have some overtime," replied Sandy. "I didn't send anyone home early all week, and on several days the production crew stayed late to prep extra for the next day. I also had to call in extra servers on both Friday and Saturday."

"Well," replied Cindy, "I understand, but accounting still said you were way over budget on our payroll. What are you going to do now?"

1. Do you think Sandy showed good judgment by increasing staffing in response to the increase in volume? Would you have done anything differently?

2. What are some reasons managers might spend more money than they originally budgeted in a specific time period? What are some reasons they might spend less money?

213

COMPARING BUDGETED TO ACTUAL PERFORMANCE

As outlined in chapter 4, an operating budget helps managers plan the financial activities related to their daily operations. A manager's operating budget is a projected financial plan for a specific period of time. It is intended to project anticipated revenue and the costs that will be incurred by a business. This provides an estimate of the profit or loss expected for the budget period. After the budget period, managers can dramatically improve the future operation of their businesses by carefully comparing budgeted financial performance to actual financial performance.

To complete an analysis of budgeted to actual performance, managers engage in specific activities:

- Review actual profit and loss (P&L) performance.
- Compare budgeted to actual performance.
- Identify significant variations from budget.
- Investigate reasons for the variations.
- Document findings.
- Identify and implement needed operational changes.
- Make recommendations for revisions to the budget.
- Present recommendations to owners for their approval.

The reasons for conducting such an analysis are many:

- To ensure revenue goals are being achieved
- To ensure expense-related goals are being achieved
- To ensure guest service standards are being met
- To ensure profit goals are being achieved
- To identify needed improvements in operational areas
- To identify areas of needed budget modification
- To evaluate the effectiveness of managers

Managers who compare actual operating results to previously projected, or budgeted, results must identify and investigate the reasons for any significant variations that occur. The methods they use to do that are addressed in this chapter. Changes in operating procedures may be required to bring actual results back in line with budgeted results. These changes are made to ensure that the operation's financial goals can be met in the future. This could be the case, for example, when excessive food waste causes food costs to increase above acceptable levels (see *Exhibit 9.1*). Factors that can cause food waste include poor storage methods, improper cooking techniques, and overportioning. Correcting these problem areas can help the operation correct its variation from budget problems.

Exhibit 9.1

Expense areas in which actual spending is below planned levels can also be cause for concern. For example, suppose labor-related costs decrease far below budgeted levels. Then guest service may suffer because too few employees would be available to cook for and serve guests. In a similar manner, if equipment maintenance is not performed as provided for in the budget, spending will be less than planned. However, the useful life of the poorly maintained equipment may be significantly reduced. This could, in the long term, result in the operation actually spending more, not less, money on equipment.

In some cases, factors beyond the control of management may be the cause of budget variations. For example, the cost of a popular menu item may increase significantly, and may not be expected to go down in the near future. In this case, the manager has several options:

- Revise quality requirements
- Search for other vendors
- Increase the price of the menu item
- Reduce the portion size of the menu item
- Revise the food cost budget
- Do nothing

Each of these actions will, in some manner, impact the budget and must be evaluated for their impact. When managers feel the need to revise operating budgets, they may need to first seek approval from their supervisor or the operation's owner.

In all cases, budgets must be attainable if they are to be valuable financial guides. Before suggesting a revision to a budget, managers must ensure they have carefully analyzed their actual operating performance. They can then determine whether a budget revision is indeed appropriate. They begin the process of doing that by measuring the difference between their operations' budgeted performance and its actual performance.

Calculating Variance Amount

To learn how managers compare actual to budgeted performance, review the information in *Exhibit 9.2*. It shows a six-month budget from January 1 to June 30, prepared for the Rain Shower Café.

Exhibit 9.2

RAIN SHOWER CAFÉ: SIX-MONTH BUDGET (JANUARY 1 TO JUNE 30)

Guests	40,000	
Sales	**Budget**	**Percentage**
Food	$ 360,000	81.8%
Beverage	80,000	18.2
Total sales	**$440,000**	**100%**
Cost of Sales		
Food	$ 126,000	35.0%
Beverage	20,000	25.0
Total cost of sales	**$146,000**	**33.2%**
Gross Profit		
Food	$ 234,000	65.0%
Beverage	60,000	75.0
Total gross profit	**$294,000**	**66.8%**
Controllable Expenses		
Salaries and wages	$ 110,000	25.0%
Employee benefits	24,000	5.5
Legal/accounting	800	0.2
Music and entertainment	5,000	1.1
Marketing	6,000	1.4
Utility services	4,000	0.9
General and administrative	8,000	1.8
Repairs and maintenance	2,500	0.6
Miscellaneous	500	0.1
Total controllable expenses	**$160,800**	**36.5%**
Fixed Expenses		
Rent	$ 42,000	9.5%
Depreciation	12,000	2.7
Licenses/permits	1,500	0.3
Insurance	7,000	1.6
Loan payments	25,000	5.7
Total fixed expenses	**$ 87,500**	**19.9%**
Profit/(Loss)*	**$ 45,700**	**10.4%**
Income Taxes	**$ 8,500**	**1.9%**
Net Earnings (Loss)	**$ 37,200**	**8.5%**

*Before income taxes.

THINK ABOUT IT...

What do you think would happen to an operation whose manager tried to save money by not spending any of the dollars designated for advertising? For staff training?

The budget was developed using the operation's preferred income statement (chapter 3) format. The format was developed after reviewing the Uniform System of Accounts for Restaurants (USAR) explained in chapter 1.

Note that the budget in *Exhibit 9.2* contains key information:

- Projected number of guests to be served
- Projected sales by revenue source (food and beverage)
- Projected cost of sales by revenue source (food and beverage)
- Projected controllable expenses
- Fixed expenses
- Projected profits or losses
- Percentage calculations for all budgeted amounts

After a business has completed operations for a budgeted time period, managers can compare their actual performance to their previously budgeted performance. This is done to identify variances between anticipated and actual operating results.

Exhibit 9.3 shows budgeted and actual performance results for the Rain Shower Café for the budget period January 1 through June 30.

The manager of the Rain Shower Café would obtain actual operating results from a variety of sources:

- The operation's POS system
- The operation's income statements, or P&Ls
- Accounts payable (AP) records
- Accounts receivable (AR) records

When budgeted and actual operating results are known, managers subtract to determine areas of variance using the following formula:

$$\text{Actual results} - \text{Budgeted results} = \text{Variance}$$

The variance formula is used to identify the dollar difference between budgeted and actual operating performance. *Exhibit 9.4* on page 218 shows the amount of variance in each line item to be reviewed (see more about line item review in chapter 7).

Note from *Exhibit 9.4* that variances can be positive or negative. A **positive variance** is one in which actual performance is greater than budgeted performance. In this example, the number of guests served results in a positive variance:

$$\text{Actual guests} - \text{Budgeted guests} = \text{Guest variance}$$

Exhibit 9.3

RAIN SHOWER CAFÉ: BUDGETED AND ACTUAL PERFORMANCE (JANUARY 1 TO JUNE 30)

Guests	40,000		43,826	
Sales	**Budget**	**Percentage**	**Actual**	**Percentage**
Food	$ 360,000	81.8%	$ 375,125	81.5%
Beverage	80,000	18.2	85,050	18.5
Total sales	**$440,000**	**100%**	**$460,175**	**100%**
Cost of Sales				
Food	$ 126,000	35.0%	$ 142,000	37.9%
Beverage	20,000	25.0	18,000	21.2
Total cost of sales	**$146,000**	**33.2%**	**$160,000**	**34.8%**
Gross Profit				
Food	$ 234,000	65.0%	$ 233,125	62.1%
Beverage	60,000	75.0	67,050	78.8
Total gross profit	**$294,000**	**66.8%**	**$300,175**	**65.2%**
Controllable Expenses				
Salaries and wages	$ 110,000	25.0%	$ 132,000	28.7%
Employee benefits	24,000	5.5	25,250	5.5
Legal/accounting	800	0.2	500	0.1
Music and entertainment	5,000	1.1	6,000	1.3
Marketing	6,000	1.4	8,000	1.7
Utility services	4,000	0.9	4,650	1.0
General and administrative	8,000	1.8	9,200	2.0
Repairs and maintenance	2,500	0.6	250	0.1
Miscellaneous	500	0.1	410	0.1
Total controllable expenses	**$160,800**	**36.5%**	**$186,260**	**40.5%**
Fixed Expenses				
Rent	$ 42,000	9.5%	$ 42,000	9.1%
Depreciation	12,000	2.7	12,000	2.6
Licenses/permits	1,500	0.3	1,500	0.3
Insurance	7,000	1.6	7,600	1.7
Loan payments	25,000	5.7	25,000	5.4
Total fixed expenses	**$ 87,500**	**19.9%**	**$ 88,100**	**19.1%**
Profit/(Loss)*	**$ 45,700**	**10.4%**	**$ 25,815**	**5.6%**
Income Taxes	**$ 8,500**	**1.9%**	**$ 4,880**	**1.1%**
Net Earnings (Loss)	**$ 37,200**	**8.5%**	**$ 20,935**	**4.5%**

*Before income taxes.

Exhibit 9.4

RAIN SHOWER CAFÉ: BUDGETED AND ACTUAL PERFORMANCE VARIANCE AMOUNTS (JANUARY 1 TO JUNE 30)

Guests	40,000		43,826		3,826
Sales	**Budget**	**Percentage**	**Actual**	**Percentage**	**Variance**
Food	$ 360,000	81.8%	$ 375,125	81.5%	$ 15,125
Beverage	80,000	18.2	85,050	18.5	5,050
Total sales	**$440,000**	**100%**	**$460,175**	**100%**	**$20,175**
Cost of Sales					
Food	$ 126,000	35.0%	$ 142,000	37.9%	$ 16,000
Beverage	20,000	25.0	18,000	21.2	(2,000)
Total cost of sales	**$146,000**	**33.2%**	**$160,000**	**34.8%**	**$14,000**
Gross Profit					
Food	$ 234,000	65.0%	$ 233,125	62.1%	($ 875)
Beverage	60,000	75.0	67,050	78.8	7,050
Total gross profit	**$294,000**	**66.8%**	**$300,175**	**65.2%**	**$ 6,175**
Controllable Expenses					
Salaries and wages	$ 110,000	25.0%	$ 132,000	28.7%	$ 22,000
Employee benefits	24,000	5.5	25,250	5.5	1,250
Legal/accounting	800	0.2	500	0.1	(300)
Music and entertainment	5,000	1.1	6,000	1.3	1,000
Marketing	6,000	1.4	8,000	1.7	2,000
Utility services	4,000	0.9	4,650	1.0	650
General and administrative	8,000	1.8	9,200	2.0	1,200
Repairs and maintenance	2,500	0.6	250	0.1	(2,250)
Miscellaneous	500	0.1	410	0.1	(90)
Total controllable expenses	**$160,800**	**36.5%**	**$186,260**	**40.5%**	**$25,460**
Fixed Expenses					
Rent	$ 42,000	9.5%	$ 42,000	9.1%	$ 0
Depreciation	12,000	2.7	12,000	2.6	0
Licenses/permits	1,500	0.3	1,500	0.3	0
Insurance	7,000	1.6	7,600	1.7	600
Loan payments	25,000	5.7	25,000	5.4	0
Total fixed expenses	**$ 87,500**	**19.9%**	**$ 88,100**	**19.1%**	**$ 600**
Profit/(Loss)*	**$ 45,700**	**10.4%**	**$ 25,815**	**5.6%**	**($ 19,885)**
Income Taxes	**$ 8,500**	**1.9%**	**$ 4,880**	**1.1%**	**($ 3,620)**
Net Earnings (Loss)	**$ 37,200**	**8.5%**	**$ 20,935**	**4.5%**	**($ 16,265)**

*Before income taxes.

In this example,

43,826	−	40,000		3,826
Actual guests		**Budgeted guests**		**Guest variance**

The operation served more guests than forecasted. A **negative variance** is one in which actual performance is less than the budgeted performance. In this example, profit/(loss) results in a negative variance:

Actual profit/(loss) − Budgeted profit/(loss) = Profit/(loss) variance

In this example,

25,815	−	45,700	=	(19,885)
Actual profit/(loss)		**Budgeted profit/(loss)**		**Profit/(loss) variance**

The operation generated fewer profits than previously estimated. The result is a negative variance. In many cases, accountants use special techniques to highlight negative variances for the readers of financial reports:

- Marking negative variance amounts in red; for example $100 to represent a $100 negative variance

- Placing a negative (−) sign in front of the variance, for example −$100 to represent a $100 negative variance

- Placing the amount of the variance in parentheses; for example ($100) to represent a $100 negative variance

- Placing the amount of the variance in parentheses and in red; for example ($100) to represent a $100 negative variance

As shown in *Exhibit 9.4*, the Rain Shower Café experienced both positive and negative variances during this budget period. Some of the variances were a small amount, such as ($300) for legal and accounting, while others were much larger, such as $20,175 for total sales.

To compare actual to budgeted performance, managers calculate all positive and negative variances as shown in *Exhibit 9.4*. In some cases, no variance will exist. This is often the case, for example, when fixed costs are known in advance and are budgeted in the exact amounts the operation will pay. In many operations, examples would include expenses incurred for items such as rent and lease payments.

Some small variances between planned and actual results may be important to some operations, while other, even larger variances may not be so important. Consider, for example, the very small restaurant or foodservice operation that overspends its $500 monthly advertising budget by $250. Such a variance in budgeted versus actual performance is likely a **significant variance**—one that should be investigated by managers. Suppose, however, that a very large restaurant or foodservice group has an advertising budget of $250,000 for a

THINK ABOUT IT . . .

What could cause positive (exceeded budget) variations in an expense category?

What could cause negative (less than budget) variations in an expense category?

specific time period. A variation of $250 or even more in actual spending may not constitute a significant variance. Because the size of a variance is related to the size of the amount originally budgeted, experienced managers know it is always a good idea to calculate their operations' variance percentages.

Calculating Variance Percentages

Managers want to know the size of the variance they experience relative to the amount originally budgeted. They use the following formula to calculate their variance percentages:

$$\textbf{Variance} \div \textbf{Budgeted results} = \textbf{Variance percentage}$$

Exhibit 9.5 shows the variance percentages for each budget line item at the Rain Shower Café.

The manager of the Rain Shower Café calculates the operation's variance percentages using the formula shown previously. For example,

$$\textbf{Variance sales: beverages} \div \textbf{Budgeted sales: beverages} = \begin{array}{c}\textbf{Variance}\\ \textbf{percentage}\end{array}$$

In this example:

$$\begin{array}{ccccc}\$5,050 & \div & \$80,000 & = & 6.3\%\\ \textbf{Variance sales: beverages} & & \textbf{Budgeted sales: beverages} & & \begin{array}{c}\textbf{Variance}\\ \textbf{percentage}\end{array}\end{array}$$

MANAGER'S MATH

OPEN FOR BUSINESS

A manager created the following operating budget and achieved the actual results shown. For each line item, calculate the variance and the variance percentage.

Sales	Budget	Percentage	Actual	Percentage	Variance	Percentage
Food	$525,000	77.8%	$541,000	80.0%	_____	_____
Beverage	150,000	22.2	135,000	20.0	_____	_____
Total sales	$675,000	100%	$676,000	100%	_____	_____

1. Did the operation's sales increase?

2. What is your assessment of this operation's sales-related performance during this budget period?

3. What would you do if you were this operation's manager?

3. Find the cause for the dropoff in beverage sales.)

1. Yes, by a very small amount ($1,000); 2. Food sales were good, beverage sales were not so good;

Sales	Budget	Percentage	Actual	Percentage	Variance	Percentage
Food	$525,000	77.8%	$541,000	80.0%	$16,000	3.05%
Beverage	150,000	22.2	135,000	20.0	−15,000	−10.00
Total sales	$675,000	100%	$676,000	100%	$ 1,000	0.15%

(Answers:

Exhibit 9.5

RAIN SHOWER CAFÉ: BUDGETED AND ACTUAL PERFORMANCE VARIANCE PERCENTAGES

Guests	40,000		43,826		3,826	9.6%
Sales	**Budget**	**Percentage**	**Actual**	**Percentage**	**Variance**	**Percentage**
Food	$ 360,000	81.8%	$ 375,125	81.5%	$ 15,125	4.2%
Beverage	80,000	18.2	85,050	18.5	5,050	6.3
Total sales	**$440,000**	**100%**	**$460,175**	**100%**	**$20,175**	**4.6%**
Cost of Sales						
Food	$ 126,000	35.0%	$ 142,000	37.9%	$ 16,000	12.7%
Beverage	20,000	25.0	18,000	21.2	(2,000)	(10.0)
Total cost of sales	**$146,000**	**33.2%**	**$160,000**	**34.8%**	**$14,000**	**9.6%**
Gross Profit						
Food	$ 234,000	65.0%	$ 233,125	62.1%	($ 875)	(0.4%)
Beverage	60,000	75.0	67,050	78.8	7,050	11.8
Total gross profit	**$294,000**	**66.8%**	**$300,175**	**65.2%**	**$ 6,175**	**2.1%**
Controllable Expenses						
Salaries and wages	$ 110,000	25.0%	$ 132,000	28.7%	$ 22,000	20.0%
Employee benefits	24,000	5.5	25,250	5.5	1,250	5.2
Legal/accounting	800	0.2	500	0.1	(300)	(37.5)
Music and entertainment	5,000	1.1	6,000	1.3	1,000	20.0
Marketing	6,000	1.4	8,000	1.7	2,000	33.3
Utility services	4,000	0.9	4,650	1.0	650	16.3
General and administrative	8,000	1.8	9,200	2.0	1,200	15.0
Repairs and maintenance	2,500	0.6	250	0.1	(2,250)	(90.0)
Miscellaneous	500	0.1	410	0.1	(90)	(18.0)
Total controllable expenses	**$160,800**	**36.5%**	**$186,260**	**40.5%**	**$25,460**	**15.8%**
Fixed Expenses						
Rent	$ 42,000	9.5%	$ 42,000	9.1%	$ 0	0.0%
Depreciation	12,000	2.7	12,000	2.6	0	0.0
Licenses/permits	1,500	0.3	1,500	0.3	0	0.0
Insurance	7,000	1.6	7,600	1.7	600	8.6
Loan payments	25,000	5.7	25,000	5.4	0	0.0
Total fixed expenses	**$ 87,500**	**19.9%**	**$ 88,100**	**19.1%**	**$ 600**	**0.7%**
Profit/(Loss)*	**$ 45,700**	**10.4%**	**$ 25,815**	**5.6%**	**($19,885)**	**(43.5%)**
Income Taxes	**$ 8,500**	**1.9%**	**$ 4,880**	**1.1%**	**($ 3,620)**	**(42.6%)**
Net Earnings (Loss)	**$ 37,200**	**8.5%**	**$ 20,935**	**4.5%**	**($16,265)**	**(43.7%)**

*Before income taxes.

Determining Significant Variance

Exhibit 9.5 shows Rain Shower Café's budget, actual operating performance, variance, and percentage variances. Managers must determine in which areas there is significant variation from the budget.

The significance of a variation must be assessed based both on its dollar amount and the size of percentage variance from budget. In some cases, a small dollar amount of variance may also represent a fairly small percentage change. In *Exhibit 9.5* this is illustrated by the line item for insurance. In this case, a $600 variance represents an 8.6 percent variance. In other cases, a similar-sized dollar amount of variance may represent a much larger percentage variance. In *Exhibit 9.5* this is illustrated by the line item for utility service. In that case, a $650 difference represents a 16.3 percent variance.

In some cases, a small dollar amount of difference may represent a large percentage change. In *Exhibit 9.5* this is illustrated by the line item for legal/accounting. In that case, a ($300) (negative) variance represents a percentage change from the original budget of 37.5 percent. However, in other cases, a different amount that is many times larger may represent only a small percentage change. In *Exhibit 9.5* this is illustrated by the line item for sales: food. In that case, a $15,125 difference represents only a 4.2 percent difference from the original budget.

Comparing budgeted to actual performance is useful in identifying potential areas of concern. Any variance between actual amounts and the budget could indicate that something unexpected has occurred. For instance, actual sales amounts might be lower than expected due to bad weather conditions or emergency road repairs in front of the operation (*Exhibit 9.6*). It is easy to see how such unforeseen conditions would have affected sales. In addition, variances might indicate that assumptions made during creation of the budget were inaccurate.

Comparing budgeted to actual performance is the most common way to assess operating performance. However, it is not the only way. Many operations will have preestablished operating standards to compare to as well. These standards are usually the basis of the operation's original budget. General operating standards often reflect accepted ranges, targets, or thresholds for certain costs within the restaurant and foodservice industry. These standards are not an exact measurement because every restaurant and foodservice operation is unique. It is important to make sure the values being compared actually fit the nature of an operation. For example, a fine-dining establishment will spend more for labor than a quick-service restaurant (QSR). If the fine-dining manager's goal is to have better service than any other establishment in the area, then that

Exhibit 9.6

operation would expect to have labor costs that are higher than the industry standard. If an operation is part of a chain, there will likely be company standards to compare against. A **chain** is an operation in which multiple restaurants share the same name and operating systems.

Company standards are used as a guide for how the operation can and should be run. This includes percentages of costs related to food and beverages. It also could be broken down more specifically into specific food items. Often, other controllable and fixed expenses can be addressed by company standards as well. Still another way to analyze differences between budgeted and actual operating results is to compare them with historical data from the same operation. This can be done for an individual unit or across multiple properties.

Areas of significant variation must be investigated. In some cases, the explanation for them may be well known and easily understandable. In *Exhibit 9.5* this is illustrated by the line item for insurance. Here, the actual cost of the operation's insurance policy simply exceeded the amount originally budgeted for it. In every case of significant variance, however, the cause of the variance should be determined.

If revenue is higher than originally budgeted, it stands to reason variable costs such as food and labor will also increase. In *Exhibit 9.5* this is illustrated by the line item for cost of sales: food. It is important to note that, in some cases, significant decreases in costs should be of as much concern to managers as are significant increases in costs. In *Exhibit 9.5* this is illustrated by the line item for repairs and maintenance. If needed repair and routine maintenance work is not completed, the costs in this area may increase at an even greater rate in the future (*Exhibit 9.7*).

Exhibit 9.7

Investigating Variances

After managers have determined which variances are significant, it becomes their job to take specific steps to investigate the reasons for variations from budget. They must identify and implement needed operational changes and, if necessary, make recommendations for revisions to the budget.

The process of identifying the potential causes of line item variances can be examined in the same order that the major financial performance areas are presented in the accounting formula:

$$\text{Revenue} - \text{Expense} = \text{Profits}$$

THINK ABOUT IT . . .

Have you ever delayed an automobile repair only to find that the delay cost you more in the long run than the repair? Do you think the same thing could happen with restaurant and foodservice equipment?

THINK ABOUT IT . . .

Do you think managers should be most concerned about significant variances that occur in revenue or expense categories? How would variances in these areas affect an operation's profits?

Assessing Variance in Revenue

Assessing revenue variance can be more challenging than it first appears. This is so because revenue generation is affected by two variables:

1. Number of guests served
2. Amount spent per guest

Changes in the two variables can produce the results shown in *Exhibit 9.8*.

Exhibit 9.8

REVENUE VARIABLES ANALYSIS

Number of Guests Served	Amount Spent per Guest	Resulting Impact on Revenue
Increases	Increases	Increases
Increases	Decreases	May increase or decrease
Decreases	Increases	May increase or decrease
Decreases	Decreases	Decreases

In *Exhibit 9.5*, the number of guests served was 9.6 percent higher than budgeted (3,826 ÷ 40,000 = 9.6%). Food revenue increased 4.2 percent and beverage revenue increased 6.3 percent. Total sales increased 4.6 percent.

In many respects these results are good because revenue is increasing. *Exhibit 9.9*, however, shows that the average sale per guest was less than budgeted. Recall from chapter 8 that the formula for calculating average sale per guest is:

$$\text{Sales} \div \text{Guests served} = \text{Average sale per guest}$$

Exhibit 9.9

REVENUE ANALYSIS: RAIN SHOWER CAFÉ

	Budget	Actual	Variance
Number of guests served	40,000	43,826	3,826
Food sales	$360,000	$375,125	$15,125
Beverage sales	$ 80,000	$ 85,050	$ 5,050
Food sales per guest	$ 9.00	$ 8.56	($ 0.44)
Beverage sales per guest	$ 2.00	$ 1.94	($ 0.06)
Total sales per guest	$ 11.00	$ 10.50	($ 0.50)

When revenues increase, but the amount spent by each customer declines, managers will have served more guests to achieve the revenue increase (*Exhibit 9.10*). When they do they will likely incur additional labor expense. In this example, the manager would seek to identify the reasons for the decline in per-guest spending. There are four fundamental reasons revenue per guest served can decline, and thus be below budgeted expectations:

- Guests choosing to buy fewer items
- Guests selecting less expensive items
- Guests choosing fewer and less expensive items
- Theft of revenue

If the sale per guest amount is less than budgeted, managers must identify the causes and take appropriate corrective action. Potential corrective actions related to below-budgeted actual revenue levels can be varied:

- Assess food quality levels for adherence to standards.
- Assess service quality levels for adherence to standards.
- Assess marketing efforts.
- Assess service staff selling efforts.
- Confirm revenue security controls are in place.

Assessing Variance in Expense

As shown in earlier in *Exhibit 9.5*, variance in expenses can be positive or negative. A positive variance means expenses were higher than budgeted. In *Exhibit 9.5* this is illustrated by the line items for food: beverages and marketing, as well as others.

A negative variance means the expense was less than anticipated. In *Exhibit 9.5* this is illustrated by the line items for legal/accounting and repair and maintenance.

As a general rule, when revenue increases above budgeted amounts, variable costs will increase as well. In *Exhibit 9.5* this is illustrated by the line item for cost of sales: food. As a general rule, when revenue increases above budgeted amounts, the dollar amount of fixed cost will not change. In *Exhibit 9.5* this is illustrated by the line items for rent and loan payments.

Note that in the Rain Shower Café example cost of sales: food, as a percentage of revenue, was higher than budgeted—35.0 percent budgeted, 37.9 percent actual. While variable cost dollar amounts increase with increased sales, in this case this variable cost increased beyond what would be expected. The causes should be investigated and corrected.

Exhibit 9.10

Manager's Memo

Suggestive selling is a revenue enhancing strategy whereby servers provide guests opportunities to purchase related or higher-priced products that the guest wants. The purpose of this is to make a larger sale. A common example of suggestive selling happens when a QSR employee asks a guest who has just purchased a hamburger, "Would you like fries with that?"

Suggestive selling can be a powerful strategy that significantly impacts an operation's total sales. In a restaurant or foodservice operation, suggestive selling should maximize guest satisfaction and increase the average sale per guest, resulting in increased profitability. The success of suggestive selling requires that managers employ talented servers with in-depth product knowledge, effective communication skills, and appropriate sales training.

Cost of sales: beverage, as a percentage of revenue, was lower than budgeted—25.0 percent budgeted, 21.2 percent actual. This is a potential problem area because the costs are below expectations. That may indicate the quality of drinks served to guests is below the operation's quality standards because too little alcohol is being used to prepare guests' drinks. It could also mean that the right amount of alcohol is being served but the revenue that should have been generated from the sales has not been collected or secured. In either case, the cause should be investigated and corrected.

In this example, the line item for marketing is one that should be reviewed because its costs are well *above* the amount budgeted. In this example the line item for repair and maintenance is one that should be reviewed because its costs are well *below* the amount budgeted. That may mean the operation did not experience any equipment breakdowns or that needed repairs or preventive maintenance on equipment is not being performed. Again, it is the job of the manager to investigate each significant expense variance, determine its cause, and take appropriate corrective action.

Potential corrective actions related to higher than budgeted expense levels can be varied:

Exhibit 9.11

- Assess increases in variable expense to ensure they are in line with increased revenue.
- If variable expense related to food and beverage products exceed what is expected by increased revenue:
  - Review purchasing procedures.
  - Review receiving procedures (*Exhibit 9.11*).
  - Review storage procedures.
  - Review production procedures.
  - Review portioning procedures.
  - Review service procedures.
- Assess accounts payable (AP) procedures.
- Assess all revenue security procedures.
- Assess accounts receivable (AR) procedures.

Potential corrective actions related to lower than budgeted expense levels also can be varied:

- Assess decreases in variable cost areas to determine if they are lower due to lower than budgeted revenue.
- If variable expense reductions related to food and beverage products exceed those expected by reduced revenue:
  - Review purchasing procedures to ensure quality standards are met.
  - Review production procedures to ensure preparation and portion size standards are met.

Assessing Variance in Profit

Variances in budgeted revenue and expense will lead to deviations in an operation's profitability. In *Exhibit 9.5* this is illustrated by the line items for profit/(loss) and net earnings. As shown in *Exhibit 9.5*, the impact on profit of greater than budgeted sales levels of $20,175 was more than offset by above budgeted total controllable expenses of $25,460 and total fixed expenses of $600. The final result was more income, but also a reduction in budgeted profit of $19,885.

Exhibit 9.12 summarizes the impact on profitability of variance in revenue and expense categories.

Potential corrective actions related to lower than budgeted profits can be varied:

- Assess marketing efforts.
- Assess product quality.
- Assess product security programs.
- Assess service quality.
- Assess all revenue security programs.

Taking Corrective Action

After problems such as significant variances between planned and expected operating results are identified, they must be managed. Managers use a corrective action process to do so. Effective managers recognize that it is their responsibility to address problems that hinder the attainment of financial goals. This philosophy of being in control may seem obvious, but some managers think they are already doing the best they can and it is not possible to improve.

Managers are busy. Therefore, they must address the most important concerns first. Which is more important, enhancing revenue or controlling costs? Is it a higher priority to address food costs, labor costs, or another type of

Exhibit 9.12

IMPACT OF OPERATING VARIANCE ON PROFITS

Area of Variance	Operating Variance	Impact on Profits
Revenue	Exceeds budget	Increases
Revenue	Below budget	Decreases
Expenses	Exceeds budget	Decreases
Expenses	Below budget	Increases

MANAGER'S MATH

OPEN FOR BUSINESS

A manager had the following operating budget and achieved the actual results shown. Calculate the variance and variance percentage for each line item. Then answer the questions that follow.

Sales	Budget	Actual	Variance	Percentage
Food	$500,000	$550,000	_____	_____
Beverage	$150,000	$165,000	_____	_____
Total sales	$650,000	$715,000	_____	_____
Total controllable expense	$450,000	$495,000	_____	_____
Total fixed expense	$135,000	$135,000	_____	_____
Profit (Loss)	$ 65,000	$ 85,000	_____	_____

1. What is your assessment of this operation's expense control performance during this budget period?

2. Why are managers who are skilled at controlling expenses in such high demand in the hospitality industry?

(Answers:)

Sales	Budget	Actual	Variance	Percentage
Food	$500,000	$550,000	$50,000	10%
Beverage	$150,000	$165,000	$15,000	10%
Total sales	$650,000	$715,000	$65,000	10%
Total controllable expense	$450,000	$495,000	$45,000	10%
Total fixed expense	$135,000	$135,000	$ 0	0%
Profit (Loss)	$ 65,000	$ 85,000	$20,000	30.8%

1. Variable expense control was excellent in this period. 2. They are in high demand because when revenue increases and variable costs are well controlled, profit increases can be substantial.

cost? If these questions were asked of students on a class exam, the correct answer would be all of the above. However, busy managers must set priorities.

Exhibit 9.13 gives some suggestions about how to do this.

Exhibit 9.13

PRIORITIZING PROBLEMS: ASSESS THE ECONOMIC IMPACT

A. Would you rather increase revenue or decrease variable costs? (*Answer:* Ideally both!) What about in the following example?

Priority: To increase revenue by $2,000 or to decrease variable costs by $2,000.

Assume	Current Data	Increase Revenue by $2,000	Decrease Variable Costs by $2,000
Revenues	$12,000	$14,000	$12,000
Variable costs (70%)	(8,400)	(9,800)	(6,400)
Fixed costs (20%)	(2,400)	(2,400)	(2,400)
"Profit"	$1,200	$1,800	$3,200

Increasing revenue by $2,000 yields only a $600 increase in profit ($1,800 – $1,200); decreasing variable costs by $2,000 increased profit by $2,000 ($3,200 – $1,200).

B. Which of the following costs would you first "manage"?

  (*Answer:* Hopefully both at the same time!) In other words, which is the priority?

	Budget	Actual	Difference
Food cost	34%	36%	(2%)
Beverage cost	26%	31%	(5%)

At first examination, it appears "obvious" that beverage costs represent the biggest problem: a 5 percent variance from expected costs compared to only 2 percent variance for food costs. However, after we learn more details, our opinion of the largest problem changes:

Food	Actual	Budget	Difference	Beverage	Actual	Budget	Difference
Food revenue	$450,000	$450,000		Beverage revenue	$105,000	$105,000	
Food cost %	36%	34%		Beverage cost %	31%	26%	
Food cost	$162,000	$153,000	($9,000)	Beverage cost	$32,550	$27,300	($5,250)

As seen, a 2 percent variance in food costs represents $9,000 in higher-than-expected costs (and lower profits). By contrast, a 5 percent variance in beverage costs results in $5,250 in higher-than-expected costs (and lower profits). Clearly, after any "quick fix" with the beverage operation, the manager's attention must be directed to food control activities.

After managers have determined a problem to address, they can employ a decision-making process to address the issue.

Exhibit 9.14 shows an example of how managers can reduce problems identified in the financial analysis process.

Exhibit 9.14

EXAMPLE OF DECISION-MAKING PROCESS

Step	Examples
Step 1: Define the problem.	Revenue is below budget because average sale per guest has been declining for each of the last three months.
Step 2: Determine solution alternatives.	• Use suggestive selling. • Evaluate the menu to determine if changes can increase revenues. • Check for errors in procedures to calculate customer check average. • Check for revenue theft by employees.
Step 3: Evaluate solution alternatives.	• Manager does not observe suggestive selling; training is needed to implement suggestive selling program. • Menu is recently redesigned; customer counts are up slightly. • An auditor has found no bookkeeping problems that suggest an error or employee theft.
Step 4: Select the best alternative.	Implement a suggestive selling program.
Step 5: Implement the alternative.	Train service staff; implement a contest, such as all servers achieving a specified average sale per guest win a prize.
Step 6: Evaluate the solution.	Determine how much the average sale per guest increases after the suggestive selling program is implemented.

Some basic principles are used in the steps shown in *Exhibit 9.14*:

1. **Define the problem:** Sometimes problems such as lower revenue levels and increasing costs are obvious. At other times it is more difficult to identify the revenue or cost-related problem. Consider the view of some managers that customers are spending less because of a slowed overall economy in their operating areas. If this is the case, there may be components of this issue that make it hard to specifically identify the problem.

   To help define the problem, some managers ask themselves, What would the situation be like in the absence of the problem? Their answer helps suggest a situation different from the present and allows them to think about the problem in a different way. Unfortunately, in the busy world of restaurant and foodservice operations, problems do not occur one at a time. Instead, managers are often faced with several or more problems at the same time, and must prioritize their response to them.

2. **Determine solution alternatives:** What can be done to address the problem? The manager should have some answers, but the employees may as well. For example, a problem with increased costs due to rising prices paid for ingredients may be addressed by the manager, servers, cooks, or others who can provide potential solutions.

3. **Evaluate solution alternatives:** Factors including costs, ease of implementation, and impact on other work processes can help evaluate the solution alternatives.

4. **Select the best alternative:** Often, the best solution involves using aspects of several possible alternatives generated in step 2.

5. **Implement the alternative:** Changes in the food and beverage items purchased, employee training (*Exhibit 9.15*), purchase of necessary equipment or tools, and changes in work procedures are among the tactics that may be useful to implement the chosen alternative.

6. **Evaluate the solution:** If the manager has considered what the situation would be like if the problem no longer existed (step 1), this step becomes easier. Sometimes, solutions help but do not totally resolve the problem. In other words, it may still exist, but as a result of the decision-making process, its impact is reduced. If the problem is still significant relative to others, the manager may repeat the decision-making process to identify and implement other solution alternatives. This could reduce the problem's impact still further.

Exhibit 9.15

In many cases, the corrective actions that must be taken to address budgetary and financial issues are people related as much as they are numbers related. This is because responses to variations from budget may call for significant changes in operations. Examples include specific employee actions required to reduce food waste, or changed work schedules to lessen labor costs. When that is the case, managers may face employee resistance to the needed changes.

Employees who are used to doing something one way may resist changes in procedures. Their response to proposed change may be "We have always done it this way!" or "We have never done it that way!" They may be uncertain about how they will be affected by the change, and they may not want to take time, if necessary, to learn new ways of doing things. They may also be concerned about the closer supervision that may come as the change is implemented and evaluated. If this human nature to resist change is understood and addressed, the manager is more likely to be successful in the change effort.

There are a number of tactics a manager can use to overcome resistance to change. All will be more effective if there is a history of involving employees and explaining, defending, and justifying why the change is necessary. It is also helpful if the manager has historically been right. That is, situations have usually been better after a change than before it was made.

There are specific actions managers can take to help reduce resistance to change:

- Explain the circumstances, such as changes in revenue or expense assumptions that created the need for change.
- Involve employees in the decision-making process used to address the change. Seeking employee input prior to making changes makes the implementation of corrective actions easier. This is because the decision involved the employees rather than just the manager.
- Inform employees in advance about changes that will impact them.
- Select an appropriate time to implement the change. Trying something new during an extremely busy shift is never a good idea.
- Share past successes. Review related changes that have benefited the employees and the organization.
- Reward employees for sharing ideas in the decision-making process that benefit the restaurant and the employees.

Managers who truly believe in the quality management process will be leading their staff members through a plan of **continuous quality improvement (CQI)**. This involves ongoing efforts to better meet or exceed the customers' expectations and thus achieve the financial goals of the operation. Managers define ways to perform work with better, less costly, and faster methods (*Exhibit 9.16*).

They recognize that, regardless of how small a change may be, the operation is better. Any change that helps the organization better meet its mission and goals is good. Employees working within a CQI environment will be conditioned for change. They will look forward to it because they know its benefits, and will be active participants in it. Another advantage is that CQI typically works from the bottom up, since the employees closest to the situation are likely to have improvement suggestions.

Exhibit 9.16

REVISING THE BUDGET

Just as managers initiate needed operational changes in response to the financial performance of their operations, they should consider their budgets to be active and sometimes changing documents. Budgets should be regularly reviewed and modified as new and better information replaces that which was available when the original budget was developed. This is especially true when the new data significantly affect the revenue and expense assumptions used to create the budget.

The budget should be reviewed as actual operating results become available. It should also be reviewed anytime it is believed that the basic assumptions upon which it is based are unfounded. For example, suppose an establishment's owner employs 25 full-time staff members. Each staff member is covered under a group health insurance policy. Last year, the owner, who pays 50 percent of the insurance cost, paid $300 per month for each employee. The total monthly cost of the insurance contribution is calculated as follows:

25	×	$300	=	$7,500
Total employees		**Cost per employee**		**Total monthly cost**

When the budget was developed, the manager estimated a 5 percent increase in health insurance premiums. If the premiums actually rose 10 percent, employee benefit costs will be greater than projections each month. The manager or owner faces several choices.

- Modify the budget.

- Change the amount contributed to stay within the budget.

- Reduce health insurance benefits or coverage to stay within the costs allocated.

Regardless of the decision, the budget, if affected, should be modified. *Exhibit 9.17* shows some situations that illustrate why operating budgets may need to be modified.

When considering revisions to their operating budgets, managers first review their actual operating results. They then calculate variance amounts and percentages as illustrated earlier in this chapter. After reviewing any relevant historical or industry data, managers must review their assumptions in two areas: revenue and expenses. These areas directly affect budgets and the profitable operation of the businesses.

Exhibit 9.17

FACTORS THAT MAY REQUIRE BUDGET REVISIONS

- The opening or closing of a major and direct competitor
- A significant and long-term or permanent increase or decrease in the price of major menu ingredients
- Significant and unanticipated increases in fixed expenses such as utilities, insurance, or taxes
- A management change that significantly alters the skill level of the management team
- Unplanned road construction that significantly affects customers' abilities to reach the restaurant
- Natural disasters, such as floods, hurricanes, or severe weather that significantly affects forecasted revenues
- A significant change in the establishment's operating hours
- Permanent changes in service style that appreciably affect labor costs
- Changes in financial statement formats and/or bases for allocation of financial resources
- Significant changes in the prices of controllable expenses
- Changes in fixed expenses
- The loss of especially skilled or talented employees

Revenue Assumptions

When it is the manager's assumption that the number of guests to be served in a budget period, or the amount to be spent per guest in the period, will vary significantly from previous estimates, a revision of the revenue budget may be appropriate. Forecasting revenue for a revised budget is not an exact process, but to increase accuracy several steps can be taken:

1. **Review revenue records from previous years:** If a restaurant or foodservice operation has been open for an extended period of time, its revenue history may help predict future revenue levels. If it is a newly opened operation, records from previous years will not be available.

2. **Evaluate internal changes:** Some activities undertaken by the managers or staff can affect revenue projections. Consider, for example, a significant change in the type, quantity, or direction of marketing efforts. Improvements in server training programs can be a source of potential revenue increases. This is because suggestive selling efforts can lead to labor cost reductions due to increased productivity. Other activities such as a renovation may affect seating capacity, and create times when the operation will be disrupted.

3. **Evaluate external changes:** New establishments that open and others that close in the same market can impact revenues, as can road improvements or construction. Also, economic downturns can reduce what potential customers can spend during fewer dining-out occasions.

4. **Estimate the impact of selling price changes:** Some managers think an increase in menu selling prices automatically results in revenue increases. However, if menu prices increase and the number of guests served decrease, revenues will decline. This is due to the law of supply and demand—economic beliefs about the supply of an item and its price relative to its demand. Often, as the price of an item increases, the demand for the item decreases. Similarly, as the price of an item goes down, the demand for the item increases.

5. **Estimate the effect of menu changes on revenues:** Some managers expand or revise menu offerings to increase revenues. Sometimes these efforts are successful, and long-term increases in revenues are achieved. In other cases, however, short-term increases in revenues are achieved, but longer-term revenues do not increase. This is because the same customers who had previously purchased other menu items purchase the new items.

It is not possible to forecast a restaurant or foodservice operation's exact revenues for a budget period. With practice and good information, however, managers can revise revenue budget forecasts to be very close to the actual results that will be achieved.

MANAGER'S MATH

OPEN FOR BUSINESS

A manager is considering the relationship between increased revenue, fixed expenses, and profits at various estimated revenue levels. Calculate the following:

• The variable expense at each revenue estimate level

• The profit achieved at each revenue estimate level

• The profit percentage achieved at each revenue estimate level

Then answer the questions that follow.

Revenue Estimate	70% Variable Expense	Fixed Expense	Profit	Profit Percentage
$ 75,000	_____	$20,000	_____	_____
100,000	_____	20,000	_____	_____
125,000	_____	20,000	_____	_____
150,000	_____	20,000	_____	_____

1. What is the impact of increased revenue on variable expenses?

2. Why do managers seek to carefully control variable expenses?

3. What is the impact of increased revenue on profits?

4. What is the impact of increased revenue on the profit percentage achieved by an operation?

(Answers:)

Revenue Estimate	70% Variable Expense	Fixed Expense	Profit	Profit Percentage
$75,000	$52,500	$20,000	$2,500	3.3%
100,000	70,000	20,000	10,000	10.0
125,000	87,500	20,000	17,500	14.0
150,000	105,000	20,000	25,000	16.7

1. As revenue increases, variable expenses increases. 2. They seek to control variable expenses because as revenue increases and variable expense is controlled, profit amounts increase dramatically; 3. As revenue increases, profits increase in a disproportionally large amount; 4. If variable costs are controlled, profit percentage increases along with increases in revenue.)

Expense Assessment

In nearly all cases, initial operating budgets are prepared using both estimated and known costs. Variable costs, for example, are estimated based on the amount of revenue that will be achieved. These costs are also estimated based on known prices to be paid. To illustrate, consider the manager who assumes that 15 percent of the total revenue generated in an operation will be spent on meat products. If the manager estimates future sales of $100,000, the estimated amount to be spent for meat would be $15,000. If sales forecasts increase, the amount spent for meat will increase in direct proportion. Changes in variable expenses of this type are the result of any modification to the revenue budget.

The amount spent for variable expense can also change based on prices paid for products and services. Returning to the previous example, if the manager learned that the price of meat would increase by 20 percent during the budget period, the new amount to be budgeted for meat would be $18,000. That amount would be calculated as follows:

$$\underset{\substack{\text{Original} \\ \text{amount}}}{\$15,000} + \underset{\text{Increase amount}}{(\$15,000 \times 0.2)} = \underset{\substack{\text{Revised} \\ \text{amount}}}{\$18,000}$$

Manager's assumptions about variable costs in key expense areas such a food, beverages, and labor costs should be carefully assessed for their potential to require a budget modification. When changes in noncontrollable fixed costs become known, however, these changes should result in the immediate modification of the operating budget.

Profit Forecast Modification

In most cases, changes in revenue forecasts and expense forecasts will result in modifications of profit forecasts. Recall that the accounting formula is:

$$\text{Revenue} - \text{Expenses} = \text{Profits}$$

Stated another way, the accounting formula is:

$$\underset{\substack{\text{Guests} \\ \text{served}}}{} \times \underset{\substack{\text{Amount spent} \\ \text{per guest}}}{} - \left(\underset{\text{expenses}}{\text{Variable}} + \underset{\text{expenses}}{\text{Fixed}} \right) = \text{Profits}$$

Stated in this way, it is easy to see that modifications to projected profits may need to be initiated. This is in response to changing management assumptions about each component of the accounting formula:

- Guests served
- Amount spent per guest
- Variable expenses
- Fixed expenses

After sales trends and expense trends have been analyzed and their impact on profits has been assessed, managers modify their operating budgets. If the manager is also the owner of the operation, the modified budget will be put in place immediately. In other cases, the managers recommended budget modification will be submitted to a supervisor for approval.

In most cases, the supervisor will want to know the reason for the recommended budget change. He or she may also want to know what corrective actions the manager has taken, or will take, in response to them. When these questions are addressed appropriately, the manager's recommended budget modifications will likely be approved.

SUMMARY

1. **Explain the purposes for comparing budgeted results to actual operating results.**

   Managers conduct reviews of budgeted results to actual operating results for several reasons. These include ensuring that revenue goals are being achieved and that expenses are being kept in line with projections or standards. The review can also help ensure that guest service standards are being met. In addition, a thorough review of actual performance can help managers determine if their profit goals are being achieved and what must be done if they are not. If appropriate, the review can also help identify areas in which future budgets should be modified.

2. **Describe the way managers calculate budget variances and budget variance percentages.**

   Managers use two basic formulas to determine the size of budget variances. To calculate the dollar amount of variance, managers use the formula: Actual results − Budgeted results = Variance. To determine budget percentage variances, managers use the formula: Variance ÷ Budgeted results = Variance percentage. Both the actual amount and the percentage amount of variance must be carefully examined if managers are to identify areas of significant budget variation.

OPEN FOR BUSINESS

RESTAURANT TECHNOLOGY

Tech-savvy restaurant and foodservice managers can make use of many fully automated and easy-to-understand budgeting software programs on the market today. Primarily spreadsheet-based, these specially-developed programs provide instant and accurate reports on an operation's financial performance. These include actual sales-to-date versus budgeted sales-to-date comparisons, by both dollar amounts and percentages.

Additional features include cost of sales analysis and analysis of other variable cost expenditures. The best programs also display labor budget dollar amounts, and actual over- or underbudget tables and charts. They can also provide overall profitability projections based on actual to-date operating performance.

3. **Identify reasons for variation in revenue, expense, and profit line items.**

Reasons for variations in revenue include the serving of more or fewer guests. In addition, the size of the average sale per guest directly affects revenue levels.

Increases in revenue will result in increases in variable expense categories. Reasons for variation in all expense categories include changes in the price of products or services purchased, as well as shortcomings in expense management.

Because profits are the result of the formula: Revenue − Expenses = Profits, any variations in revenue and/or in expenses will directly affect an operation's ability to generate its budgeted profits.

4. **State factors that could result in revenue or expense-related budget revisions.**

Revenue is determined by the number of customers served and the amount each guest buys. When permanent changes in the estimated number of guests to be served occur, revenue budgets should be revised. If the amount spent by each guest changes, revenue budgets should also be revised.

Variable expense budgets are revised in response to permanent changes in the cost of goods or services purchased by an operation. Variable expense budgets may also require adjustment if changes in menus or service levels result in significant operating cost differences. Fixed expense budgets should be revised as changes in fixed expense amounts to be paid are known.

5. **State factors that could result in profit-related budget revisions.**

Profits are the amount remaining from revenue when all operating expenses have been subtracted. As a result, profit budgets should be revised any time revisions are made to revenue budgets, expense budgets, or both.

In general, when revenue budgets are reduced, budgeted profits will be reduced. When revenue budgets are increased, profit budgets will likely be increased, despite the fact that variable expense budget amounts will be increased as well. This is because increases in revenue result in decreases in fixed expenses when calculated as a percentage of sales.

APPLICATION EXERCISE

A manager is preparing a revenue budget for next month.

The following is the manager's current month actual operating results.

ACTUAL OPERATING RESULTS CURRENT MONTH

Revenue Source	Number of Guests	Average Sale per Guest	Sales
Restaurant	3,492	$ 20.50	$ 71,586
Lounge	515	12.00	6,180
Banquet room	388	28.50	11,058
Total	**4,395**	**$20.21**	**$88,824**

Create the revenue forecast for next month based on the following assumptions:

A. Restaurant guest counts will be 3,600 with an average sale per guest of $21.00.

B. Lounge guests to be served are estimated at 525 with a 10 percent increase in average sale per guest.

C. The banquet room will serve 425 customers and generate $12,750 in sales.

NEXT MONTH BUDGET

Revenue Source	Number of Guests	Average Sale per Guest	Sales
Restaurant			
Lounge			
Banquet room			
Total			

1. What will be the manager's revenue forecast for next month?

2. What will be the manager's average sale per guest forecast for next month?

3. What is the overall percentage increase in the revenue forecast when compared to the current month's actual operating results?

4. What are some factors that would cause the manager of an operation to create a sales forecast for the next month that exceeds the operation's current month actual operating results?

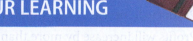

REVIEW YOUR LEARNING

Select the best answer for each question.

1. If an operation experienced a significant negative variance in variable labor costs in an accounting period,

   A. guest service levels would likely have declined in that accounting period.

   B. guest service levels would likely have been improved in that accounting period.

   C. the number of guests served would likely be more than previously estimated.

   D. the average sale per guest would likely be less than previously estimated.

2. If the dollar amount spent for food in an operation is significantly higher than budgeted, but the operation's food cost percentage is exactly as budgeted, then

   A. revenue is below budgeted levels.

   B. revenue is above budgeted levels.

   C. food waste in the operation is significant.

   D. the prices paid for food have increased significantly.

3. An operation projected it would serve 10,000 guests at an average sale per guest of $11 in a specific budget period. In that period, the operation actually served 11,000 guests and achieved revenue of $100,000. What was the operation's variance in revenue for the period?

   A. $1,000
   B. $1,100
   C. $10,000
   D. $11,000

4. An operation budgeted $8,000 for labor costs. In the actual performance, labor costs were $10,000. What was the percentage variance in labor costs for the period?

   A. 20%
   B. 25%
   C. 30%
   D. 35%

5. The two factors that directly impact an operation's revenue generation are the average sale per guest and

   A. the operation's menu prices.
   B. the number of seats in the operation.
   C. the weekly hours the operation is open.
   D. the number of guests served by the operation.

6. An operation served more customers than it forecast and met its beverage cost percentage target. What will be true about the dollars budgeted for beverages and the actual cost of beverages for this operation?

   A. The difference between budgeted and actual beverage costs will be zero.
   B. The dollars spent for beverages will be less than the budgeted amount.
   C. The dollars spent for beverages will exceed the budgeted amount.
   D. The dollars spent for beverages will equal the budgeted amount.

7. What happens to fixed cost as a percentage of sales when revenues exceed forecasted levels?

   A. Fixed cost as a percentage of revenue goes down.
   B. Fixed cost as a percentage of revenue goes up.
   C. Fixed cost as a percentage of revenue stays the same.
   D. Fixed cost as a percentage of revenue increases in direct proportion to the increase in revenue.

8. What would be the impact on the budget of a projected increase in the number of guests served?

   A. Increased sales and increased fixed expense
   B. Increased sales and increased variable expense
   C. Increased sales and decreased variable expense
   D. Increased sales and decreased profits

9. A manager originally budgeted $85,500 in sales with a 38% food cost target. The revenue budgeted is revised upward to $100,000. What would be the amount projected for food cost in the new budget?

   A. $3,420
   B. $3,800
   C. $34,200
   D. $38,000

10. What would be the impact on profits of an increase in total sales of 10% if variable expenses, as a percentage of total sales, are unchanged?

    A. Profits will be unchanged.
    B. Profits will increase by 10%.
    C. Profits will increase by less than 10%.
    D. Profits will increase by more than 10%.

FIELD PROJECT

Visit a commercial or noncommercial restaurant or foodservice operation. Ask the manager some questions about the operation's budget and the operation's actual operating performance.

1. Is a formal budget prepared for the operation?

2. Who prepares the budget?

3. When is the budget prepared?

4. For what accounting periods is the budget prepared?

5. How often are actual performance results compared to budgeted results?

6. Who performs the analysis of actual to budgeted results?

7. What factors would be considered before a budget revision would be initiated?

8. Who has the final authority for determining when the operating budget will be revised?

10

Accounting and Finance Issues for Restaurant Owners

CHAPTER LEARNING OBJECTIVES

After completing this chapter, you should be able to:

- Explain the purpose of a balance sheet.

- Describe the three main components of a balance sheet.

- Describe the importance of managing cash flow in restaurant and foodservice operations.

- Explain the process used to prepare a capital budget.

- Discuss the major differences between leasing and buying a capital item.

- Explain the impact of effective tax management and planning.

KEY TERMS

balance sheet, p. 242

book value, p. 243

capital improvement, p. 258

capital items, p. 253

cost–benefit analysis, p. 254

current assets, p. 243

current liabilities, p. 243

current ratio, p. 247

economic study, p. 255

furnishings, fixtures, and equipment (FF&E), p. 253

lease, p. 257

liquidated, p. 248

long-term debt, p. 245

owner's equity ratio, p. 248

payables, p. 245

payback period, p. 255

personal property, p. 257

prepaid expenses, p. 243

rate of return, p. 254

ratio analysis, p. 247

real property, p. 257

return on investment (ROI), p. 254

solvency ratio, p. 248

statement of cash flows, p. 251

tax management, p. 263

tax planning, p. 263

CASE STUDY

"Let's just buy a new catering van," said Steve, the catering manager at the Tea Rose restaurant. "How many times are we going to be late on a setup because the van keeps breaking down?"

Steve was telling Jerri, the general manager of the Tea Rose, that the van used for off-site catering had overheated again. It had to be towed and the set up crew was late getting to the restaurant's most recent catered event. It was not the first time the van had caused trouble.

"It's not in the budget," said Jerri.

"Well, what will we do if it just keeps breaking down?" Steve asked. "It must be in the budget to fix it. We're wasting money and we're making our catering customers unhappy."

"I'll call the owner and let her know what's happening with the van. But money is tight right now. I really don't know what she'll say," replied Jerri.

"If buying one is out of the question," said Steve, "maybe we could rent one. We have four off-site events next week, and I don't think our old van will even make it that long—if its not still in the shop!"

1. Why is it important for restaurant and foodservice owners and managers to plan in advance for large purchases, such as the van replacement requested by Steve?

2. If you were the owner of this operation, what specific questions would you ask Jerri when she presents her request for a new van?

Manager's Memo

Liabilities are the amounts owed to creditors and investors who have provided cash or its equivalent to a business. As a source of funds, creditors and investors allow a business to continue or expand its operations. If creditors and investors are hesitant about their ability to recover invested money, the businesses' chances of securing their future investments will be limited.

Assets, on the other hand, represent the company's use of funds. A business uses cash or other funds provided by creditors and investors to obtain assets. Assets include all things of value that are owned by the business.

Liabilities represent a company's obligations to creditors. Owner's equity represents the owner's funding of the company. In fact, creditors and owners alike are investors in the company. The only real difference is the timeframe in which they expect repayment.

BALANCE SHEETS

Managers are most often interested in the operating results shown on monthly and annual income statements, or P&Ls. Investors and owners of businesses, however, are also interested in additional financial statements. Among the most important of these is the balance sheet. A **balance sheet** reports the assets, liabilities, and owner's equity of a business at a specific point in time. Also called the statement of financial position, the balance sheet provides owners with a variety of information about their businesses that is not found on the income statement:

- Assets owned by the business
- Debts owed by the business
- Cash on hand
- The ability to pay bills in a timely manner
- Owner's equity in the business

The basic purpose of a balance sheet is to provide its readers the information they must have to determine if the business is financially strong and economically efficient. The balance sheet is a snapshot of the company's financial standing at a point in time. The individual entries listed on a balance sheet change from day to day, reflecting the activities of the business. For example, while cash is an asset listed on a balance sheet, the actual amount of cash on hand in an operation will vary daily. This is because each day, guests pay their bills (*Exhibit 10.1*), bank deposits are made, vendors are paid for goods and services, and employees are paid for their work. As a result, analyzing how the balance sheet changes over time helps owners better understand their businesses trends.

Balance Sheet Components

Recall from chapter 1 that accountants use the accounting formula to express the relationship between a business's assets, liabilities, and owner's equity. The accounting formula is shown here:

$$\text{Assets} = \text{Liabilities} + \text{Owner's equity}$$

The components of the balance sheet are designed to provide detailed information about the areas listed to the left and to the right of the equal sign in the accounting formula. As a result, the name balance sheet is appropriate, because both sides of the accounting formula must always be equal, or in balance.

A balance sheet will contain the same basic information regardless of a company's size, or even the number of units

Exhibit 10.1

it operates. However, balance sheets can and do vary in the amount of detail provided. A balance sheet should contain the level of detailed desired by a company's owners or others who may rely on the information to make important decisions.

Professional accountants typically assist owners in making decisions about the amount of detail that is appropriate for their business's balance sheets. In all cases, the balance sheet consists of three main categories or sections:

- Assets
- Liabilities
- Owner's equity

When constructing a balance sheet, a company's assets and liabilities are listed in a specific order. Assets are listed in descending order, with cash and assets most like cash listed first. Liabilities are listed in the order in which the debts are due. Those due soonest are listed first. **Current liabilities** are those liabilities that must be paid within the next 12 months. Those liabilities owed to owners, known as owner's equity, that may or may not be paid out are listed last.

Exhibit 10.2 on the following page is an example of a balance sheet for an establishment owned by a partnership. It is prepared according to recommendations contained in the Uniform System of Accounts for Restaurants (USAR).

The methods used to perform a detailed analysis of balance sheets are beyond the scope of this book. However, some terms used in a balance sheet are important for all owners and managers to understand:

- **Current assets:** Cash and assets that will be converted to cash in one year or less.

- **Accounts receivable (AR):** Money due from customers as a result of selling inventory or services on credit.

- **Inventory:** An itemized list of goods and products, their on-hand quantity, and their monetary value.

- **Prepaid expenses:** When cash is used to purchase a good or service, the benefits of which will be realized or received within the current year; for example, the money paid at the beginning of the year for an annual insurance policy.

- **Property and equipment:** Physical assets that have life in excess of one year, including all land, buildings, equipment, furniture, dishware, and kitchen utensils owned by the business.

- **Accumulated depreciation:** Also known as the **book value**, this is calculated as the purchase price of an asset, less the accumulated depreciation (the sum of the amounts charged because the asset will wear out over its lifetime).

THINK ABOUT IT . . .

In what sense are vendors, who sell on credit items that managers need, also investors in a business? What would make vendors want to continue to invest in an operation? What could make them stop?

THINK ABOUT IT . . .

What are some parties that do not own a business who would be interested in details about its strength in a balance sheet? What level of detail do you think these parties would want?

Exhibit 10.2	

SAMPLE BALANCE SHEET: PARTNERSHIP

Sample Balance Sheet: Partnership

ASSETS		LIABILITIES AND OWNER'S EQUITY	
Current Assets		**Current Liabilities**	
Cash on Hand	$ 1,000	Accounts Payable (AP)	$22,000
Cash in Banks	68,500	Payroll Taxes Payable	5,500
Accounts Receivable (AR)	8,500	Sales Taxes Payable	8,000
Food Inventory	4,000	Gift Cards Payable	4,300
Beverage Inventory	3,500	Accrued Expenses	7,000
Supplies Inventory	2,500	Deposits on Banquets	1,500
Prepaid Expenses	17,000	Current Portion Long-Term Debt	18,200
Total Current Assets	**$105,000**	**Total Current Liabilities**	**$ 66,500**
Property and Equipment		**Due to Owners/Partners**	**$ 85,000**
Leasehold Improvements	$225,000	**Long-Term Debt Net of Current Portion**	**$118,500**
Furnishings, Fixtures, and Equipment	80,000		
Tableware, Kitchen Utensils	5,500	**Total Liabilities**	**$270,000**
Less: Accumulated Depreciation	(30,500)		
Total Property and Equipment— Net	**$280,000**	**Owner's Equity (Partnership)**	
		Partner 1	$45,000
Other Assets		Partner 2	45,000
		Partner 3	45,000
Cost of Liquor License	$ 20,000	Partner 4	5,000
Lease and Utility Deposits	5,000		
Total Other Assets	**$ 25,000**	**Total Owner's Equity**	**$140,000**
TOTAL ASSETS	**$410,000**	**TOTAL LIABILITIES AND OWNER'S EQUITY**	**$410,000**

- **Total other assets:** Assets that are not cash, property, or equipment.
- **Current liabilities:** Debts owed by the company that must be repaid within one year.
- **Long-term debt:** The portion of a long-term loan that does not have to be paid within the next year.
- **Current portion of long-term debt:** The principal portion of a long-term loan that is due within the next 12 months.
- **Total liabilities:** All money owed by the company that must be repaid.
- **Owner's equity:** The value of a company's assets minus its liabilities.

To better use and analyze balance sheets, it is important to understand each component:

- Assets
- Liabilities
- Owner's equity

ASSETS

Assets are all the things of value that are owned by a business. Cash is the asset listed first on the balance sheet. Other assets are listed in the order in which they could most easily be turned into cash. Cash includes all cashier banks and petty cash funds on hand, as well as any cash held in the company's bank accounts.

Current assets, which include cash and those assets that are most likely to be turned into cash in one year or less, are listed first. As a result, a company's assets are listed on the balance sheet in a specific order:

- Cash
- Accounts receivable (AR)
- Inventories, to be sold for cash
- Prepaid expenses
- Property and equipment, used to generate cash
- Other assets

LIABILITIES

Managers must list the operations' assets and liabilities on a balance sheet to give owners the detailed information needed to assess the operation's financial standing (*Exhibit 10.3*). Liabilities are often called **payables**. Current liabilities also include the amount of deposits guests have put down for meals or events that have not yet taken place. **Long-term debt** is any obligation, or loan, that will be paid back in a period longer than 12 months. It can be owed to investors, banks, or other lenders.

Exhibit 10.3

RESTAURANT TECHNOLOGY

Software for the preparation of balance sheets is one of the most common types on the market. Monthly and annual balance sheet preparation is a good idea for nearly every business, and advanced technology makes their preparation easy.

Owners can save money and spend valuable time operating their business, rather than doing accounting, by using computerized balance sheet programs. Most owners can produce their own balance sheets when they have all of the financial records needed for the sheets' preparation. Regardless, it is always a good idea to have balance sheets and other important financial reports reviewed by a qualified accountant.

MANAGER'S MATH

An establishment owner has $20,000 cash on hand, and additional current assets of $50,000. The value of the property and equipment less accumulated depreciation is $320,000. Other assets are valued at $10,000. The owner has total current liabilities of $70,000 and the owner's balance sheet shows a "Long-term Debt Net of Current Portion" of $210,000.

1. What would the balance sheet show as total assets for this operation?

2. What would the balance sheet show as total liabilities for this operation?

3. What would the balance sheet show as owner's equity for this operation?

(Answers: 1. $400,000; 2. $280,000; 3. $120,000)

OWNER'S EQUITY

The presentation of the owner's equity section of the balance sheet will vary based on the legal entity operating the business. *Exhibit 10.2* shows the form it would take in a partnership with four entities. Hospitality accountants somewhat vary the format of the owner's equity portion of the balance sheet, when the entity that owns the business is a corporation or a sole proprietorship. Regardless of the manner in which owner's equity is presented, the form of a business's balance sheet can be summarized as shown in *Exhibit 10.4*.

Exhibit 10.4	

BALANCE SHEET FORMAT SUMMARY

Business Balance Sheet	
Owns	**Owes**
Cash	Debts that must be paid within one year
Assets that will turn into cash within one year	Debts that will not be paid within one year
Assets that may never be turned into cash	Obligations owed to the owners of the business, known as owner's equity
Total Assets	**Liabilities and Owner's Equity**

READING THE BALANCE SHEET

One convenient way to assess the information gained from reading a balance sheet is by considering the balance sheet's three main parts:

- Assets
- Liabilities
- Owner's equity

Assets

Balance sheet readers must exercise caution when interpreting the information listed in the asset section of a balance sheet. To better understand why, consider the entries Cash on Hand and Cash in Banks shown earlier in *Exhibit 10.2*. In this example, the total available cash is $69,500 ($1,000 cash on hand + $68,500 cash in banks = $69,500 total cash). Note that the number alone does not indicate whether the amount of cash on hand is sufficient to allow the operation to pay its bills as they come due.

In a small operation, $69,500 may be exactly the right amount of cash to have available. In a very large operation, the same $69,500 may not provide sufficient cash for an operation to pay its bills in a timely manner.

Similarly, *Exhibit 10.2* shows the value of food and beverage inventory as $7,500:

Exhibit 10.5

$$\underset{\substack{\text{Food} \\ \text{inventory}}}{\$4,000} + \underset{\substack{\text{Beverage} \\ \text{inventory}}}{\$3,500} = \underset{\substack{\text{Food and beverage} \\ \text{inventory}}}{\$7,500}$$

Again, in some operations this might well be the proper amount of inventory to keep on hand. In other operations, however, it may represent too many, or too few, products in inventory.

The value of assets in an operation should be relative to the size of the business. Therefore, many owners use ratio analysis to gain a better sense of their operation's asset positions. **Ratio analysis** is the comparison of financial information found on the balance sheet, income statement, or other financial statement. Ratio analysis can be complex, but when assessing the asset portion of a balance sheet, the **current ratio** is a useful and easy calculation. The current ratio gives an indication of a business's ability to pay its bills in a reasonable time period (*Exhibit 10.5*). The formula used to compute a current ratio is:

Total current assets ÷ Total current liabilities = Current ratio

Using the information found in *Exhibit 10.2*, the current ratio for this business would be calculated as:

$$\underset{\substack{\text{Total current} \\ \text{assets}}}{\$105,000} \div \underset{\substack{\text{Total current} \\ \text{liabilities}}}{\$66,500} = \underset{\substack{\text{Current} \\ \text{ratio}}}{1.58}$$

A current ratio of 1.58 means this business has $1.58 available to pay each $1.00 of its liabilities that will soon require payment. Acceptable levels of current ratio vary somewhat. As a general rule, the easier it is to turn current assets into cash, the smaller the current ratio could be without cause for concern. For many restaurant and foodservice operations, a 1.58 current ratio would be very acceptable. As the number approaches or falls below 1.00, an owner would need to take a very close look at the business. He or she must determine if cash and inventory levels are sufficient to allow the business to pay its bills as they come due. In addition, some lenders require managers to maintain a minimum current ratio level to maintain favorable loan status.

Liabilities

Liabilities listed on the balance sheet indicate the amount of a business's indebtedness. *Exhibit 10.2* indicates that for this business total liabilities equal $270,000. The amount of a company's liabilities alone may not provide much information to the reader of a balance sheet. For example, $270,000 for a very small business might be a great amount of debt. For a very large business, however, that same amount might indicate a very low level of debt.

OPEN FOR BUSINESS

MANAGER'S MATH

Last year an establishment owner's balance sheet showed $40,000 cash, and additional current assets of $150,000. The operation's current liabilities for the same period were $175,000.

This year the same operation's balance sheet shows current liabilities of $200,000. The operation has $80,000 cash and additional current assets of $190,000.

1. What was the operation's current ratio last year?

2. What is the operation's current ratio this year?

3. What are reasons that might explain this business's change in current ratio?

(Answers: 1. 1.09; 2. 1.35; 3. Student answers will vary, but should indicate profits generated in the prior year and/or an increase in asset values.)

When assessing the liability portion of a balance sheet, the solvency ratio is a useful and easy ratio to calculate. It gives an indication of a business's ability to pay its longer-term financial obligations as they become due. The formula used to compute a solvency ratio is:

Total assets ÷ Total liabilities = Solvency ratio

Using the information found in *Exhibit 10.2*, the solvency ratio for this business would be calculated as:

$410,000	÷	$270,000	=	1.52
Total assets		**Total liabilities**		**Solvency ratio**

The solvency ratio measures the ability of a business to pay its obligations with its assets. To the degree that this number exceeds 1.00, the business has a good chance to sell its assets at values large enough to pay all of its debts. Like the current ratio, some lenders may require a business to maintain a minimum solvency ratio such as 1.5, 2, or even 3, to remain creditworthy.

Owner's Equity

Owner's equity represents the difference between a business's assets and its liabilities. The owner's equity ratio, which for a corporation is called the shareholder's equity ratio, gives an indication of how much the owners of a business would receive in the event the business was liquidated. A company is liquidated when all of its assets are sold and it ceases operations. The formula used to compute the owner's equity ratio is:

Total owner's equity ÷ Total assets = Owner's equity ratio

Using the information found in *Exhibit 10.2*, the owner's equity ratio for this business would be calculated as:

$140,000	÷	$410,000	=	0.341
Total owner's equity		**Total assets**		**Owner's equity ratio**

In this case, the owners would receive $140,000 if the business was liquidated and all assets were sold at their balance sheet values:

$410,000	×	0.341	=	$140,000 (rounded)
Total assets		**Owner's equity ratio**		**Equity remaining after asset liquidation**

If the assets could not be sold at their balance sheet values, owners would, of course, receive less. In either case, the greater the owner's equity ratio, the more owners would receive after all assets were sold. The lower the owner's equity ratio, the less owners would receive after all assets are liquidated.

Every manager wants his or her operation to stay busy serving guests (*Exhibit 10.6*), but being busy is no guarantee that an operation is financially healthy. Balance sheet analysis provides a better idea of the true financial success of a business. Owners prepare and read balance sheets to gain greater insight into businesses and their operations. Using ratios such as those introduced in this chapter is a good way to assess the information in the balance sheet. Note, however, that owners use information from the balance sheet along with other financial documents, such as the income statement and statements related to cash management. Doing so allows owners to gain an understanding of the financial strength of their businesses.

Exhibit 10.6

CASH MANAGEMENT

"Cash is king" is a favorite saying among business owners. It means that the amount of cash (see chapter 5) a business has, and how that cash is managed, is of utmost importance. In fact, the management of cash is one of the most important skills that can be learned by a restaurant or foodservice business owner or manager. While some operations accept only currency as payment for the products they sell, others accept credit cards, debit cards, or checks. Some even extend credit to selected customers in the form of accounts receivable.

Restaurant and foodservice operations use the cash they receive to pay their operating expenses. As a result, the cash held by a business must be sufficient to pay its bills as they are incurred. If expenses consistently exceed revenue, there may not be enough cash available to pay all bills.

Various actions taken by an owner or manager can affect the amount of cash held by a restaurant or foodservice business. Some significant actions that influence the amount of cash available to an operation are shown in *Exhibit 10.7.*

Exhibit 10.7

ACTIONS THAT IMPACT AVAILABLE CASH

Action	Increase Available Cash	Decrease Available Cash
Additional purchases of food or beverage inventories		X
Repayment of long-term or short-term loans		X
Purchases of supplies, equipment, or other assets		X
Increase in accounts receivable (AR)		X
Decrease in accounts payable (AP)		X
Loans are obtained	X	
Food or beverage inventories are reduced in size	X	
Assets are sold	X	
Decrease in accounts receivable (AR)	X	
Increase in accounts payable (AP)	X	

It is important to recognize that, in the short term, it is possible for a business to lose cash through operating activities but maintain adequate cash levels through borrowing. This can be the case, for example, with a new business that is just getting started. In the long-term, however, most business owners must make sure that operating activities produce sufficient cash to pay the operation's normal operating expenses before depreciation expenses.

When a business generates more cash than is needed to pay its operating expenses, the owners of the business can use the excess cash for other purposes. These include expanding the business, purchasing new equipment, or paying long-term loans that were obtained to start the business. These may also include cash payments to the owners, partners, or stockholders of the operation.

If a business consistently generates less cash than is needed to pay its operating expenses, the owners of the business may be able to borrow money or sell assets. It is not realistic to assume, however, that a business that does not generate cash will be able to continue selling assets or borrowing money indefinitely.

Owners must assess the ideal amount of cash that should be kept on hand. Some factors that can influence this include the average size of food and beverage purchases, the size and frequency of payrolls, the amount of accounts receivable owed to the business, and the frequency of large annual payments that may be difficult to pay without additional cash reserves.

Many actions can affect cash flowing into and out of a business. One critical financial document regularly prepared for owners is the statement of cash flows. The **statement of cash flows** is a summary of the changes, or flows, in cash available to a business during a designated accounting period.

There are three activities that directly affect overall cash flow, and the statement of cash flows details each one:

1. **Operating activities:** This includes the cash generated from sales and the expenses incurred to generate the sales. When sales exceed expenses, operating activities will generate cash, causing a cash inflow to the business. When expenses exceed revenues, cash levels will be reduced, causing an outflow of cash (see *Exhibit 10.8*).

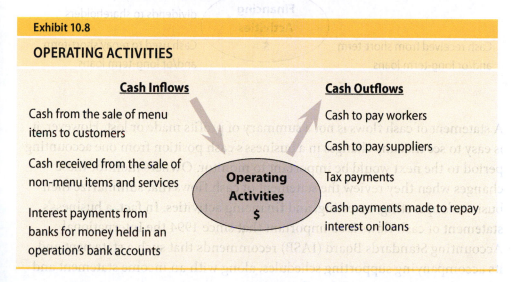

Exhibit 10.8

OPERATING ACTIVITIES

Cash Inflows	**Cash Outflows**
Cash from the sale of menu items to customers	Cash to pay workers
	Cash to pay suppliers
Cash received from the sale of non-menu items and services	Tax payments
Interest payments from banks for money held in an operation's bank accounts	Cash payments made to repay interest on loans

Operating Activities $

2. **Investing activities:** When business assets, such as land, buildings, or equipment, are purchased for cash, the amount of available cash is reduced. When assets are sold for cash, cash levels increase (see *Exhibit 10.9*).

Exhibit 10.9

INVESTING ACTIVITIES

Cash Inflows	**Cash Outflows**
Cash from the sale of business assets such as furnishings and equipment	Cash to buy business assets such as furnishings and equipment
Cash from the sale of marketable securities	Cash to buy marketable securities
Cash collected from the repayment of loans made to others	Cash used to make loans to others

Investing Activities $

3. **Loan or financing activities:** When loans are received by a business, its cash levels increase. As loans are repaid, cash levels will decline (see *Exhibit 10.10*).

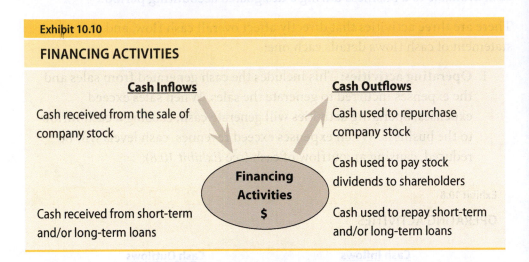

Exhibit 10.10

FINANCING ACTIVITIES

Cash Inflows	Cash Outflows
Cash received from the sale of company stock	Cash used to repurchase company stock
	Cash used to pay stock dividends to shareholders
Cash received from short-term and/or long-term loans	Cash used to repay short-term and/or long-term loans

A statement of cash flows is not a summary of profits made or lost. However, it is easy to see that any changes in a business's cash position from one accounting period to the next would be important to monitor. Owners monitor these changes when they review the statement of cash flows that summarize their business's operating, investing, and financing activities. In fact, a business's statement of cash flows is so important that since 1994 the International Accounting Standards Board (IASB) recommends that such a statement and its accompanying supporting schedules, along with an income statement and a balance sheet, be created for all companies.

THE IMPORTANCE OF CAPITAL BUDGETING

Every operation will have spending needs that fall outside its daily costs of operation. At times, major purchases, such as those for replacement equipment or facility repairs, are necessary just to keep the operation in business. Other times, an operation might need to spend money on large projects, like remodeling or expansion. Such work can be costly, but it can help an operation maintain its competitive edge. Improvements and upgrades that are carefully planned and budgeted for can help an operation realize its profit potential. They can also help the operation avoid becoming obsolete in the marketplace.

How do owners plan for this spending? How does the owner or manager ensure that these major expenses do not negatively affect the operation's income statement? The answers to these questions lie in the effective planning and use of a capital budget.

A capital budget (see chapter 4) is a spending plan specifically for major purchases that will be used over a long period of time. Such expensive purchases are often referred to as **furnishings, fixtures, and equipment (FF&E)** items. FF&E items are also known as capital items. **Capital items** often require financial commitment that extends into the future. Generally, if the item being purchased is expected to last beyond one year, it would be considered a capital item. Many FF&E items, such as a gas range (*Exhibit 10.11*), are considered capital items because they often require a financial commitment that extends over a long period of time. Operations may specify actual limits for categorizing an item as a capital item. For example, any purchase greater than $500, or greater than $5,000, might be a guideline.

It is important to note the difference between items included on the capital budget versus items that fall into the operating budget. A capital budget does not include day-to-day operating expenses such as food, labor, or rent. Capital spending is not reported on an operation's income statement. This is because the substantial costs of many capital items could easily cause the profitability reported on that statement to be skewed.

Exhibit 10.11

Preparing the Capital Budget

Preparing a capital budget is a fairly straightforward process. However, the more careful effort that is made during this process, the more efficient the budget will be. There are three essential steps in creating a capital budget:

- Assessing capital needs
- Evaluating identified needs
- Prioritizing and justifying needs

A capital budget that has not gone through the important steps of analysis, prioritizing, and planning for the future runs the risk of being inadequate.

ASSESSING CAPITAL NEEDS

The first thing managers must do when creating a capital budget is to evaluate the operation to determine what capital needs exist. *Exhibit 10.12* lists some sample questions that managers should ask when evaluating the capital needs at their operation. The process of performing this evaluation results in a wish list of capital items for the operation.

Exhibit 10.12

ASSESSING CAPITAL NEEDS

Capital Category	Questions to Ask
Furnishings and fixtures	What repairs or replacements need to be made to furniture, such as chairs, tables, or countertops?
	Does anything require professional cleaning or replacement, such as drapery or carpeting?
Equipment	Has any equipment become obsolete or significantly behind in technology?
	Are there equipment pieces that are not running efficiently and/or need frequent repair?
	Can current equipment keep up with forecasted production volumes?

REAL MANAGER

WOULD YOU INVEST IN THIS?

While I was president of one brand, there were several key initiatives that we focused on to grow the business. When I first took over, there was very little discipline within the team as to strategic planning. There was no proper analysis of strategy, goals, benchmarks, or the intended ROI.

Seeing this, I asked my financial analyst to identify these basics for a new project. He couldn't. So, I asked him to complete this analysis (working with the person within the operating team running the project) before I would agree to continue to fund it. I told the team members that after they were done with the analysis, they should come to me and give me a recommendation on whether or not we should move forward with the project—as if they were investing their own money in it. The analysis showed a negative ROI and lots of wasted resources. The team members were not interested in investing their own money in the project, and the company should not have either. We canceled the project, shifting the resources to projects that had a much greater ROI and overall benefit.

EVALUATING IDENTIFIED NEEDS

To address the capital needs of the operation, managers should compare several purchase options, as the best option is often not immediately clear. Once a list of capital needs has been prepared, each item on the list should be carefully evaluated in terms of a **cost–benefit analysis** and probably prioritized. A cost–benefit analysis examines the cost of purchasing an item in relationship to its potential cost savings. **Return on investment (ROI)** is a measurement of the financial benefits of a purchase as well. In other words, these analyses involve how much is saved or earned in the long run by making the purchase. This information helps an owner or management team make capital purchases that result in the most financial benefit to the operation. There are several options for performing cost–benefit analysis and ROI evaluations.

One of the most common ways to evaluate ROI is to compare the cost of an item in relationship to its potential cost savings. One technique used to evaluate return on investment is to calculate the anticipated rate of return. The **rate of return** is the relationship between the savings (or additional income) and the amount expended on the item. A formula is used to calculate rate of return:

$$\frac{\text{Income or savings}}{\text{generated by a project}} \div \frac{\text{Net amount}}{\text{invested in project}} = \frac{\text{Rate of}}{\text{return}}$$

To illustrate the use of a rate of return calculation, assume an establishment is considering purchasing a new dishwashing machine. In order to analyze the rate of return for this purchase, the financial information related to the purchase and potential cost savings need to be collected. This information is highlighted in *Exhibit 10.13*.

Exhibit 10.13

ECONOMY STUDY EVALUATING RETURN ON INVESTMENT

Existing dishwashing machine	New dishwashing machine
• Has a book value of $5,000	• Costs $12,000 installed
• Could be expected to last five more years	• Has an expected life of ten years
• Could be sold now for $2,000	• Has no expected salvage value after ten years
• Results in annual operating expenses (largely labor) of $20,120	• Requires fewer worker hours and additional supplies to operate, which results in annual operating expenses of $15,940

The manager has pulled together the information related to the value of the existing dishwasher, its remaining life expectancy, its value if sold today, and the labor costs it takes to operate it. For the new dishwashing machine, the manager has collected information, such as the price of the machine including installation, life expectancy, value at the end of the expected life, and labor costs for its operation. Based on the given information, the new dishwashing machine costs $12,000, and the old machine can be sold to recover $2,000. This results in a net investment of $10,000. What is the return for this $10,000 investment?

According to the information provided, the new dishwashing machine will result in a cost savings of $4,180 annually. This is figured by comparing the annual cost of operating the old machine, which is $20,120, to the annual operating costs for the new one, which is $15,940. The rate of return is stated as a percentage. In this example, the rate of return on investment is 41.8 percent, which is calculated as follows:

$4,180	÷	$10,000	=	0.418, or 41.8%
Income or savings generated by a project		Amount invested in project		Rate of return

An operation might, for example, have a standard guideline in place. This may be that capital spending with a rate of return of below 20 percent will not be approved.

Another technique used to evaluate and analyze possible capital expenditures is the payback period. The payback period is the length of time it will take to recover the amount of an investment. Generally, the shorter the period to recover the funds spent on an item, the better investment it is. The formula to calculate payback period is:

Net cash outlay for project	÷	Annual net income (or savings) for project	=	Payback period

For the example in *Exhibit 10.13*, the investment is $10,000 and the return is $4,180. The payback period is then calculated as follows:

10,000	÷	$4,180	=	2.39 years or approximately 2 years, 5 months
Net cash outlay for project		Annual net income (or savings) for project		Payback period

Based on this information, the payback period is about two years and five months. This payback period can then be compared to those of other options to determine which option will result in the shortest payback period. It can also be compared to an operation-specific guideline. For instance, some operations might not approve capital spending on any item that has a payback period of longer than two years.

Owners who make careful decisions about capital spending often use an economic study to assist them in the process. An economic study is a direct financial comparison of cost–benefit analyses for two or more alternatives.

Performing this comparison helps owners determine which option is more economically advantageous. Some important questions can be answered by an economic study:

- Which of several purchases should be made?
- Are extra features worth the cost?
- Should more expensive equipment be purchased?
- Is it financially desirable to replace equipment while it is still usable?

PRIORITIZING AND JUSTIFYING NEEDS

Rarely can an operation finance all the capital items on its wish list. Instead, owners must prioritize and justify the need to make each different purchase. Assigning these priorities also helps managers determine when to make the purchases, and in what order. However, there are some capital expenditures, such as a broken boiler or leaking roof, which must be made regardless of other considerations. In most cases, the highest priority must be given to items in a specific order.

Priority 1: These items pose an immediate safety risk, either to customers or employees—for example, broken or malfunctioning seating or equipment, or uneven flooring.

Priority 2: These items cause the operation to be in violation of local codes, such as fire codes or health regulations.

Priority 3: These items improve the operation's efficiency, such as a new piece of equipment, or its visual appearance by the addition of items such as new artwork, carpeting, or furnishings.

It is usually necessary to make capital expenditures over a period of time, rather than all at once. Therefore, it is necessary to pre-plan when this capital spending will occur. This, of course, involves the priority or necessity of the project, as well as forecasting when funds for the projects will be available. There may be years when, in order to accumulate funds for larger purchases, only very low-cost capital purchases or no capital purchases are scheduled. It may also be necessary to make unplanned capital expenditures, such as an unexpected furnace replacement. *Exhibit 10.14* is an example of a capital spending schedule.

Exhibit 10.14	
CAPITAL SPENDING SCHEDULE	
Year	**Project**
2013	New dishwashing machine
2014	Replace walk-in refrigerator
2015	Repaint and carpet dining room
2016	Repave parking lot
2017	Install new serving counter

Capital Budget Approval

Like any budget, capital budgets must be approved by the individuals who authorize such spending for the operation. This could be the owner of an operation, an area manager for a small chain, or the corporate purchasing department for a large chain. Review and approval are necessary to ensure the capital budget is realistic and appropriate.

Funds for capital budgets can come from an operation's profits, depreciation, or new investment. Operations can also plan for future capital purchases by putting aside a set amount of money on a regular basis. In addition, some types of businesses specialize in financing new construction, real estate purchases, and renovation projects for the restaurant and foodservice industry. The federal government also helps administer funding resources to help individuals and targeted groups, such as women and minorities, as well as other qualifying business owners.

LEASING

Many owners buy the real and personal property needed to operate their businesses. **Real property**, or real estate, is land and any structures permanently attached to the land. Typically this includes acreage, buildings, and parking areas. For many restaurant and foodservice operations, it may also include landscaping as well as trees, ponds, trellises, and other distinguishing features of the operation.

Personal property is that which is not permanently attached to the land. Examples include chairs and tables in a dining room as well as most kitchen equipment. These items can be easily removed from a building. Just as it is common to buy property in the hospitality industry, it is equally common for an owner to lease what is needed.

A **lease** is a legal arrangement by which property owned by one person or business is occupied or used by another person or business. Owners may legally lease real property or personal property. Because a lease is a legal arrangement, both the entity owning the property and the one leasing it should know about, and must agree on, the terms of the lease.

It is important for owners and managers to understand the differences in leasing, rather than buying, a piece of property. There are areas of special concern when owners consider leasing:

- Length of the lease
- Required lease payments, including when and how much
- Restrictions, if any, on the use of the property
- Required insurance
- Responsibility for damage
- Rights to terminate the lease
- Rights to renew the lease

Lease or Buy Decision Making

The decision to lease, rather than buy, a piece of property is an important one. The decision impacts three key areas of a business's operation:

- Cash
- Rights of use
- Continued use

IMPACT ON CASH

In many instances, the decision to lease rather than buy property is an economic one. This is because the decision impacts an operation's balance sheet, statement of cash flows, and income statement. For example, a new dishwashing machine for a high-volume operation may cost more than $50,000. Assume that the owner took out a bank loan to purchase the machine. When the loan is received, it is deposited in the operation's bank account and is counted as part of "Cash."

When the machine is purchased, the owner has made a capital improvement in the business. A **capital improvement** is the purchase of real or personal property that results in a depreciable asset. The balance sheet now lists an asset valued at $50,000. The operation's available cash has been reduced by $50,000.

The borrowing of money has impacted the operation's cash flow. In this case, repayments of the loan will not be listed as a normal or monthly business expense on the operation's income statement. Rather, the value of the machine is depreciated over a period of time consistent with GAAP and applicable deprecation rules established by the government. The portion of the loan to be repaid within one year will be listed as a current liability and the portion of the loan to be paid back in more than one year will be listed on the balance sheet as a long-term debt.

In some cases, owners elect to lease a piece of equipment rather than buy it because it is more cost-effective. For example, an operation manager may decide that it makes the most sense to lease a transportation van only for the relatively few days a year it performs off-site catering events (*Exhibit 10.15*). The owner of an operation that performs a large number of off-site catering events per year may decide, however, that purchasing a van will cost the operation much less per year than leasing one.

In some other cases, an owner may be forced to lease, rather than be allowed to buy, the property needed to operate his or her business. This would be the case, for example, for an owner who wanted to operate a business in the food court of a busy shopping mall. In this situation, the mall owner would lease the space to the manager, but would not permit the manager to buy it.

THINK ABOUT IT . . .

Some managers lease vehicles, dishwashing machines, ice machines, ranges, and/or refrigeration equipment. When might it make more sense for a restaurant or foodservice manager to rent rather than buy a piece of equipment?

Exhibit 10.15

IMPACT ON RIGHTS OF USE

The owners of leased property have the right to determine to whom they will lease (for example, the lessee may need to be of a designated age or have a specific ability) and how the leased property can be used. Lease terms related to the use of leased property can be extensive:

- How it can be used
- When it can be used
- Where it can be used
- Who is permitted to use it
- How it must be maintained during use

Managers who lease real or personal property should become very familiar with the terms of use that are identified in their leases.

IMPACT ON CONTINUED USE

An extremely important aspect of leasing is the fact that the owner retains all ownership of the leased property. Thus, the owner has the right to change the terms of a lease when it expires.

To illustrate the potential disadvantages to this arrangement, consider the establishment owner who leases space in a shopping mall. If the operation is financially successful, its owner will want to renew the lease each time it expires with as little increase in rent as possible. The mall owner, however, has no obligation to continue leasing at the same price when the old lease has expired. Therefore, the owner may be faced with significant rent increases when the lease expires. To help minimize this, the manager may insist that renewal terms limiting future rent increases be written into each lease when it is originally signed.

Manager's Memo

Hospitals, colleges, hotels, airports, and shopping malls are all very common locations for leased restaurant and foodservice operations. In many cases, the monthly or annual rent payment in these arrangements is based on the amount of revenue generated by the operation.

The most common arrangement is for the lease to require a fixed minimum amount be paid each month, regardless of the operation's achieved revenue. The amount due increases as the operation's revenue increases. For example, a lease might call for a monthly payment of $5,000 plus 5 percent of all sales in excess of a predetermined revenue amount.

OPEN FOR BUSINESS

MANAGER'S MATH

A restaurant or foodservice manager is contemplating leasing space in a shopping mall. The mall owner is asking for a monthly lease payment of $2,000 per month plus 6 percent of all revenue in excess of $50,000 per month.

1. What would this manager's monthly lease payment be if sales were $60,000 in a month?

2. What would this manager's monthly lease payment be if sales were $75,000 in a month?

3. What would this manager's monthly lease payment be if sales were $100,000 in a month?

(Answers: 1. $2,600; 2. $3,500; 3. $5,000)

Exhibit 10.16 summarizes some of the important differences between leasing and buying.

Exhibit 10.16		

DIFFERENCES IN LEASING VERSUS BUYING

Area of Difference	Leasing	Buying
Impact on balance sheet	A line item amount is entered under long-term debt (liabilities) on a balance sheet that indicates the value of future lease payments due.	Property is listed as an asset at its current value. If financed, the remaining amount owed on the item is listed as a current liability or a long-term debt.
Reporting of costs	Lease payments are considered a business expense and are listed on the income statement.	Property is depreciable in accordance with applicable income tax laws.
Ability to borrow money to make property payments	Very unlikely, because the property cannot be used for collateral.	Likely, because the property can be used for collateral.
Liability for damages to the property	Determined by the specific terms of the lease.	Owner responsible for damages.
Rights of usage	Restricted by property owner through terms of the lease.	Unlimited, but subject to any laws regulating the property's use.
Result of payment default	Property owner may terminate the lease and reclaim the property for nonpayment.	Lender may repossess if the property was purchased with borrowed money.

TAXATION

Taxes, tax management, and tax planning are issues of great importance to restaurant and foodservice owners and managers. In one respect, taxes are simply a cost of doing business that most managers must pay. Taxes must be paid and a record must be kept of tax payments. Business owners may be required to pay taxes imposed by local, state, and federal government entities.

In addition to paying taxes they owe, business owners play an important role in the collection of taxes that are to be forwarded to the government. For example, if a state institutes a tax on the purchase of food and beverages sold in restaurant and foodservice operations, the operation will collect these taxes from guests who have made the purchases. The taxes are then held and forwarded, on a regularly scheduled basis, to the state agency responsible for collecting the mandated tax. In general, taxes related to a restaurant or foodservice operation are of two types:

- Taxes due from the operation
- Taxes collected by the operation on behalf of the government

Taxes Due from the Operation

In most cases, businesses pay taxes on what they own and on what they earn. Taxes on what is owned include those assessed on real property and personal property. In most cases these taxes are assessed by local or state governments, and must be paid annually in one or more payments. In general, the higher the estimated value of a business's real and personal property, the more taxes will be due.

Taxes will also be due on what a business earns. The methods for calculating earned income for tax purposes can vary on a local or state level. Federal taxes due on earned income are detailed in the U.S. tax code. The methods used to establish the amount of earned income subject to income taxes change on a regular basis. For that reason, most business owners seek the advice of qualified tax experts when determining the amount of taxes due on their business's earned profits.

Taxes Collected by the Operation on Behalf of the Government

In addition to taxes based on what they own and earn, businesses are responsible for the collecting and forwarding of taxes to the government in two additional areas:

- Sales taxes
- Payroll-related taxes

SALES TAXES

All states and many local governments have the legal authority to tax sales made to restaurant and foodservice customers (*Exhibit 10.17*). When they exercise that authority, the collection and forwarding of the taxes due become the responsibility of the restaurant or foodservice operation. In most cases, managers will be responsible for specific actions related to sales taxes:

- Recording the amount of the business's sales subject to sales tax payment
- Recording the amount of tax charged to, and collected from, guests
- Forwarding the collected tax to the taxing authority according to the authority's required schedule
- Keeping appropriate records related to the sales tax payments made by the business

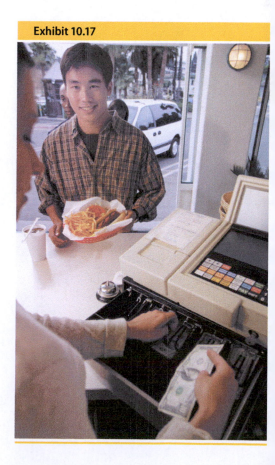

Exhibit 10.17

PAYROLL-RELATED TAXES

In addition to sales taxes, businesses are responsible for the management and payment of payroll-related taxes. In most cases, managers will be responsible for specific actions related to payroll taxes:

- Withholding from employee wages the amounts mandated by local, state, and federal taxing authorities
- Payment of withheld amounts to the appropriate taxing authority
- Payment of legally mandated payroll-related taxes imposed on the business by local, state, and federal taxing authorities
- Keeping appropriate records related to the payroll-related tax payments made by the business

The various types of taxes paid by most businesses include those summarized in *Exhibit 10.18*.

Exhibit 10.18

TYPES OF TAXES

Taxes Due from the Operation

Income taxes: These can be federal, state, or local.

Property taxes: Real property (real estate) taxes can be a major expense and may be imposed by state or local jurisdictions. They are based on the assessed value of the property.

Personal property taxes: This is a tax on the non–real estate items owned by a business and can include such categories as kitchen equipment and improvements; small wares such as china, glassware, and dining-room equipment; and construction in progress. Personal property tax does not apply to business inventories intended for resale, or to intangible property such as copyrights and trademarks.

Taxes Collected by the Operation on Behalf of the Government

Sales taxes: Most states have some type of sales and use tax. Some communities also impose a sales tax. Although customers pay these taxes, sellers collect them.

Payroll-related taxes: These can be considered in two categories. One is tax money withheld from employees' paychecks and then forwarded to the government by the employer. Other taxes or fees are paid directly by the employer.

Federal:

　Social Security taxes

　Medicare taxes

　Federal unemployment taxes (FUTA)

State:

　State unemployment taxes

　Workers' compensation insurance

Local:

　Taxes and fees vary according to the local community

Tax Management and Planning

Tax management is the process used by owners and managers to ensure they are in compliance with all of the tax-related requirements imposed on them. Typically, these include keeping detailed records related to a business and to its tax collection and payment efforts. Tax management related to the payment of taxes consists of specific activities:

- Paying real estate and property taxes in a timely manner
- Accurately reporting income earned by the business if the income is to be taxed
- Accurately reporting profit payments paid to the owners of the business
- Recording sales tax amounts collected from customers and paid to the appropriate governmental entity
- Recording payroll-related tax amounts withheld from employees
- Recording payroll-related taxes owed and paid by the business

Tax management is an activity that may be completed by managers or owners. Unlike tax management, tax planning is an activity best undertaken only by the owners of a business. **Tax planning** is a year-round activity designed to ensure that a business legally complies with the tax code, while doing so in a way that is of the most benefit to the business.

It is important to note that it is not the purpose of tax planning to illegally avoid paying taxes. Rather, the purpose of professional tax planning is to pay 100 percent of what a business legally owes, but not more than this. In addition to affecting the timely payment of taxes, there are a variety of additional ways in which effective tax planning can impact a business:

- Minimizing the use of cash
- Optimizing after-tax profits
- Gaining tax credits for engaging in specific activities
- Gaining favorable tax status for engaging in specific activities

The tax codes of local, state, and federal governments change on a regular basis. For example, in 2010 the federal government revised Section 179 of the U.S. tax code. The revision allows businesses to choose to claim certain equipment purchases as a business expense in the year they were purchased, rather than depreciating the equipment over the several years of the life of the assets. Choosing to use this available option is typical of the type of decision best made by owners who fully understand the implications of the decision. For that reason, business owners should seek the advice of qualified tax experts to assist them in their year-round tax planning efforts.

SUMMARY

1. **Explain the purpose of a balance sheet.**

   The purpose of a balance sheet is to give its readers an indication of the financial health of a business. It does so by listing key areas of interest to readers that include the amount of cash held by the business, as well as the value of assets that can reasonably be converted into cash. This gives an indication of the ability of a business to pay its bills as they come due. The balance sheet also lists the obligations, or debts, of a business. These liabilities give an indication of how much the business owes to others. Finally, the balance sheet identifies the amount of owner's equity in a business. This gives an indication of the portion of the business's assets that are held free of any debt incurred in their acquisition.

2. **Describe the three main components of a balance sheet.**

   The three main components of a balance sheet are assets, liabilities, and owner's equity. A balance sheet will contain these same components regardless of its size; however, it will vary in the amount of detail provided about each one.

   Assets are listed first on the balance sheet and consist of cash and those items owned by a business that can be readily converted to cash. These include accounts receivable (AR), inventories to be sold for cash, prepaid expenses, and the property and equipment used to generate cash. Liabilities are the debts owed by a business and these are listed second on the balance sheet and in the order in which the debts are due. Those due soonest are listed first. Liabilities that must be repaid in 12 months or less are called current liabilities or payables. Liabilities to be repaid in more than 12 months are called long-term liabilities or long-term debt. Owner's equity is the third component of the balance sheet and it is listed last. Owner's equity represent ownership's free and clear claim to business assets. It is equal to the value of a business's assets less the amount of debt owed by the business.

3. **Describe the importance of managing cash flow in restaurant and foodservice operations.**

   The management of cash in a business is critical. A business that generates more cash than needed to pay bills permits the business to use excess cash for other purposes, such as expanding, paying off long-term debt, or returning cash to its owners. If a business generates less cash than needed to pay its operating expenses, its owners may need to borrow money or sell assets to keep the business operating. Optimum cash levels must be maintained. The amount of cash available to do so will be affected by the size of a business as well as by its operating, investing, and financing activities. For this reason, business owners assess their cash position by regularly preparing and reviewing a financial summary known as the statement of cash flows.

4. **Explain the process used to prepare a capital budget.**

   Creating a capital budget is a three step process. Step 1 consists of identifying capital needs. Owners do this by asking questions to identify specific capital needs of their business. Step 2 is evaluating the needs based on established criteria that can include return on investment (ROI), rate of return, and payback periods. In the final step, owners prioritize their spending to ensure the most pressing needs are met first. These can include items that pose a safety risk, or items that must be purchased or improved to meet legal requirements that must be met by the business.

5. **Discuss the major differences between leasing and buying a capital item.**

   When owners need to undertake capital improvements in their businesses, they can often choose between buying and leasing an item or physical space. The decision will impact cash flow because in many cases leasing an item for short-term use is less expensive than buying it. When an item is leased, however, the owner of the item is allowed to establish the terms of the item's use. This may include who can use it, when it can be used, and how it can be used.

   While some leases are written for extended periods of time, the owner of an item is under no obligation to renew an expired lease. Because that is so, the leasing of a capital item, rather than its purchase, can result in unknown future costs for its continued use.

6. **Explain the impact of effective tax management and planning.**

   Tax management includes record keeping and activities designed to ensure a business is in compliance with all of their tax-related requirements. This includes keeping those records related to a business's tax collection and tax payment. Effective tax management ensures that businesses are in compliance with tax law. The managers or owners of a business can undertake tax management.

   Tax planning is an activity undertaken to ensure that a business complies with the tax code in a way that is most beneficial to the owners of the business. Tax planning by owners helps ensure that their businesses pay all taxes legally owed, but not more than legally owed. Because of its complexity, tax planning is typically done with advice from qualified tax experts.

APPLICATION EXERCISE

Ben's Garage

Lately the owner of Ben's Garage, a popular beer and burger establishment in the business district of a large town, has noticed that lunch sales have drifted steadily downward since the new 1950s-style diner opened up around the corner. The owner of Ben's Garage has not had any customer complaints and has a great, experienced staff. The diner has been in operation for only three months and is very eye-catching, with lots of neon and shiny chrome.

The owner takes a look around Ben's Garage. She notices several tables with coasters under them to keep them from wobbling, and 80 out of the 125 vinyl chairs have tears or cigarette burns on them. In addition, the skylights need professional cleaning, and the sign outside needs replacement. She also received a notice from the fire department that each tenant in her building must install a sprinkler system within 90 days in order to satisfy new fire code requirements.

The owner puts together some cost estimates on these projects.

Option	Cost	Comments
Buying new chairs	$33 per chair; $2,640 to replace 80 chairs; $4,125 to replace all 125 chairs	Chairs come with a one-year warranty for replacement.
Reupholstering current chairs	$7 per chair; $560 to repair 80 damaged chairs	Upholstery comes with a six-month warranty.
Cleaning skylights	$125 × 6 skylights = $750	
Buying new sign	$2,150 installed	
Installing new sprinkler system	$1,800 installed	
Project Total	**$ 8,825**	**Includes 125 new chairs**

The owner contacts the local bank and is approved for a small business loan of only $5,000. Given this information, answer the following questions:

1. How would you recommend the owner use the $5,000 on capital improvements for Ben's Garage?

2. Justify the recommendations. Why did you choose some options over others?

REVIEW YOUR LEARNING

Select the best answer for each question.

1. **What are the three major sections in a balance sheet?**

   A. Revenue, Expenses, and Profits

   B. Revenue, Liabilities, and Profits

   C. Assets, Expenses, and Owner's equity

   D. Assets, Liabilities, and Owner's equity

2. **The basic purpose of a balance sheet is to provide its readers with the information needed to determine if the business is financially strong and**

   A. is making a profit.

   B. has increasing sales.

   C. is economically efficient.

   D. has performed well over time.

3. **A business has $40,000 in current assets and $400,000 in total assets. It has $50,000 in current liabilities and $200,000 in total liabilities. What is the solvency ratio for the business?**

   A. 2.0

   B. 3.0

   C. 4.0

   D. 5.0

4. **In a business, cash is decreased when**

   A. assets are sold.

   B. accounts receivable are reduced.

   C. inventories are increased.

   D. accounts payable are allowed to get larger.

5. **The purpose of a capital budget is to**

   A. track profits and losses over time.

   B. measure control of selected variable costs.

   C. check the operating budget for line item accuracy.

   D. plan ahead for major improvements to the operation.

6. **Which improvement should have the highest priority on a capital budget?**

   A. POS upgrade

   B. Sidewalk repair

   C. Drapery cleaning

   D. Dining-room remodeling

7. **A capital improvement is the purchase of real or personal property that results in**

   A. the creation of a lease.

   B. a decrease in operating expenses.

   C. an increase in operating expenses.

   D. the recording of a depreciable asset.

8. **Where do accountants record the payments due on a business's long-term loans?**

   A. The income statement

   B. The statement of cash flows

   C. The liabilities segment of the balance sheet

   D. The owner's equity segment of the balance sheet

9. **Which taxes are collected by businesses on behalf of the government?**

   A. Sales taxes

   B. Income taxes

   C. Real estate taxes

   D. Personal property taxes

10. **When is the best time for an owner to engage in tax planning?**

    A. Year-round

    B. When taxes are filed

    C. At the end of the tax year

    D. At the beginning of the tax year

FIELD PROJECT

Financial Procedures Audit

This field project is designed to give you a glimpse of how the financial management processes and procedures in this book are applied in a real-world restaurant or foodservice environment. This project will give you an in-depth "reality check" regarding financial management practices in a single operation.

The Assignment

Select a restaurant or foodservice operation—it can be either commercial or noncommercial, and from any segment of the industry. Get approval from the operation's manager to perform a basic audit of the financial management processes currently in place at the operation. This audit will entail researching brief questions related to financial management practices, viewing sample forms and documents, and observing employee practices. It is estimated that you will need *at least 10 hours* of time to interact with the operation manager and staff to collect the information you need.

Prepare a report that includes the following three sections:

1. Current financial management practices
2. Analysis/Evaluation of current financial management practices
3. Recommendations for future enhancements

Use the following questions as guidelines to get you started.

1. **Current Financial Management Practices**

   Managing Cash at the Operation

   - What procedures exist for processing guest payments?
   - How are employees trained in these procedures?
   - What tools are in place to help spot counterfeit currency?
   - How does the management staff monitor the handling of cash by employees?
   - What procedures are in place to ensure cash is stored securely?
   - What tools or forms are used for cash register reconciliation?
   - What tools or forms are used for bank deposit preparation?

Managing Payables and Receivables

• What procedures are in place for managing accounts payable?

• Does a chart of accounts exist for the operation? If not, how are invoices categorized?

• Who is responsible for authorizing payment of invoices?

• What procedures are in place for managing accounts receivable?

• How are credit terms for house accounts determined?

• How does the operation identify and collect past-due accounts receivable?

Exploring Costs

• Which operating costs are controllable? Which are noncontrollable?

• Which operating costs are variable? Semivariable? Fixed?

Preparing the Operating Budget

• How are sales revenue forecasts prepared? How accurate are they?

• How are food costs forecasted? How accurate are they?

• How are labor costs forecasted? How accurate are they?

• Does the operation use a master schedule? If not, how is the hourly employee schedule determined?

• Examine an operating budget for one period. How is it organized?

Introduction to Cost Control

• How are sales and cost data collected?

• How are sales and cost data analyzed? What are the actual figures compared to?

• Which costs are more likely to be out of line?

• What corrective actions are most often needed to bring these costs back into line?

• What is the target food cost percentage?

• How is food product waste recorded and calculated?

• What is the target labor cost percentage for the operation?

• What productivity ratios are commonly used to analyze labor costs? How are these calculated?

The Profit and Loss Report

• How often are profit and loss reports created?

• What is the procedure for collecting information to generate profit and loss reports?

• What does the profit and loss report look like? How is the information organized?

• How are profit and loss reports analyzed?

The Capital Budget

- Is there a capital budget in place? If so, what items are included?
- How is the capital budget prepared?
- What information is considered when planning for capital spending (return on investment, priorities, etc.)?
- What items are being considered for future capital budgets?

2. Analysis/Evaluation of Current Financial Management Practices

- How effective are the practices and tools that are currently in place?
- Where is the operation at risk of losing money?

3. Recommendations for Future Enhancements

- What changes or improvements would you recommend? For the short term? For the long term?
- What would it cost to implement these enhancements? Propose a sample budget for implementing these recommendations.

GLOSSARY

Account code A unique number usually assigned to each of the accounts listed on the chart of accounts for expenses.

Accounting Counting, or accounting for, the money received and spent operating a restaurant or foodservice facility or company.

Accounting equation Assets minus liabilities equals owner's equity.

Accounting period Any time period for which financial records are prepared.

Accounts payable (AP) The total of all invoices that are due and payable in an operation at any point in time.

Accounts receivable (AR) Those amounts due to the operation from others, usually customers and clients.

Accrual accounting (method) An accounting method that recognizes and records revenues when they are earned, rather than when the cash is received.

Aging schedule A chart that shows the age of all receivables not yet paid.

À la carte menu A menu in which each item is priced separately.

Alternative revenue source (ARS) A source that generates money in addition to that raised from other funding sources such as loans and personal savings.

Amortization The reduction in value of an intangible asset, such as the right to use a franchise trademark.

Annual budget A budget that addresses estimated financial performance of an operation for 52 consecutive weeks.

Assets The items a business owns.

Auditing The independent verification of a business's financial records.

Audit trail The steps in the payment process that are supported by verifiable documents or other tangible proof.

Average sale per guest Total sales divided by number of guests served.

Balance sheet A document that reports the assets, liabilities, and owner's equity of a business at a specific point in time.

Beginning inventory The total value of products on hand at the beginning of the accounting period for which food cost is being calculated.

Benchmark A description of desired performance.

Benefit The advantage or favorable result obtained from purchasing a feature.

Beverage cost percentage The proportion of beverage sales spent for beverage expense.

Bleeding The process of removing cash from a cash register during the hours of operation to secure the cash in a safe.

Bonding An arrangement with an insurer in which, for a fee, the insurance company guarantees payment to an operation for a financial loss caused by the actions of the specific covered employee.

Bookkeeping The recording, but not the analyzing, of financial transactions.

Book value The purchase price of an asset, less the accumulated depreciation (the sum of the amounts charged because the asset will wear out over its lifetime).

Brand The single term that owners and managers use to describe an establishment's distinguishing features.

Break-even point The level at which the revenue achieved in an operation equals its expenses.

Budget A financial plan for operating a facility during a future time period.

Business plan A formal statement of business goals that explains how the goals can be achieved, and the detailed steps for reaching the goals.

Business transaction The act of purchasing or selling a product or service.

Capital The money, property, and other valuables that collectively represent the wealth of an individual or business.

Capital budget A budget that addresses a business's capital expenditures for a specific period of time.

Capital expenditure The purchase of an item that costs a specified amount, such as $5,000 or more.

Capital improvement The purchase of real or personal property that results in a depreciable asset.

Capital items Major purchases that require a significant financial commitment and will be used over a long period of time, also known as **Furnishings, fixtures, and equipment (FF&E)** items.

Cash The currency and coins guests use to pay their bills.

Cash accounting (method) An accounting method that recognizes business income as it is received and business expenses as they are paid.

Centralized accounting system A system in which financial information from a business is transmitted to a central location, where it may be recorded and analyzed by management.

Certified public accountant (CPA) A person who has been specially trained and, by passing a test, is certified as highly competent in the field of business accounting.

Chain (restaurant) An operation in which multiple restaurants share the same name and operating systems.

Chart of accounts A list of categories used to organize an operation's revenue and cost information.

Co-branding A situation when two companies join together to share the expense of marketing the products and services each company offers to its own customers.

Code of conduct A document that explains employee behavioral expectations including company values, rules, principles, confidentiality, and loyalty.

Coding A system of assigning actual costs listed on invoices to predetermined cost areas.

Concept statement The part of a business plan that details exactly what type of establishment will be created.

Continuous quality improvement (CQI) Ongoing efforts to better meet or exceed customers' expectations and thus achieve the financial goals of an operation.

Contracted expense The use of an outside vendor to perform a needed task or provide a needed service.

Contribution margin (CM) The amount of sales remaining after variable costs have been subtracted.

Controllable costs The costs that management can directly control, such as food cost.

Corporation A formal business structure recognized as a legal entity having its own privileges and liabilities separate from that of its owners.

Corrective actions Steps that should be taken by a manager as soon as the cause for a variance is identified.

Cost accounting The branch of accounting that specializes in recording the expenses of a business.

Cost–benefit analysis An analysis that examines the cost of purchasing an item in relationship to its potential cost savings.

Cost of sales The industry term for the food and beverage product expense incurred in the generation of sales.

Cost of sales percentage The proportion of total sales spent for the products used to create the sales.

Covers per server The number of customer meals that a server can serve in an hour.

Credit memo A written record of a proposed adjustment to a delivery invoice.

Credit terms The payment rules established for an account.

Current assets Cash and assets that will be converted to cash in one year or less.

Current liabilities Those liabilities that must be paid within the next 12 months.

Current ratio Total current assets divided by total current liabilities.

Day part A specific segment of the day.

DBA An abbreviation for "doing business as" when a sole proprietor's business is operated under a different name.

Decentralized accounting system A system in which a manager collects accounting data from an operation and then records, reports, and analyzes those data at the same site.

Delivery invoice A document used by vendors to indicate products, including quantities and prices, that are delivered to a restaurant or foodservice operation.

Demographics Information about customers such as their age, gender, race, marital status, geographic location, or other personal characteristics.

Depreciation A method of calculating and recording the reduction in value of a tangible, or physical, asset over its useful lifetime.

Distinct business principle A principle stating that a business's financial records cannot be mixed with the personal financial records of its owners.

Dogs Menu items that are unprofitable and unpopular.

Economic study A direct financial comparison of cost–benefit analyses for two or more alternatives.

Embezzlement The act of stealing financial assets, including cash, from a business.

Ending inventory The total value of products on hand at the end of the accounting period for which food cost is being calculated.

Ethics The behavior of one person toward another person, based on a person's view of what is right or wrong.

Executive summary A document that provides readers of a business plan with the highlights of the plan.

Expense (business) A cost incurred in the operation of a business.

Expense timing The proper method of reporting an operation's expenses.

Extension An arithmetic calculation made on a delivery invoice; for example, the item quantity is multiplied by the purchase unit price for each product delivered to determine the total cost for each product.

Factor pricing method Another name for the **food cost percentage pricing method**.

Feature A characteristic of the actual menu items and services sold to guests.

Finance The term managers use to describe the management of a business's money and other assets.

Financial accounting The branch of accounting that specializes in recording business transactions.

Financial plan An estimation of the cash needed to open a new business or buy an existing business, and to keep it operating until it becomes financially stable.

Fiscal year Any consecutive 12-month period.

Fixed cost A cost that remains the same regardless of sales volume.

Food cost percentage The proportion of food sales spent for food expense.

Food cost percentage pricing method The simplest of all menu pricing methods, based only on the cost of food required to make a menu item.

Food product waste A measurement of how much food product is purchased and taken from inventory, but not actually sold.

Furnishings, fixtures, and equipment (FF&E) Major purchases requiring a significant financial commitment that will be used over a long period of time, also called **capital items**.

Generally Accepted Accounting Principles (GAAP) Standards and procedures that have been widely adopted and used by those responsible for preparing business financial statements.

Gratuity A tip paid to a server.

Gross profit The amount of revenue remaining after the costs of food and beverages have been subtracted from sales.

Guest check A record listing the food and beverages purchased by a customer.

Historical costs The costs that have been incurred in the past.

House account An arrangement whereby a customer is allowed to buy products and services on credit.

Income statement The financial report that details an operation's revenue, expense, and profit for a specific time period.

Investor Someone who supplies money to a business and gets paid back in its profits.

Invoice A formal, detailed, and written request for payment, commonly called a *bill*.

Invoice scam A bill for goods and services the operation did not order or did not receive.

Labor cost The cost of payroll plus all other labor-related costs, including FICA, employer-paid health insurance premiums, vacation pay, sick leave, and so on.

Labor cost percentage Labor cost divided by sales.

Labor standard A measure determined by management that indicates what a labor cost should be.

Law of supply and demand Economic belief about the supply of an item and its price relative to its demand: as the price increases, the demand decreases; as the price goes down, the demand increases.

Lease A legal arrangement by which property owned by one person or business is occupied or used by another person or business.

Lender Someone who supplies money to a business with the legal requirement that the money, and any interest charged for it, be repaid on an agreed-upon schedule.

Liabilities The debts a business incurs in the process of doing business.

Line item review To check every item on the budget against actual figures, and to note any differences.

Liquidated A situation in which all of a business's assets are sold and it ceases operations.

Long-range budget A budget that usually addresses accounting periods of two to five years.

Long-term debt Any obligation, or loan, that will be paid back in a period longer than 12 months.

Managerial accounting The field of accounting that addresses the specific financial information that managers need to make good decisions about how to operate their businesses.

Market conditions The economic, legal, and competitive conditions faced by a business at a specific point in time.

Market share The number or value of units sold by a business during a given period, which is expressed as a percentage of the total market size.

Market size The number or value of units sold to an entire group of customers in a given time period.

Menu mix The frequency with which a menu item is ordered compared to other menu items.

Menu mix popularity percentage The percentage of total menu items that must be sold for a menu item to be considered popular.

Moving average A forecasting technique in which sales information for two or three recent and same-length periods is averaged together.

Negative variance A variance in which actual performance is less than the budgeted performance.

Net earnings The amount of after-tax income earned by a business during an accounting period.

Noncontrollable costs Those costs over which managers have little or no control, such as rent.

Occupancy cost A cost related to the expense of occupying a building that houses a restaurant or foodservice operation.

Opening cash bank The amount of money initially placed in the cash drawer.

Operating budget A projected financial plan for a specific period of time.

Over A situation where there is more money on hand in the cash drawer than is indicated by the sales report.

Overhead Expenses in addition to food and labor costs, such as utilities, marketing, equipment maintenance, and so forth.

Owner's equity The difference between what a business owns (assets) and what it owes (liabilities).

Owner's equity ratio Total owner's equity divided by total assets; the ratio indicates how much the owners of a business would receive in the event the business was liquidated.

Partnership A business structure consisting of two or more owners who agree to share in the profits and losses of a business.

Partnership agreement A contract that details the rights and responsibilities of each co-owner of a business.

Payables Another term for **liabilities**.

Payback period The length of time it will take to recover the amount of an investment.

Payment card A credit card or debit card issued by a bank or other financial institution.

Payment terms The conditions under which a supplier will complete a sale.

Payroll cost The amount of money that is spent for employee wages, both fixed and variable.

Personal property Property that is not permanently attached to the land, such as kitchen equipment.

Petty cash A fund used in case of an emergency and for small-dollar purchases.

Petty cash voucher A document used to record information about the petty cash purchase.

Plow horses Menu items that are popular but not profitable.

Point-of-sale (POS) system A machine that records guest purchases as well as other important operating data.

Portion cost The cost of creating one serving of a menu item.

Positive variance A variance in which actual performance is greater than the budgeted performance.

Prepaid expenses Using cash to purchase a good or service, the benefits of which will be realized or received within the current year; for example, the money paid at the beginning of the year for an annual insurance policy.

Prime cost The sum of food costs and labor costs.

Prix fixe menu A menu consisting of predetermined items presented as a multicourse meal and at a set price.

Profit and loss (P&L) report An alternative term for an **income statement**.

Profit per guest served Profit divided by the number of guests served.

Pro forma A detailed estimate of the revenue, expenses, and profits to be achieved by a business over a specific time period.

Purchase order (PO) A document authorizing a purchase.

Puzzles Menu items that are profitable, but not many are sold.

Random audit An audit in which auditors randomly choose a variety of AP-related financial transactions for close examination.

Rate of return The relationship between the savings (or additional income) and the amount expended on an item.

Ratio analysis The comparison of financial information found on the balance sheet, income statement, or other financial statement.

Real property Land and any structures permanently attached to the land, also known as *real estate*.

Reconciliation A comparison made to confirm that the money, checks, and credit card receipts in the cash drawer are equal to the recorded sales for a particular time period, less the amount of the opening cash bank.

Return on investment (ROI) A measurement of the financial benefits of a purchase: how much is saved or earned in the long run by making the purchase.

Revenue The amount of money generated from the sale of products and services.

Revenue source A distinct area, for example, a bar or dining room, in which sales are generated.

Secret shopper A company that sends hired customers into an establishment to check the service level of employees.

Semivariable costs Costs that go up and down as sales fluctuate, but not in direct proportion.

Service charge A service-related fee assessed and retained by an operation.

Shareholder An individual or group that owns one or more portions, or shares, of a corporation.

Short A situation where there is less money on hand in the cash drawer than is indicated by the sales report.

Short-range budget A budget that is prepared for an accounting period in the near future, often addressing financial performance for one year or less.

Shrinkage Product spoilage, product waste, or theft of inventory.

Significant variance A variance above a certain dollar amount, which should be investigated by managers.

Simple markup pricing method Another term for the **food cost percentage pricing method**.

Sole proprietorship An operating business structure in which one individual owns, and frequently operates, the business.

Solvency ratio Total assets divided by total liabilities.

Stars Menu items that are profitable and popular.

Statement of account A list of multiple invoice amounts due to a vendor.

Statement of cash flows A summary of the changes, or flows, in cash available to a business during a designated accounting period.

Step cost A fixed cost that increases to a new level in step with significant changes in activity or usage.

Stock rotation The practice of ensuring that products in storage the longest are used first.

Subtotal A list of all of a guest's purchased items and their costs added together, before sales tax is added.

Suggestive selling Recommending additional or different items to a customer.

SWOT analysis An analysis that identifies an operation's strengths and weaknesses and examines its opportunities and threats.

Targeted audit An audit that closely examines only a specific type of financial transaction.

Target market Those potential customers whose specific needs and wants the organization will seek to meet.

Tax accounting The recording and reporting of taxes to be paid.

Tax management The process used by owners and managers of an establishment to ensure they are in compliance with all tax-related requirements.

Tax planning A year-round activity designed to ensure a business legally complies with the tax code, while doing so in a way that is of most benefit to the business.

Tender The amount of cash given by a guest to an employee.

Uniform System of Accounts for Restaurants (USAR) An accounting system for collecting and reporting financial information that can be used by nearly all restaurant and foodservice operations.

Value The difference between what customers get when they buy a product or service and what they pay to get it.

Variable costs Costs that go up and down as sales fluctuate, and do so in direct proportion.

Variance The difference between the sales report and the actual cash count when there are overages or shortages.

Voucher A numbered form that has space to record the information about a payment, including the date of the payment, the check number, and the amount and recipient of the check.

Wine list An operation's menu of wine offerings.

Write-off A recorded reduction in the stated value of inventory.

INDEX

NOTES

NOTES

NOTES

NOTES

NOTES